Career Directions Handbook

Fifth Edition

Donna J. Yena
Johnson & Wales University

Mc Graw Hill

Connect
Learn
Succeed™

CAREER DIRECTIONS HANDBOOK
Published by McGraw-Hill, a business unit of The McGraw-Hill Companies, Inc., 1221 Avenue of the
Americas, New York, NY, 10020.

Some ancillaries, including electronic and print components, may not be available to customers outside the
United States.

This book is printed on acid-free paper.

1 2 3 4 5 6 7 8 9 0 WDQ/WDQ 0

ISBN 978-0-07-736308-6
MHID 0-07-736308-6

Vice president/Editor in chief: *Elizabeth Haefele*
Vice president/Director of marketing: *John E. Biernat*
Senior sponsoring editor: *Alice Harra*
Director of development: *Sarah Wood*
Developmental editor: *Jenae Grossart*
Editorial coordinator: *Vincent Bradshaw*
Senior marketing manager: *Keari Green*
Digital developmental editor: *Kevin White*
Director, Editing/Design/Production: *Jess Ann Kosic*
Senior project manager: *Jane Mohr*
Production supervisor: *Nicole Baumgartner*
Senior designer: *Srdjan Savanovic*
Cover design: *Daniel Krueger*
Typeface: *10/12 Times Roman*
Compositor: *Laserwords Private Limited*
Printer: *Worldcolor*
Cover credit: *©Iconica, Philip and Karen Smith*

Library of Congress Cataloging-in-Publication Data

Yena, Donna J.
    Career directions handbook / Donna J. Yena.—5th edtion.
        p. cm.
    ISBN 978-0-07-736308-6 (alk. paper)
    1. Vocational guidance. I. Title.
HF5381.Y46 2010
650.1—dc22
                                                                2009051803

The Internet addresses listed in the text were accurate at the time of publication. The inclusion of a Web site
does not indicate an endorsement by the authors or McGraw-Hill, and McGraw-Hill does not guarantee the
accuracy of the information presented at these sites.

www.mhhe.com

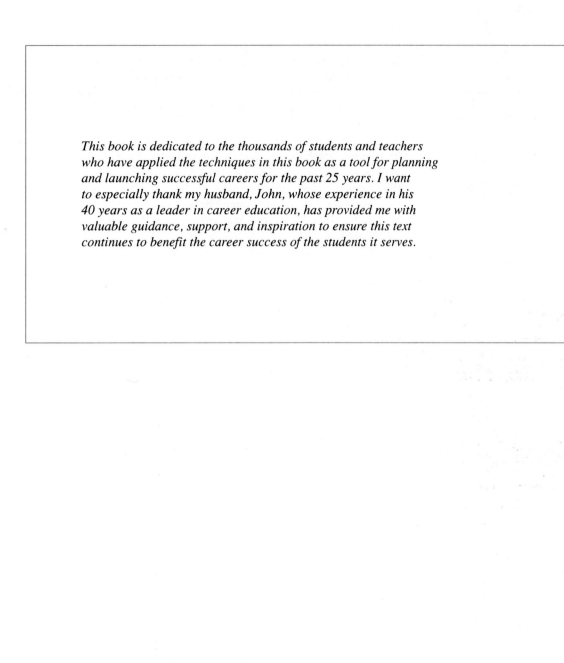

This book is dedicated to the thousands of students and teachers who have applied the techniques in this book as a tool for planning and launching successful careers for the past 25 years. I want to especially thank my husband, John, whose experience in his 40 years as a leader in career education, has provided me with valuable guidance, support, and inspiration to ensure this text continues to benefit the career success of the students it serves.

About the Author

Donna Yena

With 30 years of experience in career development and human resources, Donna Yena brings a practitioner's perspective to this book. Her experience as Vice President of Career Development at Johnson & Wales University, along with her background as a manager, instructor, and curriculum designer, contribute to the advice and techniques found in the *Career Directions Handbook* and *Career Directions: The Path to Your Ideal Career.*

Yena developed and implemented a series of career management education courses for students at Johnson & Wales University, while responsible for experiential education programs for more than 3,500 students at four campuses. For 30 consecutive years, 98 percent of Johnson & Wales University graduates were employed within 60 days of graduation, under Yena's leadership. Yena is one of the University's certified DACUM (Developing a Curriculum) facilitators. She currently serves as a member of the Board of Governors for the World Association of Cooperative Education and is a member of the Society for Human Resource Management, the Women's Foodservice Forum, and NACE, the National Association of Colleges and Employers.

Yena is a nationally recognized speaker on career development, job placement, and student success. She has led seminars for school professionals and their students across the country and has published numerous articles on a range of job search and career development topics.

Table of Contents

The *Career Directions Handbook* is a practical guide to help you manage your career throughout your lifetime. The *Career Directions Handbook* is a companion product to the *Career Directions: The Path to Your Ideal Career* textbook. The information found in the *Career Directions Handbook* is a useful resource when completing chapter activities and end of chapter reflection exercises.

Section A, "Career Paths," shows you the many career areas that exist in your chosen field of study. Some of the actual jobs available in each of these career areas are outlined to show you how your chosen career may progress over the years. Section B, "Glossary of Terms Used in Job Descriptions," defines some of the key words commonly found in job descriptions. This will help you use Section C, the "Index of Job Descriptions," which is a comprehensive list of actual job descriptions defining job titles presented in "Career Paths." These three sections work together to present you with a better understanding of the day-to-day job responsibilities in your chosen career and can be referred to periodically when making career decisions. Section D, "Bibliography," provides you with additional sources of career information that will help guide your own job search and enhance your professional development.

Section A, "Career Paths," is designed to help you decide how you want to apply your degree after graduation and then provides you direction for future career moves. It is useful for self-assessment and goal setting as you conduct periodic reviews of your own career. In almost any career field, there is a wide variety of jobs that suit interests, abilities, and personalities. The job titles listed range from high people-oriented to high task-oriented jobs. They show you that you may change jobs to try many different types of work without changing the career field you have chosen. The salary ranges listed vary according to geographic location, type of industry and employer, the overall state of the economy, and your own experience level; they should always be weighed against the relative cost of living in a given area. Understanding the overview of career paths in your career field can also help you communicate to an employer that you know your long-term professional goal, that you know the series of jobs you may need to hold before getting there, and that you realize it is necessary to start any career with an entry-level job.

In addition to helping you understand the terminology used in job descriptions, the "Glossary of Terms Used in Job Descriptions" is also a helpful tool for constructing your résumé. This section provides an additional resource for identifying words that best describe on your résumé what you bring to an employer. It is also good to review Section B of the Handbook when preparing for a job interview so you will be able to describe your specific skills to the interviewer.

Once you are aware of the career paths available to you and understand the main terms used in job descriptions, you should find that the "Index of Job Descriptions" will explain the responsibilities of the job(s) you are interested in. This information is useful in clarifying whether your perception of what a job entails is accurate and should be critical to helping you decide on your career goal. Being able to articulate to an employer, during an interview, a proper understanding of the job available to you may be important to the success of your interview. This is because employers frequently find that job candidates misunderstand what many jobs entail until an explanation is provided by the employer.

Some of the resources included can help you find information on prospective employers, refine your job search skills, and improve your professional skills. The *Career Directions Handbook* is something you will find useful at many points in your career, long after your first job.

Career Paths

In this section, you will become aware of the many career choices available to you, learn how to choose a career area, and learn how to map out a plan in order to make successful career moves. If there was ever a time to do the work that you really love, to do the kind of work that you are really attracted to, it's now. Your career training enables you to choose a variety of traditional career paths. It also opens doors to many of the new and exciting career paths emerging in the workplace.

Take some time to think about any and every career direction that exists for you. When you do this, you will feel more confident about the decisions you make because you will know that you have considered all your options. In this age of change, it will be necessary for you to consider new options periodically. Learning to be flexible now will be helpful as your world of work changes.

You have already made your first step in choosing a career area by deciding on your major or program. Unfortunately, many times students do not have access to all the information they need to decide how to best apply their professional training in the workplace. Focusing on your career means selecting an area within your field that interests you the most.

For example, if you are a retailing major, you may choose to become involved in management, buying, distribution, visual merchandising, or sales within the retail field. As a business administration/management student, you may put your professional training to work in banking, insurance, finance, human resources, retailing, advertising, production, or distribution. Your first step, then, is to look at career areas directly related to your major or program.

Don't stop there. Your talents can go to work in many other areas as well. For example, if you are pursuing professional training in accounting, you may first look into private and public accounting firms, but you should also consider accounting work in a retail firm or a hotel as possibilities. If you are pursuing a degree in information sciences, you may consider this type of work in any type of business or industry that is of interest to you. You may also want to explore jobs that allow you upward mobility into management or sales.

Most important to choosing your career area is really understanding the jobs in each area. Without a clear understanding of what a job involves, you cannot really know if it's what you want, nor can you convince a potential employer that you are right for that job. Job titles don't tell us what we need to know. They are only a start. Every day, people perform in the jobs that we think we want someday. What the job really consists of or how we would spend our time every day on the job is often something we're not familiar with. Then how can we be sure this is what we really want to do? One way to find out is to become familiar with job descriptions. Once employed in the workplace, you'll then be likely to say, "There's more to this job than you think there is."

The next section presents you with over 1,000 job titles representing 16 different career areas. The actual job descriptions for each job title can be found in the "Index of Job Descriptions," Section C. Follow the steps below (illustrated in the accompanying table) to make the most effective use of this section:

1. Consider the different career areas available in the field as presented in the overview.

2. Review the entry, mid-management/specialists, and management positions and their related salary ranges.

How to Use "Career Paths"

Fashion and Retail Management—Career Overview

			← ❶ Career Areas ❸ →		
❷ **Level**	**Management**	**Buying**	❹	**Distribution**	**Sales**
▼ Entry ($$$$)	Job titles	Job titles		Job titles	Job titles
Mid-management/specialists ($$$$)	Job titles	Job titles	▼	Job titles	Job titles
Management ($$$$)	Job titles	Job titles		Job titles	Job titles

3. Focus on the area(s) in which you have the most interest.

4. Look down that column of job titles and ask yourself what each one represents. You may wish to ask yourself, What does a merchandise analyst do every day?

5. Review the corresponding job description in the "Index of Job Descriptions" if you are unclear about the responsibilities of a particular job title. This index also opens up a whole variety of jobs available to you about which you may have had no previous knowledge.

After each career overview, the following information is presented (see details in the accompanying box).

- salaries
- experience needed
- qualifications
- where the jobs are
- trade publications
- professional associations

"Career Paths" is your beginning to understanding your own career options. *Don't stop there!* After you have obtained your first job, you will need to refer to this information periodically to decide on your next move. By understanding the jobs in the mid-management/specialists and management segments of your career, you can create a clear vision of where you are going and how long it might take to get there.

NOTES | **Important Points to Remember about Career Paths**

- The salaries listed represent only an average range for the country as a whole in 2009. In general, *salaries vary according to geographic location, types of industries and employers, the overall state of the economy, and your own experience level.* You should always weigh a salary that is offered to you as to how it compares with these variables.

- Under "Qualifications" you will find the most common and necessary traits you need to be successful in tomorrow's jobs. Those common qualifications often include

  positive attitude

  enthusiasm

  effective written and oral skills

  well-groomed appearance

  ability to work on a team

  high energy level

  flexibility

  ability to learn

  technical skills

- In "Where the Jobs Are," the most common industries where jobs exist in each career area are outlined. The industries listed are those in which entry-level jobs are most available. There may be many more types of employers depending on your level of experience and future trends in business.

- Because a successful career includes keeping up-to-date on current trends in your field and adapting to those trends, it is important to be aware of the basic trade publications and professional associations appropriate for your career.

- It should become obvious by studying the career paths outlined here that each career area is made up of a *planned sequence of related jobs.*

Accounting

Level	Public Accounting	Private/Management Accounting	Government
1. Entry ($36,000–$45,000)	Junior Staff Accountant	Junior Accountant	Revenue Officer
2. Mid-management/specialists ($45,000–$65,000)	Staff Accountant Senior Staff Accountant	Accountant Senior Accountant General Accountant Chief Internal Auditor Department Manager Tax Accountant Cost Accountant	Accountant Internal Auditor
3. Management ($65,000–$102,000)	Manager Senior Manager Partner	Vice President Treasurer Controller Chief Financial Officer	Chief Internal Auditor Chief Accountant

Public Accounting

Level	Job Title	Experience Needed
Entry	Junior Staff Accountant	Professional training
2	Staff Accountant	1–3 years
2	Senior Staff Accountant	3–4 years
3	Manager	5–7 years
3	Senior Manager	7–10 years
3	Partner	10+ years

Salaries in Public Accounting

Level	Salary	Firm
Entry	$36,000 to $40,000	Medium-sized firm
Entry	$40,000 to $45,000	Large firm
2	$45,000 to $50,000	Medium-sized firm
2	$50,000 to $55,000	Medium-sized firm
2	$55,000 to $65,000	Large firm
3	$65,000 to $80,000	Medium-sized firm
3	$70,000 to $100,000	Large firm
3	$150,000 to $200,000	Large firm

Salaries vary with the size of the firm.

Qualifications

Personal   Good communication and concentration skills. Accuracy and attention to detail. Flexibility. Objectivity. Ability to judge and make decisions. Reliability.

Professional   Writing and communication skills. Exceptional mathematical ability. Commitment to professional standards. Ability to work independently.

Where the Jobs Are
CPA firms

Public accounting is divided into tiers: the top accounting firms, and other national, regional, and local practices.

Top Accounting Firms

KPMG Peat Marwick, New York, NY

Ernst & Young, New York, NY

DeLoitte & Touche, New York, NY

Arthur Andersen, Chicago, IL

Pricewaterhouse Coopers, New York, NY

These companies have branches throughout the country.

Private/Management Accounting

Level	Job Title	Experience Needed
Entry	Junior Accountant	Professional training
2	Accountant	1–3 years
2	Senior Accountant	3–4 years
2	General Accountant	4–8 years
2	Department Manager	4–8 years
2	Chief Internal Auditor	4–8 years
2	Tax Accountant	4–8 years
2	Cost Accountant	4–8 years
3	Vice President	15+ years
3	Treasurer	15+ years
3	Controller	15+ years
3	Chief Financial Officer	15+ years

Salaries in Private/Management Accounting

Entry	$36,000 to $40,000	Medium-sized firm
Entry	$40,000 to $45,000	Large firm
2	$45,000 to $50,000	Medium-sized firm
2	$50,000 to $55,000	Medium-sized to large firm
2	$55,000 to $65,000	Large firm
3	$65,000 to $80,000	Medium-sized firm
3	$80,000 to $100,000+	Large firm

Salaries vary with the size of the firm and are higher for accountants whose jobs require extensive travel.

Qualifications

Personal   Reliability. Ability to work independently. Flexibility. Discipline.

Professional   Understanding of business and the marketplace. Willingness to increase knowledge of practical accounting techniques.

Where the Jobs Are

> Private corporations
>
> Consulting

Government

Level	Job Title	Experience Needed
Entry	Revenue Officer	Professional training
2	Accountant	1–3 years
2	Internal Auditor	1–3 years
3	Chief Internal Auditor	3–5 years
3	Chief Accountant	5–7 years

The goal of the accounting department of a typical government agency is to function within the budgetary constraints mandated by legislative action. The IRS is the largest employer of accountants in the United States.

Salaries in Government

Positions are comparable to salaries in private industry, and much of the work performed is the same. Salary rates are based on varying grade levels.

Qualifications

Personal   Reliability. Ability to work independently. Flexibility. Discipline.

Professional   Knowledge of standard accounting procedures. Ability to design accounting techniques. Interest in publishing work in professional journals.

Where the Jobs Are

Department of Agriculture

Department of Defense Audit Agencies

Department of Energy

Department of Health and Human Services

Department of the Air Force

Department of the Navy

Department of the Army

General Accounting Office

Department of the Treasury (includes the Internal Revenue Service)

Special Certifications

CIMA (Certificate in Management Accounting)   The CIMA exam is sponsored by the Institute of Management Accounting and tests decision-making capability and knowledge of business law, finance, and organization.

CIA (Certificate in Internal Auditing)   The CIA exam is sponsored by the Institute of Internal Auditors and tests the theory and practice of internal auditing. Both the CIMA and the CIA exams are open to graduating seniors, but work experience is required for certification. Multiple certification is permissible and encouraged.

CPA (Certificate in Public Accounting)   The advantages of holding the CPA are many, as it serves as tangible proof of your skill and your commitment to the profession. Public accounting firms, particularly the largest, often expect their accountants to receive certification as quickly as state law allows. Beyond the entry level, the CPA is often a requirement for advancement. Information on how to prepare for the CPA exam, as well as test dates, is available through CPA review courses.

Trade Publications

CPA Journal
New York Society of Certified Public Accountants
530 Fifth Avenue
New York, NY 10036

Government Accountant's Journal
Association of Government Accountants
2208 Mount Vernon Avenue
Alexandria, VA 22301

Journal of Accountancy
American Institute of Certified Public Accountants
1211 Avenue of the Americas
New York, NY 10036

Management Accounting
Official Magazine of the Institute of Management Accountants
Warren, Gorham, and Lamont, Inc.
10 Paragon Drive
Montvale, NY 07645

The Wall Street Journal
200 Liberty Street
New York, NY 10281

Accounting Today
P.O. Box 30468
Salt Lake City, UT 84130

CPAdirectory
CPAdirect Marketing, Inc.
2001 Grove Street
Wantagh, NY 11793

Professional Associations

American Institute of Certified Public Accountants
1211 Avenue of the Americas
New York, NY 10036-8775

American Society of Women Accountants
8405 Greensboro Drive
Suite 800
McLean, VA 22102

Association of Government Accountants
2208 Mount Vernon Avenue
Alexandria, VA 22301-1314

Institute of Internal Auditors
247 Maitland Avenue
Altamonte Springs, FL 32701-4201

National Society of Accountants
1010 North Fairfax Street
Alexandria, VA 22314

Business Administration

Level	Banking	Insurance	Finance	Human Resources
1. Entry ($33,000–$45,000) Management Trainee	Bank Officer Trainee Systems Trainee	Adjuster Trainee Claims Examiner Underwriter Trainee Actuarial Trainee Sales Trainee	Registered Representative Manager Trainee	Employment Recruiter Interviewer Human Resources Assistant Job Analyst
2. Mid-management/ specialists ($45,000–$70,000)	Assistant Loan Officer Loan Officer Department Manager Supervisor Systems Analyst Systems Consultant Senior Systems Consultant Branch Manager Loan Manager	Assistant Underwriter Underwriter Specialist Assistant Actuary Agent Actuary Senior Claims Examiner Senior Underwriter	Investment Banker Trader Purchasing Agent Research Analyst Trust Officer Financial Analyst Portfolio Manager Credit Manager	College Recruiter Training Manager Employment Manager Corporate Recruiter Personnel Manager Wage and Salary Administrator Benefits Coordinator Labor Relations Specialist Plant Safety Specialist EEO Coordinator
3. Management ($70,000–$150,000)	Manager Division Manager Vice President President	Underwriting Supervisor Office Manager Chief Actuary Regional Vice President Vice President	Treasurer/Controller Vice President President	Director of Human Resources Vice President of Human Resources

Level	Retailing	Advertising	Production	Distribution
1. Entry ($35,000–50,000) Management Trainee	Department Manager Store Manager Trainee Buyer Trainee Management Trainee	Assistant Media Planner Junior Copywriter Media Buyer Project Coordinator Account Executive Trainee	Expeditor Assistant Buyer Assistant Purchasing Agent Production Planner Assistant Quality Assurance Manager	See careers in Fashion and Retail Management.
2. Mid-management/ specialists ($50,000–$70,000)	Assistant Store Manager Sales Representative Display Coordinator Distribution Coordinator Merchandise Analyst Assistant Buyer	Copywriter Senior Copywriter Media Planner Media Director of Planning Project Director Research Account Executive Associate Research Director Account Executive Senior Account Executive Research Director Associate Media Director	Purchasing Agent Purchasing Manager Traffic Manager Inventory Manager Quality Assurance Manager Buyer	
3. Management ($70,000–$150,000)	Merchandise Manager Buyer Store Manager Operations Manager Vice President of Operations Sales Manager	Accounts Supervisor/ Manager Department Manager Copy Chief Creative Director Director of Media Advertising Research Director Project Director	Plant Manager Materials Manager Manufacturing Manager Regional Manager Operations Research Analyst Vice President of Production	

Banking

Level	Job Title	Experience Needed
Entry	Bank Officer Trainee	Professional training
Entry	Systems Trainee	Professional training
2	Assistant Loan Officer	1–2 years
2	Supervisor	1–2 years
2	Systems Analyst	2 years
2	Systems Consultant	3 years
2	Department Manager	3–5 years
2	Loan Officer	3–5 years
2	Branch Manager	3–5 years
2	Senior Systems Consultant	5 years
2	Loan Manager	5–6 years
3	Division Manager	6+ years
3	Manager	6+ years
3	Vice President	8–10 years
3	President	10+ years

Salaries in Banking

Entry	$33,000 to $45,000
2	$45,000 to $55,000
2	$55,000 to $70,000
3	$70,000 to $90,000
3	$90,000 to $150,00

Salaries are higher for those with 2- or 4-year college degrees.

Qualifications

Personal   Strong analytical skills. Strong negotiation skills. Strong interpersonal skills. Ability to work under pressure. Ability to work with figures.

Professional   Familiarity with business applications of software and hardware. Ability to analyze financial statements and do creative financial planning. Good business judgment.

Where the Jobs Are
   Credit lending
   Trusts
   Operations
   Systems

Insurance

Level	Job Title	Experience Needed
Entry	Adjuster Trainee	Professional training
Entry	Claims Examiner	Professional training
Entry	Underwriter Trainee	Professional training
Entry	Actuarial Trainee	Professional training
Entry	Sales Trainee*	Professional training
2	Assistant Underwriter	1–2 years
2	Assistant Actuary	1–2 years

Level	Job Title	Experience Needed
2	Underwriter Specialist	2–4 years
2	Agent	2–4 years
2	Actuary	3–5 years
2	Senior Underwriter	3–5 years
2	Senior Claims Examiner	3–5 years
3	Underwriting Supervisor	6+ years
3	Office Manager	5+ years
3	Chief Actuary	6+ years
3	Regional Vice President	6+ years
3	Vice President	8+ years

Salaries in Insurance
See Salaries in Banking.

*New sales workers earn about $3,000 per month during the first six months of training. Most sales workers are paid on commission. The size of the commission depends on the type and amount of insurance sold. Insurance sales workers generally pay their own automobile and travel expenses. Independent sales workers must also pay office rent, clerical salaries, and other operating expenses out of their own earnings.

Qualifications

Personal   Enthusiasm. Self-motivation. Attention to detail. Good analytical skills. Excellent communication skills. Good quantitative skills. Confidence.

Professional   Accurate thinking and writing skills. Ability to write concisely. Aptitude for computers. Ability to supervise.

Where the Jobs Are
- Home offices/headquarters
- Branch offices
- Independent agencies
- Private corporations
- Real estate

Finance

Level	Job Title	Experience Needed
Entry	Registered Representative*	Professional training
Entry	Manager Trainee	Professional training
2	Trader	1–2 years
2	Financial Analyst	2–3 years
2	Research Analyst	3–5 years
2	Investment Banker	3–5 years
2	Purchasing Agent	3–5 years
2	Portfolio Manager	5–6 years
2	Credit Manager	5–6 years
2	Trust Officer	6–8 years
3	Treasurer/Controller	6+ years
3	Vice President	8–12 years
3	President	12–15 years

Salaries in Finance
See Salaries in Banking.

*Trainees are usually paid a salary until they meet licensing and registration requirements. During training, sales workers earn $1,500 to $2,000 per month. After licensing, earnings depend on commission from sales of stocks, bonds, life insurance, or other securities.

Qualifications

Personal   Interest in economic trends. Ability to handle frequent rejection. Ability to work independently. Good grooming. Good communication skills.

Professional   State licensing and successful completion of exams prepared by securities exchanges or NASD (National Association of Securities Dealers, Inc.).

Where the Jobs Are
Financial institutions
Banks
Private corporations
Consulting firms
Government
Securities exchanges

Human Resources

Level	Job Title	Experience Needed
Entry	Interviewer	Professional training
Entry	Employment Recruiter	Professional training
Entry	Human Resources Assistant	Professional training
Entry	Job Analyst	Professional training
2	College Recruiter	1–3 years
2	Training Manager	2–4 years
2	Corporate Recruiter	3–5 years
2	Benefits Coordinator	1–3 years
2	Plant Safety Specialist	3–5 years
2	Equal Employment Opportunity Coordinator	1–3 years
2	Labor Relations Specialist	4–6 years
2	Wage and Salary Administrator	4–6 years
2	Employment Manager	4–6 years
2	Human Resources Manager	5–7 years
3	Director of Human Resources	5–7 years
3	Vice President of Human Resources	7–10 years

Salaries in Human Resources

Entry	$33,000 to $45,000
2	$45,000 to $55,000
2	$55,000 to $70,000
3	$70,000 to $85,000
3	$85,000 to $150,000

Qualifications

Personal   Excellent communication skills, especially listening skills. Ability to speak and write effectively. Ability to work under pressure.

Professional   Fair-mindedness. Good decision-making skills. Ability to enforce policies.

Where the Jobs Are
- Private corporations
- Education
- Government agencies
- Consulting firms
- Independent businesses

Retailing

See careers in Fashion and Retail Management.

Advertising

Level	Job Title	Experience Needed
Entry	Assistant Media Planner	Professional training
Entry	Media Buyer	Professional training
Entry	Junior Copywriter	Professional training
Entry	Project Coordinator	Professional training
Entry	Account Executive Trainee	Professional training
2	Copywriter	1–3 years
2	Account Executive	1–3 years
2	Research Account Executive	1–3 years
2	Media Planner	3–5 years
2	Associate Research Director	3–8 years
2	Senior Account Executive	5–8 years
2	Associate Media Director	5–7 years
2	Research Director	7–10 years
2	Senior Copywriter	7–10 years
2	Media Director of Planning	7–10 years
2	Project Director	7–10 years
3	Accounts Supervisor/Manager	10–13 years
3	Department Manager	10+ years
3	Copy Chief	10+ years
3	Creative Director	10+ years
3	Director of Media Advertising	10+ years
3	Research Director	10+ years

Salaries in Advertising

Entry	$35,000 to $50,000
2	$50,000 to $55,000
2	$55,000 to $60,000
2	$60,000 to $65,000

2	$65,000 to $70,000
3	$70,000 to $80,000
3	$80,000 to $85,000
3	$85,000 to $90,000
3	$90,000 to $150,000

Qualifications

Personal   Strong interpersonal skills. Ability to work with a team. Problem-solving mentality.

Professional   Good writing skills. Knowledge of the media. Sales ability. Negotiation skills.

Where the Jobs Are
Advertising agencies

Media

Private corporations

Consulting

Freelancing

Production

Level	Job Title	Experience Needed
Entry	Expeditor	Professional training
Entry	Assistant Buyer	Professional training
Entry	Assistant Purchasing Agent	Professional training
Entry	Production Planner	Professional training
Entry	Assistant Quality Assurance Manager	Professional training
2	Purchasing Agent	1–3 years
2	Purchasing Manager	3–5 years
2	Traffic Manager	2–4 years
2	Inventory Manager	2–4 years
2	Quality Assurance Manager	3–5 years
2	Buyer	4–6 years
3	Plant Manager	5–6 years
3	Materials Manager	5–6 years
3	Manufacturing Manager	5–6 years
3	Regional Manager	6–8 years
3	Operations Research Analyst	6–8 years
3	Vice President of Production	7–10 years

Salaries in Production
See Salaries in Banking.

Qualifications

Personal   Good organizational skills. Aptitude for figures. Ability to plan and make quick decisions. Flexibility.

Professional   Ability to interpret computer data. Ability to supervise and think ahead.

Where the Jobs Are
Manufacturing
Distribution
Private corporations

Distribution

See careers in Fashion and Retail Management.

Trade Publications

Advertising Age
Crain Communications, Inc.
711 Third Avenue
New York, NY 10017-4036

ADWeek
VNU Business Publications, Inc.
770 Broadway
New York, NY 10003-9595

ABA Banking Journal
Simmons Boardman Publishing
345 Hudson Street
12th Floor
New York, NY 10014

The Banker's Magazine
Warren, Gorham and Lamont, Inc.
395 Hudson Street
New York, NY 10158

Professional Associations

The Advertising Council Inc.
261 Madison Avenue,
11the Floor
New York, NY 10016

Advertising Research Foundation
432 Park Avenue, South
8th Floor
New York, NY 10016

The American Advertising Federation
1101 Vermont Avenue NW
Suite 500
Washington, DC 20005-6306

American Association of Advertising Agencies
405 Lexington Avenue
18th Floor
New York, NY 10174-1801

Association of National Advertisers
708 Third Avenue
New York, NY 10017-4270

Consumer Bankers Association
1000 Wilson Boulevard
Suite 2500
Arlington, VA 22209-3912

American Management Association
1601 Broadway
New York, NY 10019

Court Reporting and Related Careers

Level	Court Reporting	Hearing Reporting	Legislative Reporting	Conference Reporting	Freelance Reporting
1. Entry ($25,000–$32,000)	Court Reporter E-Reporter	Hearing Reporter	Legislative Reporter	Conference Reporter	Freelance Reporter
2. Mid-management/ specialists ($32,000–$60,000)	Legal Videographer Real-Time Court Reporter Voice Writer Paralegal Placement Director Paralegal Instructor	Research Assistant Proofreader Information Specialist Editor	Legal Assistant Legal Technician Senior Legal Assistant Paralegal Supervisor	Marketing Representative Sales Representative	Litigation Paralegal
3. Management ($60,000–$90,000)	Systems Programmer Lawyer	Program Director	Law Office Administrator Law Library Manager	Marketing Analyst	Consultant/Advisor

Court Reporting and Related Careers

Level	Job Title	Experience Needed
Entry	Court Reporter	Professional training
Entry	Hearing Reporter	Professional training
Entry	Legislative Reporter	Professional training
Entry	Conference Reporter	Professional training
Entry	E-Reporter	Professional training
Entry	Freelance Reporter	Professional training
2	Paralegal	2–4 years (with further education)
2	Legal Assistant	2–4 years
2	Legal Technician	2–4 years
2	Paralegal Instructor	2–4 years
2	Proofreader	2–4 years
2	Legal Videographer	2–4 years
2	Marketing Representative	2–4 years
2	Sales Representative	2–4 years
2	Paralegal Supervisor	4–6 years
2	Senior Legal Assistant	4–6 years
2	Real-Time Court Reporter	4–6 years

Level	Job Title	Experience Needed
2	Research Assistant	5–8 years
2	Voice Writer	5–8 years
2	Information Specialist	5–8 years
2	Litigation Paralegal	5–8 years
2	Placement Director	5–8 years
2	Editor	5–8 years
2	Systems Programmer	5–8 years
3	Law Office Administrator	8–10 years
3	Lawyer	8–10 years (with further education)
3	Law Library Manager	8–10 years
3	Program Director	8–10 years
3	Consultant/Adviser	8–10 years
3	Marketing Analyst	8–10 years

Salaries in Court Reporting and Related Careers

Entry	$25,000 to $28,000
Entry	$28,000 to $32,000
2	$32,000 to $40,000
2	$40,000 to $45,000
2	$45,000 to $60,000
3	$60,000 to $90,000

Qualifications

Personal   Strong concentration. Physical stamina. Manual dexterity. Detail oriented. Professional appearance. Ability to work under pressure.

Professional   Accurate thinking and spelling. Transcription skills. Familiarity with legal terminology. Excellent written and oral communication skills. Positive attitude. High energy level.

Where the Jobs Are

Courts

Legal firms/departments

Freelancing

Business and industry (meetings and conferences)

Conventions

Sales

Stockholders' meetings

(Also see Paralegal careers in Office Management and Support).

Trade Publication

American Bar Association Journal
321 North Clark Street
15th Floor
Chicago, IL 60651

Professional Associations

Association of Electronic Reporters and Transcribers
23812 Rock Circle
Bothell, WA 98021-8573

American Guild of Court Videographers
1628 East Third Street
Casper, WY 82601

National Court Reporters Association
8224 Old Courthouse Road
Vienna, VA 22182-3808

Criminal Justice

Level	Corrections	Forensic Science	Department of Homeland Security	Information Security
1. Entry ($30,000–$40,000)	Corrections Officer Parole Officer Juvenile Probation Officer Probation Officer	Crime Lab Technician	Border Patrol Agent Immigration Inspector	Computer Security Specialist Security Officer
2. Mid-management/ specialists ($40,000–$60,000)	Corrections Counselor Corrections Treatment Specialist Juvenile Justice Counselor Prerelease Program Corrections Counselor Prerelease Program Employment Counselor Prerelease Progam Halfway House Counselor Recreational Counselor Substance Abuse Specialist Vocational Counselor	Arson Specialist Ballistic Specialist Document Specialist Fingerprint Specialist Polygraph Specialist Serology Specialist	Adjudication Officer Deportation Officer Immigration Officer Inspector	Certified Information Systems Security Professional Cryptographer Homeland Security Specialist Information Security Analyst Phishing Attack Security Officer Security Access Manager Steganographer
3. Management ($60,000 to $120,000)	Caseworker Clinical Psychologist Warden		Criminal Investigator Detention Enforcement Officer Immigration Information Officer	Consultant for Internet Security Systems Information Security Engineer Legal Technology Specialist Network Defense Manager Network Security Manager

Level	Law Enforcement	Federal Bureau of Investigation (FBI) and Secret Service	Transportation Security Administration	Treasury Department/ Internal Revenue Service
1. Entry ($30,000–$40,000)	Private Private First Class Deputy Sheriff Police Officer Patrol Officer Traffic Officer Postal Inspector	Intelligence Support Clerk	Airport Security Officer Railroad Police Officer	Appeals Officer Computer Specialist/ Information Technology Contact Representative Security Officer
2. Mid-management/ specialists ($40,000–$60,000)	Park Ranger State Trooper Corporal Sergeant Detective Sheriff	Intelligence Support Analyst Secret Service Agent Intelligence Specialist FBI Special Agent	Air Safety Investigator Air Patrol Officer Shore Patrol Officer	IRS Agent IRS Internal Security Inspector Revenue Agent Revenue Officer Economist Engineer
3. Management ($60,000–$120,000)	Military Investigator Investigator Chief of Police Lieutenant Captain Colonel U.S. Capitol Police Officer U.S. Marshall	Secret Service Uniformed Officer Secret Service Agent	Federal Aviation Administrator Transportation Security Administrator	IRS Criminal Investigation Senior Revenue Officer Special Agent Tax Examiner Tax Law Specialist Tax Specialist

Level	U.S. Customs and Border Protection	Private Security
1. Entry ($25,000–$35,000)	Customs Aide Customs Inspector Customs Agent Document Examiner	Skip-Tracing Assistant Technician Trainee
2. Mid-management/specialists ($35,000–$55,000)	Customs Canine Enforcement Officer Customs Import Specialist Customs Patrol Officer Federal Food Inspector	Commercial Security Specialist Clerical or Office Embezzlement Investigator Criminal and Drug Investigator Customer Service Investigator Background Investigator Deadbeat Spouse Collections Investigator Identity and Social Security Identity Theft Investigator Industrial Security Specialist Institutional Security Specialist Insurance Fraud Investigator Insurance Investigation Specialist Integrity Shopping Service Investigator Internet and Web Hack Programmer Investigator Loss Prevention Specialist Medical Negligence Investigator Missing Persons Research Investigator Music and Video Piracy Investigator Nanny and Child Care Investigator Nursing Home Care Investigator Preemployment Check Specialist Protective Specialist

Criminal Justice (continued)

Level	U.S. Customs and Border Protection	Private Security
2. Mid-management/specialists ($35,000–$55,000)		Private Investigator Real Estate Fraud Investigator Retail and Cashier Fraud Investigator Sales Fraud Investigator Telemarketing and Collections Investigator Work-at-Home Scam Investigator
3. Management ($55,000–$75,000)	Consumer Product Safety Commission Investigator Customs Special Agent Customs Pilot	Administration/Manager Undercover Agent

Other criminal justice career areas are the Department of State, the Federal Emergency Management Agency, and the Department of Justice.

Corrections

Level	Job Title	Experience Needed
Entry	Corrections Officer	Professional training
Entry	Parole Officer	Professional training
Entry	Juvenile Probation Officer	Professional training
Entry	Probation Officer	Professional training
2	Corrections Counselor	2–4 years
2	Corrections Treatment Specialist	2–4 years
2	Juvenile Justice Counselor	2–4 years
2	Prerelease Program Corrections Counselor	4–6 years
2	Prerelease Program Employment Counselor	4–6 years
2	Prerelease Program Halfway House Counselor	4–6 years
2	Recreational Counselor	4–6 years
2	Substance Abuse Specialist	4–6 years
2	Vocational Counselor	4–6 years
3	Caseworker	6–8 years
3	Clinical Psychologist	6–8 years
3	Warden	6–8 years

Salaries in Corrections

Level	Salary
Entry	$30,000 to $35,000
Entry	$35,000 to $40,000
2	$40,000 to $45,000
2	$45,000 to $50,000
2	$50,000 to $60,000
3	$60,000 to $70,000
3	$70,000 to $80,000

Qualifications

Personal   Maturity. Adaptability. Good judgment. Good perception. Sobriety. Integrity. Empathy. Discipline. Good oral and written communication.

Professional   Knowledge of state regulations. Cultural awareness. Problem solving. Ethical behavior. Confidentiality.

Where the Jobs Are
  Correctional facilities
  Rehabilitation centers
  Group homes
  Courts

Forensic Science

Level	Job Title	Experience Needed
Entry	Crime Lab Technician	Professional training
2	Arson Specialist	2–4 years
2	Ballistic Specialist	2–4 years
2	Document Specialist	2–4 years
2	Fingerprint Specialist	2–4 years
2	Polygraph Specialist	4–6 years
2	Serology Specialist	4–6 years

Salaries in Forensic Science

Entry	$30,000 to $40,000
2	$40,000 to $45,000
2	$45,000 to $50,000
2	$50,000 to $60,000

Qualifications

Personal   Maturity. Adaptability. Emotional stability. Good judgment. Good perception. Integrity. Reliability. Sobriety.

Professional   Ethical behavior. Cultural awareness. Confidentiality. Knowledge to operate certain equipment.

Where the Jobs Are
  Crime labs
  Courts
  Federal and state agencies

Department of Homeland Security

Level	Job Title	Experience Needed
Entry	Border Patrol Agent	Professional training
Entry	Immigration Inspector	Professional training
2	Adjudication Officer	2–4 years
2	Deportation Officer	2–4 years
2	Immigration Officer	2–4 years
2	Inspector	2–4 years
3	Criminal Investigator	4–6 years
3	Detention Enforcement Officer	4–6 years
3	Immigration Information Officer	4–6 years

Salaries in Department of Homeland Security

Entry	$30,000 to $35,000
Entry	$35,000 to $40,000
2	$40,000 to $45,000
2	$45,000 to $50,000
2	$50,000 to $60,000
3	$60,000 to $70,000
3	$70,000 to $80,000

Qualifications

Personal   Maturity. Emotional stability. Physical stamina. Integrity. Sobriety. Good perception. Good judgment. Attention to detail.

Professional   Knowledge of state and federal law. Cultural awareness. Ethical behavior. Reliability. Problem solving. Bilingual.

Where the Jobs Are

Official U.S. ports of entry by land, sea, or air

Local and state offices of the U.S. Citizenship and Immigration Services

Offices identified as either District Offices, Sub Offices, Service Centers, and Asylum Offices by the U.S. National Benefits Centers operated by the federal government

Information Security

Level	Job Title	Experience Needed
Entry	Computer Security Specialist	Professional training
Entry	Security Officer	Professional training
2	Certified Information Systems Security Professional	2-4 years
2	Cryptographer	2-4 years
2	Homeland Security Specialist	2-4 years
2	Information Security Analyst	2-4 years
2	Phishing Attack Security Officer	2-4 years
2	Security Access Manager	2-4 years
2	Steganographer	2-4 years
3	Consultant for Internet Security Systems	4-6 years
3	Information Security Engineer	4-6 years
3	Legal Technology Specialist	4-6 years
3	Network Defense Manager	4-6 years
3	Network Security Manager	4-6 years

Salaries in Information Security

Entry	$30,000 to $35,000
Entry	$35,000 to $40,000
2	$40,000 to $50,000
2	$50,000 to $60,000
3	$60,000 to $70,000
3	$70,000 to $80,000

Qualifications

Personal   Patience. Persistence. Ability to work under pressure and meet deadlines. Ability to work with extreme accuracy. Integrity. Sobriety.

Professional   Problem solving. Ability to think logically. Capable of performing highly analytical work. Decision-making skills. Team worker.

Where the Jobs Are

IT Security Offices (divisions of IT departments in private businesses or government agencies)

Software development firms

Computer manufacturing firms

Information technology consulting firms

Law enforcement agencies

Law Enforcement

Level	Job Title	Experience Needed
Entry	Police Officer	Professional training
Entry	Parole Officer	Professional training
Entry	Private	Professional training
Entry	Private First Class	Professional training
Entry	Deputy Sheriff	Professional training
Entry	Traffic Officer	Professional training
Entry	Postal Inspector	Professional training
2	Park Ranger	2–4 years
2	State Trooper	2–4 years
2	Corporal	4–6 years
2	Sergeant	4–6 years
2	Detective	4–6 years
2	Sheriff	4–6 years
3	Military Investigator	6–8 years
3	Investigator	6–8 years
3	Chief of Police	8–10 years
3	Lieutenant	8–10 years
3	Captain	8–10 years
3	Colonel	8–10 years
3	U.S. Capitol Police Officer	8–10 years
3	U.S. Marshall	8–10 years

Salaries in Law Enforcement

Entry	$30,000 to $35,000
Entry	$35,000 to $40,000
2	$40,000 to $50,000
2	$50,000 to $60,000
3	$60,000 to $70,000
3	$70,000 to $80,000

Qualifications

Personal   Physical ability. Maturity. Good perception. Good judgment. Emotional stability. Integrity. Sobriety. Reliability. Discipline.

Professional   Leadership. Ethical behavior. Cultural awareness. Problem-solving. Confidentiality.

Where the Jobs Are
Police department
State crime lab
Registry of Motor Vehicles
State regulatory agencies
City and state municipalities
U.S. Military

Federal Bureau of Investigation (FBI) and Secret Service

Level	Job Title	Experience Needed
Entry	Intelligence Support Clerk	Professional training
2	Intelligence Support Analyst	2–4 years
2	Secret Service Agent	4–6 years
2	Intelligence Specialist	4–6 years
2	FBI Special Agent	4–6 years
3	Secret Service Uniformed Officer	6–8 years
3	Secret Service Agent	6–8 years

Salaries with the Federal Bureau of Investigation (FBI) and Secret Service

Entry	$35,000 to $45,000
2	$45,000 to $65,000
3	$65,000 to $85,000
3	$85,000 to $110,000

Qualifications

Personal   Maturity. Adaptability. Good written and oral communication skills. Good perception. Good judgment. Reliability. Integrity. Sobriety.

Professional   Knowledge of federal regulations. License to operate certain equipment and/or carry arms. Cultural awareness. Problem solving. Ethical behavior. Confidentiality.

Where the Jobs Are
Federal agencies
U.S. government

Transportation Security Administration

Level	Job Title	Experience Needed
Entry	Airport Security Officer	Professional training
Entry	Railroad Police Officer	Professional training
2	Air Safety Investigator	2–4 years
2	Air Patrol Officer	2–4 years
2	Shore Patrol Officer	6–8 years

Level	Job Title	Experience Needed
3	Federal Aviation Administrator	6–8 years
3	Transportation Security Administrator	6–8 years

Salaries in Transportation Security Administration

Entry	$30,000 to $35,000
Entry	$35,000 to $40,000
2	$40,000 to $45,000
2	$45,000 to $50,000
2	$55,000 to $60,000
3	$60,000 to $80,000
3	$80,000 to $100,000

Qualifications

Personal   Maturity. Good perception. Good judgment. Emotional stability. Integrity. Reliability. Sobriety. Physical agility. Good written and verbal communication skills.

Professional   Leadership. Confidentiality. Ethical behavior. Cultural awareness. Problem solving. Knowledge of transportation laws and regulations.

Where the Jobs Are

Airports and aviation firms

Railways

Transportation firms

Seaports

Government offices of the Transportation Security Administration

Treasury Department/Internal Revenue Service

Level	Job Title	Experience Needed
Entry	Appeals Officer	Professional training
Entry	Computer Specialist/Information Technology	Professional training
Entry	Contact Representative	Professional training
Entry	Security Officer	Professional training
2	IRS Agent	4–6 years
2	IRS Internal Security Inspector	4–6 years
2	Revenue Agent	4–6 years
2	Revenue Officer	6–8 years
2	Economist	6–8 years
2	Engineer	6–8 years
3	IRS Criminal Investigator	6–8 years
3	Senior Revenue Officer	6–8 years
3	Special Agent	8–10 years
3	Tax Examiner	8–10 years
3	Tax Law Specialist	8–10 years
3	Tax Specialist	8–10 years

Salaries in the Treasury Department/Internal Revenue Service

Entry	$30,000 to $40,000
2	$40,000 to $45,000

2	$45,000 to $50,000
2	$50,000 to $60,000
3	$60,000 to $75,000
3	$75,000 to $85,000
3	$85,000 to $100,000
3	$100,000 to 120,000

Qualifications

Personal   Accuracy and attention to detail. Flexibility. Patience. Excellent written and oral communication skills. Discipline. Ability to work under pressure and meet deadlines. Integrity. Sobriety. Confidentiality.

Professional   Ethical behavior. Exceptional math skills. Knowledge of U.S. Treasury Department regulations and tax laws.

Where the Jobs Are

Internal Revenue Service

U.S. Customs and Border Protection

Level	Job Title	Experience Needed
Entry	Customs Aide	Professional training
Entry	Customs Inspector	Professional training
Entry	Customs Agent	Professional training
Entry	Document Examiner	Professional training
2	Customs Canine Enforcement Officer	2–4 years
2	Customs Import Specialist	2–4 years
2	Customs Patrol Officer	4–6 years
2	Federal Food Inspector	4–6 years
3	Consumer Product Safety Commission Investigator	6–8 years
3	Customs Special Agent	6–8 years
3	Customs Pilot	6–8 years

Salaries in U.S. Customs and Border Protection

Entry	$30,000 to $35,000
Entry	$35,000 to $40,000
2	$40,000 to $50,000
2	$50,000 to $60,000
2	$60,000 to $70,000
2	$70,000 to $75,000
3	$75,000 to $80,000
3	$80,000 to $85,000
3	$85,000 to $100,000

Qualifications

Personal   Maturity. Adaptability. Good written and oral communication. Perception. Reliability. Integrity. Sobriety.

Professional   Knowledge of federal regulations. Cultural awareness. Ethical behavior. Confidentiality.

Where the Jobs Are

    U.S. Customs Offices

    Airports

    Seaports

    Transportation departments

    Import and export businesses

Private Security

Level	Job Title	Experience Needed
Entry	Skip Tracing Assistant	Professional training
Entry	Technician	Professional training
Entry	Trainee	Professional training
2	Commercial Security Specialist	2–4 years
2	Clerical or Office Embezzlement Investigator	2–4 years
2	Criminal and Drug Investigator	2–4 years
2	Customer Service Investigator	2–4 years
2	Background Investigator	2–4 years
2	Deadbeat Spouse Collections Investigator	2–4 years
2	Identity and Social Security Identity Theft Investigator	2–4 years
2	Industrial Security Specialist	2–4 years
2	Institutional Security Specialist	2–4 years
2	Insurance Fraud Investigator	2–4 years
2	Insurance Investigation Specialist	2–4 years
2	Integrity Shopping Service Investigator	2–4 years
2	Internet and Web Hack Programmer Investigator	2–6 years
2	Loss Prevention Specialist	2–6 years
2	Medical Negligence Investigator	2–6 years
2	Missing Persons Research Investigator	2–6 years
2	Music and Video Piracy Investigator	2–6 years
2	Nanny and Childcare Investigator	2–6 years
2	Nursing Home Care Investigator	2–6 years
2	Preemployment Check Specialist	6–8 years
2	Protective Specialist	6–8 years
2	Private Investigator	6–8 years
2	Real Estate Fraud Investigator	6–8 years
2	Retail and Cashier Fraud Investigator	6–8 years
2	Sales Fraud Investigator	6–8 years
2	Telemarketing and Collections Investigator	6–8 years
2	Work-at-Home Scam Investigator	6–8 years
3	Administrator/Manager	8–10 years
3	Undercover Agent	8–10 years

Salaries in Private Security

Entry	$25,000 to $30,000
Entry	$30,000 to $35,000
Entry	$35,000 to $45,000
2	$45,000 to $50,000
2	$50,000 to $55,000
2	$55,000 to $60,000
2	$60,000 to $65,000
3	$65,000 to $70,000
3	$70,000 to $75,000+

Qualifications

Personal   Detail-oriented. Maturity. Good judgment. Good decision-making skills. Ability to work under pressure and meet deadlines. Good written and oral skills. Emotional stability. Integrity. Physical agility.

Professional   Ethical behavior. Problem solving. Cultural awareness. Knowledge of laws and regulations pertaining to the private securities industry. Confidentiality.

Where the Jobs Are

  Insurance

  Retail

  Banking

  Manufacturing

  Real estate

  Hotel and consulting firms

  Assisted living corporations

  Law offices

  Private security firms

  Federal courts

  Government agencies

  Police departments

  Crime labs

Trade Publications

American Bar Association Journal
321 North Clark Street
15th Floor
Chicago, IL 60610

Corrections Today
Questia Media, Inc.
24 East Greenway Plaza
Suite 1000A
Houston, TX 77046

FBI Law Enforcement Bulletin
Federal Bureau of Investigation
935 Pennsylvania Avenue, NW
Washington, DC 20535-0001

Law Enforcement News
John Jay College of Criminal Justice
899 10th Avenue
New York, NY 10019

Professional Associations

International Association of Chiefs of Police
315 North Washington Street
Alexandria, VA 22314

American Society of Criminology
1314 Kinnear Road
Suite 212
Columbus, OH 43212-1156

American Criminal Justice Association
3149 Clairidge Way
Sacramento, CA 95821

National Council on Crime and Delinquency
1970 Broadway
Suite 500
Oakland, CA 94612

National Criminal Justice Association
720 Seventh Street NW
Third Floor
Washington, DC 20001-3716

Fashion and Retail Management

Level	Management	Buying	Distribution	Visual Merchandising and Design	Sales
1. Entry ($35,000–$45,000)	Manager Trainee Department Manager Assistant Store Manager Customer Service Representative	Buyer Trainee	Merchandise Planner	Window Trimmer Display Coordinator	Sales Representative
2. Mid-management/ specialists ($45,000–$65,000)	Area Manager Group Manager Divisional Manager Personnel Assistant Training Specialist Credit Manager	Junior Buyer Merchandise Analyst Fashion Coordinator	Administrative Analyst Planner MIS Specialist Coordinator of Scheduling Traffic Manager Production Coordinator Inventory Coordinator Transportation Specialist	Display Director Freelancer Fashion Writer Design Assistant (with further education) Fashion Display Specialist	Sales Manager District Sales Manager

Fashion and Retail Management (continued)

Level	Management	Buying	Distribution	Visual Merchandising and Design	Sales
3. Management ($65,000– $125,000)	Store Manager Human Resources Manager Operations Manager Director of Training Director of Human Resources Vice President of Human Resources Vice President of Operations	Buyer Merchandise Manager Vice President of Merchandising	MIS Director Transportation Manager Administrative Manager Inventory Control Manager Distribution Manager Warehousing/ Operations Manager Vice President of Operations	Consultant Fashion Designer (with further education)	Regional Sales Manager Vice President of Sales Vice President of Marketing

Management

Level	Job Title	Experience Needed
Entry	Manager Trainee	Professional training
Entry	Department Manager	Professional training
Entry	Assistant Store Manager	Professional training
Entry	Customer Service Representative	Professional training
2	Area Manager	1–3 years
2	Group Manager	2–4 years
2	Divisional Manager	3–5 years
2	Personnel Assistant	3–5 years
2	Training Specialist	3–5 years
2	Credit Manager	5–6 years
3	Human Resources Manager	6–8 years
3	Operations Manager	1–10 years
3	Store Manager	3–8 years
3	Director of Training	5–7 years
3	Director of Human Resources	7–9 years
3	Vice President of Operations	9+ years
3	Vice President of Human Resources	9+ years

Salaries vary greatly with the size and type of retail operation.

Salaries in Management

Entry	$35,000 to $45,000
2	$45,000 to $65,000
3	$65,000 to $80,000
3	$80,000 to $100,000

Qualifications

Personal   Enthusiasm. Positive attitude. Ability to learn quickly. Flexibility. Willingness to work weekends, nights, and holidays. Willingness to relocate. Diplomacy.

Professional Demonstrated leadership ability. Aptitude for dealing with figures, finances, inventories, and quotas. Team worker.

Where the Jobs Are

    Department stores

    Specialty stores

    Bookstores

    Grocery stores/supermarkets

    Boutiques

    Computer sales centers

    Government surplus organizations

Buying

Level	Job Title	Experience Needed
Entry	Buyer Trainee	Professional training
2	Junior Buyer	1–3 years
2	Merchandise Analyst	3–5 years
2	Fashion Coordinator	1–3 years
3	Buyer	5–7 years
3	Merchandise Manager	5–7 years
3	Vice President of Merchandising	7–10 years

Salaries in Buying

Entry	$35,000 to $45,000
2	$45,000 to $55,000
2	$55,000 to $65,000
3	$65,000 to $80,000
3	$80,000 to $100,000

Salaries vary greatly depending on the size and type of retail operation.

Qualifications

Personal Ability to make quick decisions. Ability to work at a fast pace. Ability to conceptualize. Good written and oral communication. Creativity. Risk taker. Negotiation skills. Willingness to travel extensively.

Professional Product knowledge. Aptitude for dealing with figures, finances, inventories, and quotas. Marketing and sales skills.

Where the Jobs Are

    Department stores

    Specialty stores buying offices

    Resident buying offices

Distribution

Level	Job Title	Experience Needed
Entry	Merchandise Planner	Professional training
2	Inventory Coordinator	1–2 years
2	Production Coordinator	1–2 years

Level	Job Title	Experience Needed
2	Traffic Manager	2–4 years
2	Transportation Specialist	2–4 years
2	Administrative Analyst/Planner	3–5 years
2	Coordinator of Scheduling	3–5 years
2	MIS Specialist	3–5 years
3	Distribution Manager	4–6 years
3	Transportation Manager	4–6 years
3	Administrative Manager	4–6 years
3	Inventory Control Manager	4–6 years
3	Warehousing/Operations Manager	4–6 years
3	MIS Director	6–10 years
3	Vice President of Operations	6–10 years

Salaries in Distribution

Entry	$38,000 to $45,000
2	$45,000 to $50,000
2	$50,000 to $55,000
2	$55,000 to $65,000
3	$65,000 to $75,000
3	$75,000 to $85,000
3	$85,000 to $100,000

Qualifications

Personal   Ability to write and speak effectively. Patience. Listening skills. Ability to get along with people. Attention to detail. Organizational skills. Initiative. Good decision-making skills.

Professional   Familiarity with computers. Ability to plan and supervise. Aptitude for figures, finances, inventories, and quotas.

Where the Jobs Are

Distribution centers

Manufacturing firms

Carriers

Public warehouses

Material handling equipment manufacturers and dealers

Consulting firms

Education

Print media

Communications

Government

Computer service organizations

Visual Merchandising and Design

Level	Job Title	Experience Needed
Entry	Window Trimmer	Professional training
Entry	Display Coordinator	Professional training
2	Fashion Display Specialist	1–3 years
2	Display Director	3–5 years
2	Freelancer	2–5 years
2	Fashion Writer	2–5 years
2	Design Assistant (with further education)	2–5 years
3	Consultant	5–7 years
3	Fashion Designer (with further education)	5–7 years

Salaries in Visual Merchandising

Entry	$35,000 to $40,000
Entry	$40,000 to $45,000
2	$45,000 to $55,000
2	$55,000 to $65,000
3	$65,000 to $75,000
3	$75,000 to $90,000
3	$90,000 to $125,000

Qualifications

Personal   Ability to conceptualize. High energy level. Ability to make quick decisions. Ability to work under pressure.

Professional   Ability to work with budget restrictions. Willingness to travel. Willingness to work long hours, including nights, weekends, and holidays. Familiarity with current trends and events.

Where the Jobs Are

> Manufacturers' showrooms
> Design houses
> Retail stores
> Advertising agencies
> Magazines
> Consulting
> Apparel manufacturers

Sales

Level	Job Title	Experience Needed
Entry	Sales Representative	Professional training
2	Sales Manager	2–5 years
2	District Sales Manager	4–6 years
3	Regional Sales Manager	5–8 years
3	Vice President of Sales	7–10 years
3	Vice President of Marketing	7–10 years

Salaries in Sales
See Salaries in Marketing.

Qualifications

Personal   Positive attitude. Enthusiasm. High energy level. Ability to take rejection. Ability to work independently. Self-motivation. Negotiation skills. Confidence. Excellent communication skills.

Professional   Product knowledge. Perception of customer needs. Willingness to learn. Diplomacy. Good grooming.

Where the Jobs Are
- Clothing manufacturers
- Design houses
- Apparel manufacturers
- Resident buying offices
- Computer manufacturers

Trade Publications

Advertising Age
Crain Communications, Inc.
711 Third Avenue
New York, NY 10017-4036

Chain Store Age
425 Park Avenue
New York, NY 10022

Journal of Retailing
Babson College
Babson Park, MA 02457

STORES Magazine
325 Seventh Street NW 1100
Washington, DC 20004

Women's Wear Daily
7 West 34th Street
New York, NY 10001

Professional Associations

American Marketing Association
311 South Wacker Drive
Suite 5800
Chicago, IL 60606

National Council of Chain Restaurants
325 Seventh Street NW 1100
Washington, DC 20004

National Retail Federation
325 Seventh Street NW 1100
Washington, DC 20004

Retail Advertising and Marketing Association
325 Seventh Street NW 1100
Washington, DC 20004

Financial Services

Level	Asset Management	Commercial Banking	Corporate Finance	Investment Banking	Securities Sales and Trading
1. Entry ($33,000–$45,000)	Stockbroker Assistant	Credit Analyst	Bookkeeping Manager Credit Analyst	Stockbroker	Securities and Sales Representative Broker
2. Mid-management/ specialists ($45,000–$90,000)	Stockbroker Sell-Side Research Analyst Private Client Services Private Banker Portfolio Banker	Branch Manager Loan Officer	Accounts Payable Manager Cash Manager Corporate Accountant Financial Analyst Internal Auditor	Stock Trader Investment Banking Researcher Investment Banking Associate Investment Banking Analyst	Senior Sales Representative Branch Manager
3. Management ($90,000–$200,000)	Fund Accountant Financial Advisor Buy-Side Research Analyst Asset Manager	Trust Officer Private Asset Manager	Chief Financial Officer Controller/Finance Director Treasurer	Investment Banker Institutional Researcher Corporate Finance Manager	Desk Trader Floor Trader

Asset Management

Level	Job Title	Experience Needed
Entry	Stockbroker Assistant	Professional training
2	Stockbroker	2–4 years
2	Sell-Side Research Analyst	2–4 years
2	Private Client Services	3–5 years
2	Private Banker	5–7 years
2	Portfolio Banker	5–7 years
3	Fund Accountant	5–7 years
3	Financial Advisor	5–7 years
3	Buy-Side Research Analyst	8–10 years
3	Asset Manager	8–10 years

Salaries in Asset Management

Entry	$33,000 to $40,000
Entry	$40,000 to $45,000
2	$45,000 to $55,000
2	$55,000 to $70,000
2	$70,000 to $90,000
3	$90,000 to $120,000
3	$120,000 to $160,000
3	$160,000 to $200,000

Qualifications

Personal   Interest in economic trends. Ability to handle frequent rejection. Ability to work independently. Professional appearance. Excellent written and oral communication skills. Ability to make complex decisions quickly.

Professional   Certifications. Understanding of the marketplace. Familiarity with industry terminology and practices.

Where the Jobs Are
- Financial institutions
- Banks
- Private corporations
- Consulting firms
- Government
- Retail brokerage firms
- Securities exchanges

Commercial Banking

Level	Job Title	Experience Needed
Entry	Credit Analyst	Professional training
2	Branch Manager	3–5 years
2	Loan Officer	3–5 years
3	Trust Officer	5–8 years
3	Private Asset Manager	6–10 years

Salaries in Commercial Banking

Entry	$33,000 to $45,000
2	$45,000 to $60,000
2	$60,000 to $75,000
2	$75,000 to $90,000
3	$90,000 to $100,000
3	$100,000 to $150,000

Qualifications

Personal   Enthusiasm. Self-motivation. Attention to detail. Good analytical skills. Excellent communication skills. Good quantitative skills. Confidence.

Professional   Accurate thinking and writing skills. Excellent planning and organizational skills. Computer skills. Ability to lead and supervise.

Where the Jobs Are
- Home offices/headquarters
- Branch offices
- Independent agencies
- Private corporations
- Real estate

Corporate Finance

Level	Job Title	Experience Needed
Entry	Bookkeeping Manager	Professional training
Entry	Credit Analyst	Professional training

Level	Job Title	Experience Needed
2	Accounts Payable Manager	2–4 years
2	Cash Manager	2–4 years
2	Corporate Accountant	5–7 years
2	Financial Analyst	5–7 years
2	Internal Auditor	5–7 years
3	Chief Financial Officer	8–10 years
3	Controller/Finance Director	8–10 years
3	Treasurer	8–10 years

Salaries in Corporate Finance

Entry	$33,000 to $40,000
2	$40,000 to $65,000
2	$50,000 to $80,000
2	$80,000 to $90,000
3	$90,000 to $100,000
3	$100,000 to $150,000
3	$150,000 to $200,000

Qualifications

Personal   Interest in economic trends. Attention to detail. Accurate thinking skills. Ability to work independently. Professional appearance. Excellent oral and written skills.

Professional   Computer skills. Knowledge of current accounting principles and practices.

Where the Jobs Are
- Financial institutions
- Banks
- Private business corporations
- Small business firms
- Consulting firms

Investment Banking

Level	Job Title	Experience Needed
Entry	Stockbroker	Professional training
2	Stock Trader	2–4 years
2	Investment Banking Researcher	2–4 years
2	Investment Banking Associate	2–4 years
2	Investment Banking Analyst	2–4 years
3	Investment Banker	5–7 years
3	Institutional Researcher	5–7 years
3	Corporate Finance Manager	8–10 years

Salaries in Investment Banking

Entry	$33,000 to $45,000
2	$45,000 to $60,000
2	$60,000 to $80,000
3	$80,000 to $100,000
3	$100,000 to $150,000

Qualifications

Personal Interest in economic trends. Strong oral and written communication skills. Strong decision-making skills. Good judgment. Professional appearance.

Professional Knowledge of current industry trends and practices. Excellent quantitative skills. Computer skills.

Where the Jobs Are

- Financial institutions
- Banks
- Private corporations
- Consulting firms
- Government
- Securities exchanges

Securities Sales and Trading

Level	Job Title	Experience Needed
Entry	Securities Sales Representative	Professional training
Entry	Broker	Professional training
2	Senior Sales Representative	2–4 years
2	Branch Manager	4–6 years
3	Desk Trader	6–8 years
3	Floor Trader	8–10 years

Salaries in Securities Sales and Trading

Entry	$33,000 to $40,000
Entry	$40,000 to $45,000
2	$45,000 to $65,000
2	$65,000 to $90,000
3	$90,000 to $100,000
3	$100,000+

Qualifications

Personal Ability to persuade and influence. Excellent oral and written communication skills. Professional appearance. Ability to make complex decisions quickly.

Professional Product knowledge. Computer skills. Selling skills. Negotiation skills.

Where the Jobs Are

    Financial institutions

    Banks

    Private corporations

    Consulting firms

    Securities exchanges

    Stock markets

Trade Publications

Business Finance Magazine
P.O. Box 3438
Loveland, CO 80539

Financial Planning
Mondo Code LLC
P.O. Box 1288
Boulder, CO 80306

Global Finance
411 Fifth Avenue
Seventh Floor
New York, NY 10016

National Tax Institute, Inc.
87 Terrace Hall Avenue
Burlington, MA 01803

Wall Street Journal Online
4300 North Route 1
South Brunswick, NJ 08852

Professional Associations

American Association of Finance and Accounting
225 West 34th Street
Suite 1800
New York, NY 10122

American Bankers Association
1120 Connecticut Avenue NW
Washington, DC 20036

American Finance Association
Haas School of Business
University of California
Berkeley, CA 94729-1900

Association of Financial Professionals
4520 East West Highway
Suite 750
Bethesda, MD 20814

National Association of Personal Financial Advisors
3250 North Arlington Heights Road
Suite 109
Arlington Heights, IL 60004

Healthcare

Level	Dentistry	Education	Emergency Medical Services
1. Entry ($30,000–$45,000)	Dental Lab Technician Dental Assistant	Instructor	Medical Transcriptionist
2. Mid-management/ specialists ($45,000–$65,000)	Claims Examiner Claims Representative Clinical Dental Assistant Administrative Dental Assistant Research Assistant	Academic Department Head Medical Librarian	Medical Assistant Medical Records and Health Information Technician Physician's Assistant Emergency Medical Technician (EMT) Paramedic
3. Management ($65,000–$142,000)	Dental Hygienist (with further education) Office Manager Research Analyst Dentist (with further education)	School Director Administrator/Educator	Medical and Health Services Manager

Level	Medical Offices/Labs	Nursing	Pharmacy
1. Entry ($30,000–$45,000)	Medical Transcriptionist Medical Billing Clerk Medical Coding Clerk	Nurse's Assistant	Pharmacy Aide
2. Mid-management/ specialists ($45,000–$65,000)	Medical Assistant Cardiovascular Technician Surgical Technician Physician's Assistant Phlebotomist Lab Technician Claims Examiner Claims Representative Clinical Medical Assistant Administrative Medical Office Assistant	Emergency Room (ER) Nurse Teaching Nurse Corporate Nurse Visiting Nurse Licensed Practical Nurse (LPN) Licensed Vocational Nurse (LVN) Head Nurse School Nurse Private Nurse Operating Room (OR) Nurse Long-Term Care Nurse Certified Registered Nurse Registered Nurse Nurse	Pharmacy Technician
3. Management ($65,000–$130,000)	Office Manager Lab Manager Health Care Administrator Medical Records Administrator	Nurse Anesthesiologist Administrator of Healthcare Services Vice President of Healthcare Administration	Pharmacist

Level	Radiology	Marketing and Sales	Therapy Services
1. Entry ($35,000–$45,000)	Cardiovascular Technician	Sales Representative Account Representative	Physical Therapist Assistant Occupational Therapist Assistant Massage Therapist
2. Mid-management/ specialists ($45,000–$80,000)	Cardiovascular Technologist Diagnostic Technologist Nuclear Medicine Technologist	Sales Manager Account Manager	Occupational Physical Therapist Recreational Physical Therapist

Level	Radiology	Marketing and Sales	Therapy Services
	Radiologic Technologist		Respiratory Physical Therapist Speech–Language Therapist
3. Management ($80,000–$250,000)	Radiologist (with further education)	Director of Marketing and Sales	Physical Therapist

Dentistry

Level	Job Title	Experience Needed
Entry	Dental Lab Technician	Professional training
Entry	Dental Assistant	Professional training
2	Claims Examiner	1–2 years
2	Claims Representative	1–2 years
2	Clinical Dental Assistant	2–4 years
2	Administrative Dental Assistant	2–4 years
2	Research Assistant	3–5 years
3	Dental Hygienist (with further education)	2–4 years
3	Office Manager	3–5 years
3	Research Analyst	7–10 years
3	Dentist (with further education)	7–10 years

Salaries in Dentistry

Entry	$30,000 to $35,000
Entry	$35,000 to $45,000
2	$45,000 to $50,000
2	$50,000 to $55,000
2	$55,000 to $60,000
2	$60,000 to $65,000
3	$65,000 to $80,000
3	$80,000 to $100,000
3	$100,000 to $142,000

Qualifications

Personal   Patience. Attention to detail. Empathy. Caring. Good patient relations. Good judgment. Ability to make complex decisions. Ethical behavior.

Professional   Technical knowledge and skill. Awareness of industry regulations and standards. Awareness of current trends and new technologies. Computer skills.

Where the Jobs Are

Private practices

Hospitals

Health maintenance organizations

State and local public health departments

Government agencies

Education

Level	Job Title	Experience Needed
Entry	Instructor	Professional training
2	Academic Department Head	2–5 years
2	Medical Librarian	2–5 years
3	School Director	5–10 years
3	Administrator/Educator	8–10 years

Salaries in Education

Entry	$30,000 to $45,000
2	$45,000 to $65,000
3	$65,000 to $80,000+

Qualifications

Personal   Positive attitude. High energy level. Strong written and oral skills. Strong planning and organization skills.

Professional   Mastery of subject matter. Strong presentation and facilitation skills. Ability to explain complex concepts. Ability to motivate others.

Where the Jobs Are

Colleges and universities

Nursing schools

Technical career schools

Emergency Medical Services

Level	Job Title	Experience Needed
Entry	Medical Transcriptionist	Professional training
2	Medical Assistant	1–4 years
2	Medical Records and Health Information Technician	2–4 years
2	Physician's Assistant	3–6 years
2	Emergency Medical Technician (EMT)	3–6 years
2	Paramedic	5–7 years
3	Medical and Health Services Managers	7–10 years

Salaries in Emergency Medical Services

Entry	$30,000 to $45,000
2	$45,000 to $50,000
2	$50,000 to $65,000
3	$65,000 to $80,000+

Qualifications

Personal   Reliability. Flexibility. Emotional stability. Physical and mental strength. Empathy. Caring. Ability to make complex decisions. Ethical behavior. Multilingual skills.

Professional   Technical knowledge. Certification. Awareness of policies and laws in the healthcare field.

Where the Jobs Are
- Physicians' group practices
- Physicians' private practices
- Clinics
- Freestanding emergency centers
- Hospitals
- Nursing homes

Medical Offices/Labs

Level	Job Title	Experience Needed
Entry	Medical Transcriptionist	Professional training
Entry	Medical Billing Clerk	Professional training
Entry	Medical Coding Clerk	Professional training
2	Medical Assistant	Professional training
2	Cardiovascular Technician	1–3 years
2	Surgical Technician	1–3 years
2	Physician's Assistant	1–3 years
2	Phlebotomist	1–3 years
2	Lab Technician	1–3 years
2	Claims Examiner	2–4 years
2	Claims Representative	2–4 years
2	Clinical Medical Assistant	3–5 years
2	Administrative Medical Office Assistant	3–5 years
3	Office Manager	5–7 years
3	Lab Manager	5–7 years
3	Healthcare Administrator	7–10 years
3	Medical Records Administrator	7–10 years

Salaries in Medical Offices/Labs

Entry	$30,000 to $35,000
Entry	$35,000 to $45,000
2	$45,000 to $50,000
2	$50,000 to $55,000
2	$55,000 to $60,000
2	$60,000 to $65,000
3	$65,000 to $75,000
3	$75,000 to $85,000
3	$85,000 to $100,000+

Qualifications

Personal   Positive attitude. Empathy. Caring. Ethical behavior. Detail oriented. Good listening skills.

Professional   Technical knowledge. Certification. Budget skills. Computer skills. Time management skills.

Where the Jobs Are

Physicians' group practices

Physicians' private practices

Clinics

Freestanding emergency centers

Hospitals

Nursing homes

Health care centers

Rehabilitation centers

Health maintenance organizations

Medical supply companies

Pharmaceutical houses

Nursing

Level	Job Title	Experience Needed
Entry	Nurse's Assistant	Professional training
2	Emergency Room Nurse	2–4 years
2	Teaching Nurse	2–4 years
2	Corporate Nurse	2–4 years
2	Visiting Nurse	2–4 years
2	LPN-Licensed Practical Nurse	2–4 years
2	LVN-Licensed Vocational Nurse	2–4 years
2	Head Nurse	2–4 years
2	School Nurse	2–4 years
2	Private Nurse	3–5 years
2	Operating Room Nurse	3–5 years
2	Long-Term Care Nurse	3–5 years
3	Registered Nurse	5–7 years
3	Certified Registered Nurse	5–7 years
3	Nurse Anesthesiologist	5–7 years
3	Administrator of Healthcare Services	7–10 years
3	Vice President of Healthcare Administration	7–10 years

Salaries in Nursing

Entry	$40,000 to $45,000
2	$45,000 to $50,000
2	$50,000 to $55,000
2	$55,000 to $60,000
2	$60,000 to $65,000
3	$65,000 to $75,000
3	$75,000 to $80,000
3	$80,000 to $100,000+

Qualifications

Personal   Caring. Empathy. Sense of responsibility. Detail oriented. Emotional stability.

Professional   Strong leadership skills. Technical knowledge. Awareness of current issues in medical field. Awareness of legal issues in the medical field. Ability to make complex, critical decisions.

Where the Jobs Are
- Emergency rooms
- Home health care
- Hospitals
- Health maintenance organizations
- Schools
- Long-term care facilities
- Military
- Staffing firms

Pharmacy

Level	Job Title	Experience Needed
Entry	Pharmacy Aide	Professional training
2	Pharmacy Technician	2–5 years
3	Pharmacist	3–7 years

Salaries in Pharmacy

Entry	$35,000 to $45,000
2	$45,000 to $65,000
3	$65,000 to $80,000
3	$80,000 to $100,000
3	$100,000 to $130,000

Qualifications

Personal   Detail oriented. Ability to assess customers' needs and make appropriate recommendations. Good judgment. Ethical behavior.

Professional   Product knowledge. Knowledge of medical terminology. Knowledge of current trends in the medical field. Knowledge of and commitment to professional standards.

Where the Jobs Are
- Consulting practices
- Freestanding pharmacies
- Managed care facilities
- Hospitals
- Retail drug stores
- Colleges and universities

Radiology

Level	Job Title	Experience Needed
Entry	Cardiovascular Technician	1-4 years
2	Cardiovascular Technologist	1–4 years
2	Diagnostic Technologist	2–4 years
2	Nuclear Medicine Technologist	4–7 years
2	Radiologic Technologist	5–8 years
3	Radiologist (with further education)	7–10 years

Salaries in Radiology

2	$40,000 to $45,000
2	$45,000 to $65,000
2	$65,000 to $80,000
2	$65,000 to $80,000+
3	$150,000 to $250,000+

Qualifications

Personal   Detail oriented. Ability to communicate complex issues. Emotional stability. Ethical behavior. Caring. Empathy.

Professional   Technical skill. Knowledge of and commitment to professional standards.

Where the Jobs Are

Physicians' group practices

Physicians' private practices

Hospitals

Healthcare organizations

Colleges and universities

Laboratories

Clinics

Research firms

Marketing and Sales

Level	Job Title	Experience Needed
Entry	Sales Representative	Professional training
Entry	Account Representative	Professional training
2	Sales Manager	2–4 years
2	Account Manager	3–5 years
3	Director of Marketing and Sales	5–10 years

Salaries in Marketing and Sales

Entry	$40,000 to $45,000
Entry	$45,000 to $50,000
2	$50,000 to $60,000
2	$60,000 to $70,000
3	$70,000 to $80,000
3	$80,000 to $110,000

Qualifications

Personal   Strong oral communication skills. Confidence. Enthusiasm. Professional appearance. Ability to work independently. Self-motivation. Flexibility.

Professional   Ability to make quick decisions. Ability to perceive customers' needs. Computer skills. Time management skills. Strong follow-up skills.

Where the Jobs Are
- Medical supply houses
- Pharmaceutical houses
- Health maintenance organizations

Therapy Services

Level	Job Title	Experience Needed
Entry	Physical Therapist Assistant	Professional training
Entry	Occupational Therapist Assistant	Professional training
Entry	Massage Therapist	Professional training
2	Occupational Physical Therapist	2–4 years
2	Recreational Physical Therapist	2–4 years
2	Respiratory Physical Therapist	3–6 years
2	Speech–Language Therapist	3–6 years
3	Physical Therapist	4–8 years

Salaries in Therapy Services

Level	Salary
Entry	$35,000 to $40,000
Entry	$40,000 to $45,000
2	$45,000 to $55,000
2	$55,000 to $60,000
3	$70,000 to $85,000
3	$85,000 to $100,000

Qualifications

Personal   Positive attitude. Empathy. Caring. Physical and emotional stamina. Patience. Flexibility. Ability to communicate well with patients. Ethical behavior.

Professional   Product knowledge. Technical skill. Certification. Knowledge of and commitment to professional standards.

Where the Jobs Are
- Private practices
- Hospitals
- Private corporations
- Self-employment
- Government contract
- Franchises
- Colleges and universities
- Foundations and trusts

Trade Publications

American Journal of Nursing
8515 Georgia Avenue
Suite 400
Silver Spring, MD 20910

Journal of the American Medical Association (JAMA)
American Medical Association
P.O. Box 10946
Chicago, IL 60610-0946

Journal of the American Dental Association
American Dental Association
211 East Chicago Avenue
Chicago, IL 60611-2678

Healthcare Executive Magazine
Health Administration Press
Suite 1700
One North Franklin Street
Chicago, IL 60606-4425

Modern Healthcare
Crain Communications, Inc.
711 Third Avenue
New York, NY 10017-4036

Nurse Week
Nurse Week Publishing
6860 Santa Teresa Blvd.
San Jose, CA 95119

Professional Associations

American Academy of Medical Administrators
701 Lee Street
Suite 600
Des Plaines, IL 60016-4516

American Academy of Nurse Practitioners
2600 Via Fortuna #100
Austin, TX 78746

American Association of Medical Assistants
20 North Wacker Drive
Suite 1575
Chicago, IL 60606

American College of Healthcare Executives
One North Franklin Street
Suite 1700
Chicago, IL 60606-4425

American Dental Association
211 East Chicago Avenue
Chicago, IL 60611-2678

American Healthcare Association
1201 L Street NW
Washington, DC 20005

American Medical Association (AMA)
515 North State Street
Chicago, IL 60610

Hospitality Management

Level	Rooms Division	Food and Beverage	Event Planning	Sports and Entertainment/ Facilities Management
1. Entry ($30,000–$40,000)	Guest Services Agent Reservationist Information Specialist Head Cashier Concierge Front Desk Supervisor Inspector/ress Assistant Manager (Front Office) Assistant Housekeeper Housekeeper Team Leader (Floor Supervisor)	See Careers in Culinary Arts and Food and Beverage Management	Event Coordinator Sales Representative	Box Hand Box Coordinator Customer Service Representative Facilities Coordinator
2. Mid-management/ specialists ($40,000–$70,000)	Front Office Manager Rooms Attendant Executive Housekeeper Superintendent of Services Rooms Division Supervisor		Business Event Planner Corporate Event Planner Education Event Planner Social Event Planner Sports Event Planner Trade Show Event Planner	Assistant Concession Manager Assistant Catering Manager Assistant Club Manager Assistant Stadium Manager Field Operations Manager Sports Safety Coordinator
3. Management ($70,000–$100,000+)	Resident Manager Assistant Hotel Manager Vice President/ Operations General Manager		Director of Special Events Events Consultant Owner/Operator of Events Services Business	Business Director for Sports Performance Center Catering Manager Concessions Manager Club Manager Director of Operations Facilities Manager General Manager Stadium Manager

Hospitality Management (continued)

Level	Sports and Entertainment Marketing, Media, and Public Relations	Recreation, Health, and Fitness	Travel Tourism Management
1. Entry ($25,000 − $30,000)	Account Representative Advertising Sales Representative Proofreader Membership Sales Representative Ticket Sales Representative Sponsorship Sales	Fitness Instructor Fitness Center Sales Representative Program Coordinator	See Careers in Travel Tourism Management
2. Mid-management/ specialists ($30,000 − $60,000)	Assistant Manager of Membership Sales Assistant Product Manager/ Sports Apparel Corporate Ticket Sales Representative Group Event Sales Specialist Sports Broadcaster Sports Writer	Assistant Coach Fitness Consultant Group Exercise Manager Massage Therapist Nutrition Consultant Personal Trainer Spa Technician	
3. Management ($40,000 − $80,000)	Account Executive Director of Public Affairs Director of Public Relations Marketing Art Director Manager of Membership Sales Sales Manager Show Manager Sports Team Promoter Sports Agent	Athletic Director Coach Physical Therapist Program Director Spa Director Owner/Operator Wellness Center	

Rooms Division

Level	Job Title	Experience Needed
Entry	Guest Services Agent	Professional training
Entry	Reservationist	Professional training
Entry	Information Specialist	Professional training
Entry	Head Cashier	Professional training
Entry	Concierge	Professional training
Entry	Front Desk Supervisor	Professional training
Entry	Inspector/ress	Professional training
Entry	Assistant Manager (Front Office)	Professional training
Entry	Assistant Housekeeper	Professional training
Entry	Housekeeper	Professional training
Entry	Team Leader (Floor Supervisor)	Professional training
2	Front Office Manager	1–2 years
2	Rooms Attendant	1–2 years
2	Executive Housekeeper	2–4 years
2	Superintendent of Services	4–6 years

Level	Job Title	Experience Needed
2	Rooms Division Supervisor	4–6 years
3	Resident Manager	6–8 years
3	Assistant Hotel Manager	6–8 years
3	Vice President of Operations	8–10 years
3	General Manager	8–10 years

Salaries in Rooms Division

Entry	$30,000 to $40,000
2	$40,000 to $60,000
3	$60,000 to $70,000
3	$70,000 to $80,000
3	$80,000 to $90,000
3	$90,000 to $100,000+

Salaries in Rooms Division vary widely according to the type of hotel. In many large or luxury hotels, top management positions are salaried over $100,000. Special combinations of bonus, housing, meals, clothing allowance, company car and the like are often in addition to salary.

Qualifications

Personal Positive attitude. Enthusiasm. High energy level. Diplomacy. Courtesy. Confidence. Ability to make quick decisions and work independently. Good grooming and professional appearance. Ability to handle pressure. Excellent communication skills.

Professional Computer knowledge. Aptitude for figures, finances, inventories, and quotas. Knowledge of and commitment to professional standards. Team worker. Ability to plan, organize, and forecast.

Where the Jobs Are

Hotels

Motels

Resorts

Inns

Bed and breakfast operations

Events Planning

Level	Job Title	Experience Needed
Entry	Event Coordinator	Professional training
Entry	Sales Representative	Professional training
2	Business Event Planner	2–4 years
2	Corporate Event Planner	2–4 years
2	Education Event Planner	2–4 years
2	Social Event Planner	2–4 years
2	Sports Event Planner	2–4 years

Level	Job Title	Experience Needed
2	Trade Show Event Planner	2–4 years
3	Director of Special Events	5–7 years
3	Events Consultant	5–7 years
3	Owner/Operator Events Services Business	8–10 years

Salaries in Events Planning

Entry	$30,000 to $40,000
2	$40,000 to $45,000
2	$45,000 to $60,000
3	$60,000 to $65,000
3	$65,000 to $70,000
3	$70,000 to $85,000

Qualifications

Personal   Positive attitude. Enthusiasm. High energy level. Strong planning and organizational skills. Time management skills. Strong interpersonal skills.

Professional   Presentation skills. Sales skills. Product knowledge. Ability to manage budgets. Ability to work independently.

Where the Jobs Are

- Consulting firms
- Convention centers
- Corporations
- Government
- Professional associations
- Trade associations
- Schools
- Stadiums

Sports and Entertainment/Facilities Management

Level	Job Title	Experience Needed
Entry	Box Hand	Professional training
Entry	Box Coordinator	Professional training
Entry	Customer Service Representative	Professional training
Entry	Facilities Coordinator	Professional training
2	Assistant Concession Manager	1–4 years
2	Assistant Catering Manager	1–4 years
2	Assistant Club Manager	1–4 years
2	Assistant Stadium Manager	1–4 years
2	Field Operations Manager	2–5 years
2	Sports Safety Coordinator	2–5 years
3	Business Director for Sports Performance Center	2–5 years
3	Catering Manager	2–5 years

Level	Job Title	Experience Needed
3	Concession Manager	2–5 years
3	Club Manager	6–8 years
3	Director of Operations	6–8 years
3	Facilities Manager	6–8 years
3	General Manager	8–10 years
3	Stadium Manager	8–10 years

Salaries in Sports and Entertainment/Facilities Management

Entry	$25,000 to $30,000
2	$30,000 to $35,000
2	$35,000 to $45,000
2	$45,000 to $60,000
3	$60,000 to $70,000
3	$70,000 to $80,000

Qualifications

Personal   Positive attitude. Enthusiasm. High energy level. Confidence. Ability to make quick decisions and work independently. Professional appearance. Ability to handle pressure. Excellent communication skills.

Professional   Knowledge of and commitment to professional standards. Team worker. Aptitude for finances, inventories, and budgets. Perception of customer needs.

Where the Jobs Are

- Civic centers
- Clubs
- Convention centers
- Recreation sites
- Sports arenas
- Stadiums

Sports and Entertainment/Marketing, Media, and Public Relations

Level	Job Title	Experience Needed
Entry	Account Representative	Professional training
Entry	Advertising Sales Representative	Professional training
Entry	Membership Sales Representative	Professional training
Entry	Proofreader	Professional training
Entry	Sponsorship Sales	Professional training
Entry	Ticket Sales Representative	Professional training
2	Assistant Manager of Membership Sales	2–4 years
2	Assistant Product Manager/Sports Apparel	2–4 years
2	Corporate Ticket Sales Representative	2–4 years
2	Group Event Sales Specialist	2–4 years
2	Sports Broadcaster	4–6 years

Level	Job Title	Experience Needed
2	Sports Writer	4–6 years
3	Account Executive	6–8 years
3	Director of Public Affairs	6–8 years
3	Director of Public Relations	6–8 years
3	Marketing Art Director	6–8 years
3	Manager of Membership Sales	6–8 years
3	Sales Manager	6–8 years
3	Show Manager	8–10 years
3	Sports Team Promoter	8–10 years
3	Sports Agent	8–10 years

Salaries in Marketing, Media, and Public Relations

Entry	$25,000 to $28,000
Entry	$28,000 to $30,000
2	$30,000 to $33,000
2	$33,000 to $36,000
2	$36,000 to $40,000
3	$40,000 to $50,000
3	$50,000 to $60,000
3	$60,000 to $70,000+

Qualifications

Personal   Positive attitude. Enthusiasm. High energy level. Ability to respond quickly. Excellent verbal and written communication skills.

Professional   Industry knowledge. Team worker. Ability to conceptualize. Marketing and sales skills. Presentation skills.

Where the Jobs Are

Advertising agencies

Civic centers

Clubs

Consulting firms

Convention centers

Corporations

Government

Internet marketing firms

Magazines

Newspapers

Professional associations

Recreation sites

Resorts and hotels

Sports arenas

Stadiums

Theaters

Ticket agencies

Trade associations

Recreation, Health, and Fitness

Level	Job Title	Experience Needed
Entry	Fitness Instructor	Professional training
Entry	Fitness Center Sales Representative	Professional training
Entry	Program Coordinator	Professional training
2	Assistant Coach	Professional training
2	Fitness Consultant	Professional training
2	Group Exercise Manager	Professional training
2	Massage Therapist	Professional training
2	Nutrition Consultant	Professional training
2	Personal Trainer	Professional training
2	Spa Technician	Professional training
3	Athletic Director	2–5 years
3	Coach	2–5 years
3	Physical Therapist	2–5 years
3	Program Director	3–6 years
3	Spa Director	3–6 years
3	Owner/Operator Wellness Center	6–10 years

Salaries in Recreation, Health, and Fitness

Entry	$25,000 to $28,000
Entry	$28,000 to $30,000
2	$30,000 to $35,000
2	$35,000 to $40,000
2	$40,000 to $45,000
2	$45,000 to $50,000
2	$50,000 to $60,000
3	$60,000 to $70,000
3	$70,000 to $80,000
3	$80,000 to $90,000

Qualifications

Personal   Positive attitude. Enthusiasm. High energy level. Perception of customers' needs. Empathy. Self-motivation. Physical stamina.

Professional   Technical knowledge. Product knowledge. Knowledge of and commitment to professional standards. Ethical behavior.

Where the Jobs Are

- Spas
- Wellness centers
- Fitness centers
- Schools
- Corporations
- Resorts
- Hotels

Trade Publications

Club Management Magazine
Finan Publishing Company
107 West Pacific Avenue
St. Louis, MO 63119-3776

Cornell Hotel and Restaurant Administration Quarterly
School of Hotel Administration
Cornell University
Ithaca, NY 14853

Events Solutions Magazine
Event Publishing LLC
4667 South Lakeshore Drive
Suite 2
Tempe, AZ 85282

Hotel and Motel RedBook
American Hotel and Lodging Association Directory
1201 New York Avenue NW #600
Washington, DC 20005-3931

Leisure Management Magazine
The Leisure Media Company
Portmill House
Portmill Lane
Hitchin, Herts SGE-IDJ, UK

Lodging Hospitality
Mondo Code, LLC.
P.O. Box 1288
Boulder, CO 80306

Nation's Restaurant News
Lebhar-Friedman, Inc.
425 Park Avenue
New York, NY 10022

Restaurants and Institutions
Cahners Business Publications
Reed Business Information
360 Park Avenue, South
New York, NY 10010-1710

Special Events Magazine
17383 West Sunset Boulevard
Suite A220
Pacific Palisades, CA 90272

Sports Management Magazine
The Leisure Media Company
Portmill House
Portmill Lane
Hitchin, Herts SGE-1DJ, UK

Professional Associations

American Association for Leisure and Recreation
1900 Association Drive
Reston, VA 20191-1598

American Hotel and Motel Association
1201 New York Avenue NW, #600
Washington, DC 20005-3931

American Therapeutic Recreation Association
629 North Mainstreet
Hattiesburg, MS 39401

Aerobics & Fitness Association of America
15250 Ventura Boulevard
Sherman Oaks, CA 91403

Association of Luxury Suite Directors
10017 McKelvey Road
Cincinnati, OH 45231

Club Managers Association of America
1733 King Street
Alexandria, VA 22314-2720

Council on Hotel, Restaurant, and Institutional Education (CHRIE)
2810 North Parham Road
Suite 230
Richmond, VA 23294

Hotel Sales and Marketing Association International
1760 Old Meadow Road
Suite 500
McLean, VA 22102

International Association for the Leisure and Entertainment Industry
10 Briarcrest Square
Hershey, PA 17033

International Food Service Executives Association
500 Ryland Street
Suite 200
Reno, NV 89502

National Executive Housekeepers Association of America, Inc.
1001 Eastwind Drive
Suite 301
Westerville, OH 43081

National Restaurant Association
1200 17th Street NW
Washington, DC 20036

Outdoor Industry Association
310 Broadway
Laguna Beach, CA 92651

Culinary Arts/Food Service

Level	Beverage Service	Education and Training	Food Production	Marketing and Sales	Media
1. Entry ($30,000–$45,000)	Assistant Steward Brewer Cellar Hand Lab Technician Mixologist Riddler Waiter Wine Taster Wine Tasting Specialist	Chef Instructor Instructor Training Assistant	Broiler Cook Butcher Certified Culinarian Commis Chef Garde-Manger Line Cook Pantry Person Prep Cook Roasting Cook Roundsman/ Swing Cook Sauce Cook Seafood Cook Soup Cook Vegetable Cook	Sales Representative Account Representative	Culinary Event Demonstrator Copyeditor
2. Mid-management/specialists ($45,000–$70,000)	Assistant Winemaker Beverage Manager Business Development Manager Coffee Technologist Distributor Master Brewer Production Hand Wine Portfolio Consultant Wine Steward	Assistant Professor Associate Professor Assistant Department Head Department Head Home Economics Teacher Training Manager	Assistant Chef Banquet Manager Cafeteria Chef Catering Chef Certified Sous-Chef Chef Chef Manager Food Production Manager Head Chef Kitchen Manager Personal Chef Private Chef Sous-Chef	Consumer Product Sales Equipment Sales Representative District Sales Manager Franchise Sales Manager Marketing and Promotion Manager Real Estate Sales Manager Sales and Marketing Specialist Sales Manager	Food Writer Promotions Manager Public Relations Specialist
3. Management ($70,000–$120,000)	Cellar Master Enologist Sommelier Winemaker/ General Manager	Assistant Dean Certified Culinary Educator Dean of Culinary Education Food Service Consultant School Director Vice President of Training and Development President	Certified Executive Chef Certified Master Chef Chef de Cuisine Executive Chef Personal Certified Executive Chef	Account Executive Director of Marketing and Advertising Regional Sales Manager Vice President of Marketing Vice President of Sales	Author Celebrity Chef Food Photographer Food Service Publisher Public Relations Manager

Level	Nutrition	Operations Management	Pastry Arts	Research and Development, Food Technology, and Product Development
1. Entry ($30,000– $45,000)	Administrative Dietitian Culinary Nutrition Assistant Dietitian	Purchasing Assistant Manager Trainee	Baker Cake Decorator Pastry Cook	Assistant Product Manager
2. Mid- management/ specialists ($45,000– $70,000)	Culinary Nutrition Specialist Clinical Dietitian Community Dietitian Dietetic Technician Management Dietitian Menu Planner Nutritionist Pharmaceutical Sales Registered Dietitian Spa Chef	Accountant Assistant Food and Beverage Manager Assistant Manager Computer Specialist Food Service Manager Merchandising Supervisor Night Auditor Production Manager Purchasing Agent Purchasing Manager Quality Control Manager Restaurant Manager Storeroom Supervisor Unit Manager Vending Manager	Assistant Manager Assistant Pastry Chef Certified Pastry Chef Finisher Pastry Chef Pastry Production Manager	Culinologist Director of Recipe Development Facilities Designer Food Service Engineer Food Technologist Research and Development Food Technologist Packaging Specialist Product Development Chef Product Development Technologist Product Manager Quality Assurance Specialist Research and Development Specialist Sensory Analyst Techno Chef Test Kitchen Chef
3. Management ($70,000– $120,000)	Clinical Nutrition Manager Consultant Dietitian Culinary Nutrition Manager Director of Nutrition Services Nutrition Consultant	Controller District Manager Food and Beverage Manager Food Service Director General Manager Maitre d'Hotel Regional Vice President Owner/Operator	Certified Executive Pastry Chef Certified Master Pastry Chef Consultant Executive Pastry Chef Manager Owner/Operator	Corporate Research Chef Food Research Scientist Food Service Regulator Research Chef

Beverage Service

Level	Job Title	Experience Needed
Entry	Assistant Steward	Professional training
Entry	Brewer	Professional training
Entry	Cellar Hand	Professional training
Entry	Lab Technician	Professional training
Entry	Mixologist	Professional training

Level	Job Title	Experience Needed
Entry	Riddler	Professional training
Entry	Waiter	Professional training
Entry	Wine Taster	Professional training
Entry	Wine Tasting Specialist	Professional training
2	Assistant Winemaker	2–4 or 4–6 years
2	Beverage Manager	2–4 or 4–6 years
2	Business Development Manager	4–6 years
2	Coffee Technologist	4–6 years
2	Distributor	4–6 years
2	Master Brewer	4–6 years
2	Production Hand	4–6 years
2	Wine Portfolio Consultant	4–6 years
2	Wine Steward	4–6 years
3	Cellar Master	8–10 + years
3	Enologist	8–10 + years
3	Sommelier	8–10 + years
3	Winemaker/General Manager	8–10 + years

Salaries in Beverage Service

Entry	$30,000 to $45,000
2	$45,000 to $55,000
2	$55,000 to $70,000
3	$70,000 to $80,000
3	$80,000 to $100,000

Qualifications

Personal   Positive attitude. Enthusiasm. High energy level. Confidence. Diplomacy. Accuracy and attention to detail. Reliability. Excellent communication skills. Ability to work under pressure. Ability to handle stress. Time management skills. Good grooming and hygiene habits. Professional appearance.

Professional   Knowledge of and commitment to professional standards. Team worker. Perception of customer needs. Creative talent. Ability to conceptualize. Excellent sensory perception.

Where the Jobs Are

- Beverage distributors
- Beverage product manufacturers
- Microbreweries
- Retail beverage stores
- Restaurants
- Wineries

Education and Training

Level	Job Title	Experience Needed
Entry	Chef Instructor	Professional training
Entry	Instructor	Professional training
Entry	Training Assistant	Professional training
2	Assistant Professor	2–4 years
2	Associate Professor	2–4 years
2	Assistant Department Head	2–4 years
2	Department Head	4–6 years
2	Home Economics Teacher	4–6 years
2	Training Manager	4–6 years
3	Assistant Dean	6–8 years
3	Certified Culinary Educator	6–8 years
3	Dean of Culinary Education	6–8 years
3	Food Service Consultant	6–8 years
3	School Director	8–10 years
3	Vice President of Training and Development	8–10 years
3	President	10+ years

Salaries in Education and Training

Level	Salary
Entry	$30,000 to $45,000
2	$45,000 to $50,000
2	$50,000 to $60,000
2	$60,000 to $70,000
3	$70,000 to $80,000
3	$80,000 to $100,000+

Qualifications

Personal   Patience. Excellent oral and written communication skills. Ethical behavior. Positive attitude. Enthusiasm. Attention to detail. Confidence. Ability to handle pressure.

Professional   Technical knowledge. Teaching skills. Planning and organizational skills. Time management skills. Presentation skills. Training skills.

Where the Jobs Are

Colleges

Secondary schools

Universities

Vocational schools

Technical schools

Corporations

Food Production

Level	Job Title	Experience Needed
Entry	Broiler Cook	Professional training
Entry	Butcher	Professional training

Level	Job Title	Experience Needed
Entry	Certified Culinarian	Professional training
Entry	Commis Chef	Professional training
Entry	Garde-Manger	Professional training
Entry	Line Cook	Professional training
Entry	Pantry Person	Professional training
Entry	Prep Cook	Professional training
Entry	Roasting Cook	Professional training
Entry	Roundsman/Swing Cook	Professional training
Entry	Sauce Cook	Professional training
Entry	Seafood Cook	Professional training
Entry	Soup Cook	Professional training
Entry	Vegetable Cook	Professional training
2	Assistant Chef	2–4 or 4–6 years
2	Banquet Manager	2–4 or 4–6 years
2	Cafeteria Chef	2–4 or 4–6 years
2	Catering Chef	2-4 years
2	Catering Manager	2–4 or 4–6 years
2	Certified Sous-Chef	4–6 or 6–8 years
2	Chef	4–6 or 6–8 years
2	Chef Manager	4–6 or 6–8 years
2	Food Production Manager	4–6 or 6–8 years
2	Head Chef	4–6 or 6–8 years
2	Kitchen Manager	4–6 or 6–8 years
2	Personal Chef	4–6 or 6–8 years
2	Private Chef	4–6 or 6–8 years
2	Sous-Chef	4–6 or 6–8 years
3	Certified Executive Chef	8–10+ years
3	Certified Master Chef	8–10+ years
3	Chef de Cuisine	8–10+ years
3	Executive Chef	8–10+ years
3	Personal Certified Executive Chef	8–10+ years

Years of experience needed vary based on both size of the food service operation and volume of business.

Salaries in Food Production

Entry	$30,000 to $40,000
Entry	$40,000 to $45,000
2	$45,000 to $50,000
2	$50,000 to $60,000
2	$60,000 to $70,000
3	$70,000 to $80,000
3	$80,000 to $95,000
3	$95,000 to $120,000+

Salaries vary widely according to the size, type, and location of the food service operation. In many large or fine dining establishments and luxury hotels, top management positions are salaried well over $100,000.

Some positions, including executive chef, banquet chef, and banquet manager, earn bonuses and/or commissions based on sales volume. Chefs' salaries are frequently based on food cost percentages and labor cost percentages.

Special combinations of bonus, housing, meals, clothing allowance, company car, and the like, are often offered in addition to salary.

Qualifications

Personal   Positive attitude. Enthusiasm. High energy level. Confidence. Diplomacy. Accuracy and attention to detail. Reliability. Excellent communication skills. Ability to work under pressure. Ability to handle stress. Good grooming and hygiene habits. Professional appearance.

Professional   Knowledge of and commitment to professional standards. Team worker. Perception of customer needs. Creative talent. Ability to conceptualize. Aptitude for finances, figures, inventories, and budgets.

Where the Jobs Are

Catering firms

Clubs

Education

Fast-food operations

Franchises

Government

Hotels

Managed services companies (schools, universities, business, hospitals, health care facilities, etc.)

Motels

Private businesses

Private homes

Resorts

Restaurants

Marketing and Sales

Level	Job Title	Experience Needed
Entry	Sales Representative	Professional training
Entry	Account Representative	Professional training
2	Consumer Product Sales Representative	2–4 years
2	Equipment Sales Representative	2–4 years
2	District Sales Manager	3–6 years
2	Franchise Sales Manager	3–6 years
2	Marketing and Promotion Manager	6–8 years
2	Real Estate Sales Manager	6–8 years
2	Sales & Marketing Specialist	6–8 years
2	Sales Manager	6–8 years
3	Account Executive	6–8 years

Level	Job Title	Experience Needed
3	Director of Marketing & Advertising	6–8 years
3	Regional Sales Manager	8–10 years
3	Vice President of Marketing	8–10 years
3	Vice President of Sales	8–10 years

Salaries in Marketing and Sales

Entry	$35,000 to $40,000
Entry	$40,000 to $45,000
2	$45,000 to $50,000
2	$50,000 to $55,000
2	$55,000 to $60,000
2	$60,000 to $65,000
3	$65,000 to $70,000
3	$70,000 to $80,000
3	$80,000 to $90,000
3	$90,000 to $100,000+

Qualifications

Personal   Positive attitude. Enthusiasm. Excellent oral and written communication skills. Good judgment and decision-making skills. Accuracy and attention to detail. Well-groomed appearance. Ability to work independently.

Professional   Knowledge of and commitment to professional standards. Technical knowledge. Product knowledge. Strong marketing and sales skills. Perception of customer needs. Creative talent. Ability to conceptualize. Team worker.

Where the Jobs Are

    Catering firms
    Corporate restaurant firms
    Clubs
    Education
    Government
    Hotels
    Managed service firms
    Franchises
    Manufacturers of food products
    Motels
    Resorts
    Restaurant equipment suppliers
    Transportation
    Wholesalers

Media

Level	Job Title	Experience Needed
Entry	Culinary Event Demonstrator	Professional training
Entry	Copyeditor	Professional training

Level	Job Title	Experience Needed
2	Food Writer	3–5 years
2	Promotions Manager	3–5 years
2	Public Relations Specialist	6–8 years
3	Author	6–8 years
3	Celebrity Chef	6–8 years
3	Food Photographer	6–8 years
3	Food Service Publisher	8–10 years
3	Public Relations Manager	8–10 years

Salaries for Media

Entry	$30,000 to $35,000
Entry	$35,000 to $40,000
2	$40,000 to $45,000
2	$45,000 to $50,000
2	$50,000 to $60,000
3	$60,000 to $70,000
3	$70,000 to $80,000
3	$80,000 to $90,000
3	$90,000 to $100,000

Qualifications

Personal   Positive attitude. Enthusiasm. Excellent oral and written communication skills. High energy level. Self-motivation. Ability to work independently. Persistence. Physical stamina. Professional appearance. Punctuality. Dependability. Flexibility.

Professional   Perception of audience needs. Professional social skills. Ethical decision making. Product knowledge. Time management skills.

Where the Jobs Are

- Advertising firms
- Internet
- Newspapers
- Product manufacturers
- Nonprofit organizations
- Professional associations
- Publishing houses
- Radio
- Television
- Trade shows

Nutrition

Level	Job Title	Experienced Needed
Entry	Administrative Dietitian	Professional training
Entry	Culinary Nutrition Assistant	Professional training
Entry	Dietitian	Professional training
2	Culinary Nutrition Specialist	2–4 years

2	Clinical Dietitian	2–4 years
2	Community Dietitian	2–4 years
2	Dietetic Technician	2–4 years
2	Management Dietitian	2–5 years
2	Menu Planner	2–5 years
2	Nutritionist	3–6 years
2	Pharmaceutical Sales	3–6 years
2	Registered Dietitian	3–6 years
2	Spa Chef	3–6 years
3	Clinical Nutrition Manager	6–8 years
3	Consultant Dietitian	6–8 years
3	Culinary Nutrition Manager	6–8 years
3	Director of Nutrition Services	8–10 years
3	Nutrition Consultant	8–10 years

Salaries in Nutrition

Entry	$35,000 to $40,000
Entry	$40,000 to $45,000
2	$45,000 to $50,000
2	$50,000 to $55,000
2	$55,000 to $60,000
2	$60,000 to $65,000
2	$65,000 to $70,000
3	$70,000 to $80,000
3	$80,000 to $90,000
3	$90,000 to $120,000

Qualifications

Personal   Positive attitude. Enthusiasm. High energy level. Empathy. Courtesy. Ethical behavior. Attention to detail. Ability to handle pressure. Excellent communications skills. Good judgment, and decision-making skills. Patience.

Professional   Knowledge of and commitment to professional standards. Ability to analyze. Confidentiality. Perception of customer's needs. Technical knowledge. Product knowledge.

Where the Jobs Are

Assisted-living operations

Hospitals

Government

Professional associations

Schools

Spas

Test kitchens

Restaurants

Product manufacturers

Managed services

Operations Management

Level	Job Title	Experience Needed
Entry	Purchasing Agent	Professional training
Entry	Manager Trainee	Professional training
2	Accountant	2–4 years
2	Assistant Food and Beverage Manager	2–4 years
2	Assistant Manager	2–4 years
2	Computer Specialist	2–4 years
2	Food Service Manager	3–5 years
2	Merchandising Supervisor	3–5 years
2	Night Auditor	3–5 years
2	Production Manager	3–5 years
2	Purchasing Agent	3–5 years
2	Purchasing Manager	3–5 years
2	Quality Control Manager	3–5 years
2	Restaurant Manager	3–5 years
2	Storeroom Supervisor	3–5 years
2	Unit Manager	3–5 years
2	Vending Manager	3–5 years
3	Controller	5–7 years
3	District Manager	5–7 years
3	Food and Beverage Manager	5–7 years
3	Food Service Director	5–7 years
3	General Manager	7–10 years
3	Maitre d'Hotel	7–10 years
3	Regional Vice President	7–10 years
3	Owner/Operator	7–10 years

Salaries in Operations Management

Entry	$35,000 to $40,000
Entry	$40,000 to $45,000
2	$45,000 to $50,000
2	$50,000 to $55,000
2	$55,000 to $60,000
2	$60,000 to $65,000
2	$65,000 to $70,000
3	$70,000 to $80,000
3	$80,000 to $90,000
3	$90,000 to $120,000

Qualifications

Personal   Positive attitude. Enthusiasm. Ability to make quick and accurate decisions. Attention to detail. Excellent written and oral communication skills. Confidence. Ability to handle pressure.

Professional   Demonstrated leadership ability. Aptitude for dealing with figures, finances, inventories, and quotas. Team worker. Product knowledge. Perception of customer's needs. Planning and organizational skills. Ability to manage budgets.

Where the Jobs Are
Catering firms
Clubs
Drinking establishments
Fast-food operations
Franchises
Hotels
Government
Managed services
Motels
Restaurants
Resorts

Pastry Arts

Level	Job Title	Experience Needed
Entry	Baker	Professional training
Entry	Cake Decorator	Professional training
Entry	Pastry Cook	Professional training
2	Assistant Manager	2–4 years
2	Assistant Pastry Chef	2–4 years
2	Certified Pastry Chef	2–4 years
2	Finisher	2–4 years
2	Pastry Chef	4–6 years
2	Pastry Production Manager	4–6 years
3	Certified Executive Pastry Chef	6–8 years
3	Certified Master Pastry Chef	6–8 years
3	Consultant	8–10 years
3	Executive Pastry Chef	8–10 years
3	Manager	8–10 years
3	Owner/Operator	8–10 years

Salaries in Pastry Arts

Entry	$30,000 to $35,000
2	$35,000 to $40,000
2	$40,000 to $45,000
2	$45,000 to $50,000
3	$50,000 to $55,000
3	$55,000 to $65,000
3	$65,000 to $75,000
3	$75,000 to $100,000

Qualifications

Personal   Attention to detail. Creative ability. Ability to conceptualize. Persistence. Patience.

Professional   Technical knowledge. Product knowledge. Professional appearance. Ability to manage budgets. Self-motivation.

Where the Jobs Are
Catering firms
Clubs
Hotels
Managed services
Retail outlets
Restaurants
Resorts
Wholesalers

Research and Development, Food Technology, and Product Development

Level	Job Title	Experience Needed
Entry	Assistant Product Manager	Professional training
2	Culinologist	3–5 years
2	Director of Recipe Development	3–5 years
2	Facilities Designer	3–5 years
2	Food Service Engineer	3–5 years
2	Food Technologist	3–5 years
2	Research and Development Food Technologist	3–5 years
2	Packaging Specialist	3–5 years
2	Product Development Chef	5–7 years
2	Product Development Technologist	5–7 years
2	Product Manager	5–7 years
2	Quality Assurance Specialist	5–7 years
2	Research and Development Specialist	5–7 years
2	Sensory Analyst	8–10 years
2	Techno Chef	8–10 years
2	Test Kitchen Chef	8–10 years
3	Corporate Research Chef	8–10 years
3	Food Research Scientist	8–10 years
3	Food Service Regulator	8–10 years
3	Research Chef	8–10 years

Salaries in Research and Development, Food Technology, and Product Development

Entry	$35,000 to $40,000
Entry	$40,000 to $45,000
2	$45,000 to $50,000
2	$50,000 to $55,000
2	$55,000 to $60,000
2	$60,000 to $65,000
3	$65,000 to $70,000
3	$70,000 to $80,000
3	$80,000 to $90,000
3	$90,000 to $100,000+

Qualifications

Personal   Attention to detail. Accuracy. Analytical skills. Ability to conceptualize. Creative ability. Patience. Flexibility.

Professional   Technical knowledge. Product knowledge. Ability to develop and work with formulas. Knowledge of and commitment to professional standards.

Where the Jobs Are

Chain restaurants

Hotels

Food manufacturers

Education

Ingredient supply houses

Test kitchens

Consulting firms

Trade Publications

Beverage Retailer
307 West Jackson Avenue
Oxford, MS 38655

Chef Magazine
20 W. Kinzie Street
Suite 1200
Chicago, IL 60654

Culinary Trends
503 Vista Bella
Suite 12
Oceanside, CA 92057

Food Arts Magazine
Food Arts Publishing, Inc.
387 Park Avenue South
New York, NY 10016

Food and Nutrition
U.S. Department of Agriculture
Food and Nutrition Service
Alexandria, VA 22302

Food Management
Penton Media, Inc.
249 W. 17th Street
New York, NY 10011

Pastry Art and Design
Haymarket Group Ltd.
45 West 34th Street
Suite 600
New York, NY 10001

Nation's Restaurant News
Lebhar-Friedman Inc.
425 Park Avenue
New York, NY 10022

Restaurants and Institutions
Reed Business Information
2000 Clearwater Drive
Oak Brook, IL 60523

Professional Associations

American Culinary Federation
180 Center Place Way
St. Augustine, FL 32095

CHRIE
2810 North Parham Road
Suite 230
Richmond, VA 23294

Foodservice Consultants Society International
1261 Don Mill Road
Suite 99
Toronto, Ontario M3B 2W7

International Association of Culinary Professionals
1100 Johnson Ferry Rd.
Suite 300
Atlanta, GA 30342

International Foodservice Executives Association
500 Ryland Street
Suite 200
Reno, NV 89502

Multicultural Foodservice Alliance
1144 Narragansett Boulevard
Providence, RI 02905

National Restaurant Association (NRA)
1200 17th Street NW
Washington, DC 20036

The American Institute of Wine and Food
1303 Jefferson Street
Suite 100-B
Napa, CA 94559

Women's Foodservice Forum
1650 West 82nd Street
Suite 650
Bloomington, MN 55431

Travel/Tourism

Level	Travel Agencies	Corporate Travel	Tourist Bureaus and Offices	Convention and Visitors Bureaus
1. Entry ($25,000–$32,000)	Travel Counselor Reservationist Travel Agent Receptionist	Reservationist Travel Agent Receptionist Travel Counselor	Information Coordinator	Coordinator of Travel Information Center Coordinator of Membership Sales

Travel/Tourism (continued)

Level	Travel Agencies	Corporate Travel	Tourist Bureaus and Offices	Convention and Visitors Bureaus
2. Mid-management/ specialists ($32,000–$50,000)	Incentive Travel Specialist Outside Sales Agent Employment Interviewer	Travel Specialist	Attractions Specialist Research Analyst Surveyor Assistant Marketing Director Interpreter	Destinations Promoter Public Relations Specialist Convention Sales Manager Convention Center Manager Finance Manager Director of Transportation
3. Management ($50,000–$80,000)	Travel Director Travel Agency Manager Human Resources Manager Owner/Operator	Travel Director Corporate Travel Manager	Director of Marketing and Sales State Travel Director Chief Tourism Officer Deputy Commissioner of Tourism Development Commissioner of Tourism	Executive Director Vice President of Sales and Marketing

Level	Chambers of Commerce	Department of Economic Development	Education	Tour Operations
1. Entry ($25,000–$32,000)	Membership Coordinator	Information Coordinator	Instructor	Tour Guide Tour Escort Tourist Information Assistant
2. Mid-management/ specialists ($30,000–$50,000)	Sales Manager Research Analyst Program Coordinator	Economic Development Coordinator Demographer Urban Planner Director of Public Safety	Academic Department Head	Tour Operator Director of Escort Services Director of Tour Guides Tour Director
3. Management ($50,000–$80,000)	Executive Director Vice President of Marketing and Sales	Executive Director	School Director/ Administrator Education Consultant	Manager of Tour Operations

Level	Associations	Conference and Meeting Planning	Hotels, Motels, and Resorts	Public Relations
1. Entry ($25,000–$32,000)	Sales Representative Coordinator of Membership Sales	Assistant Meeting Planner Assistant Conference Planner Assistant Convention Planner Assistant Front Office Manager Assistant Special Events Coordinator Assistant Conference Services Coordinator Assistant Sales Manager	See Careers in Hotels, Motels, and Resorts	Account Representative

Level	Associations	Conference and Meeting Planning	Hotels, Motels, and Resorts	Public Relations
2. Mid-management/ specialists ($30,000–$45,000)	Public Relations Specialist Research Analyst Meeting Planner Special Events Coordinator Sales Manager	Meeting Planner Conference Planner Convention Planner Front Office Manager Mail and Information Coordinator Special Events Coordinator Conference Service Coordinator		Account Manager Speaker Informer Researcher and Evaluator Special Events Coordinator Press Coordinator Communications Technician
3. Management ($45,000–$80,000)	Director of Marketing and Sales Executive Director Vice President of Marketing and Sales	Group Sales Manager Convention Sales Manager		Account Executive Director of Public Relations Vice President of Communications

Level	Travel Writing	Airlines and Airports	Car Rental Agencies	Cruise Lines
1. Entry ($25,000–$32,000)	Travel Writer	Reservationist Customer Service Representative Flight Attendant Ticket Agent Sales Representative	Customer Service Agent Rental Sales Representative	Sales Representative Reservationist
2. Mid-management/ specialists ($32,000–$45,000)	Proofreader Coder Freelancer	Airport Operations Agent Passenger Service Agent Ramp Agent Customs Inspector	Station Manager Lead Agent	Activities Coordinator Health Club Director Recreation Director
3. Management ($45,000–$70,000)	Travel Editor	Supervisor of Gate Services Airline Schedule Analyst Airport Manager Airport Security Officer Schedule Planning Manager	City Manager	Cruise Director Director of Sales and Marketing

Travel Agencies

Level	Job Title	Experience Needed
Entry	Travel Counselor	Professional training
Entry	Reservationist	Professional training
Entry	Travel Agent	Professional training
Entry	Receptionist	Professional training
2	Incentive Travel Specialist	1–2 years
2	Outside Sales Agent	1–2 years

Level	Job Title	Experience Needed
2	Employment Interviewer	2–4 years
3	Travel Director	4–6 years
3	Travel Agency Manager	4–6 years
3	Human Resources Manager	4–6 years
3	Owner/Operator	Varies

Salaries in Travel Agencies

Entry	$25,000 to $28,000
Entry	$28,000 to $30,000
2	$30,000 to $45,000
3	$45,000 to $60,000+

Qualifications

Personal   Positive attitude. High energy level. Enthusiasm. Ability to work with budgets. Negotiation skills. Good communication skills. Effective interpersonal skills. Flexibility. Patience.

Professional   Familiarity with computers. Familiarity with geographic areas and destinations. Strong marketing and sales skills.

Where the Jobs Are

- Hotels
- Travel agencies
- Department stores

Corporate Travel

Level	Job Title	Experience Needed
Entry	Reservationist	Professional training
Entry	Travel Agent	Professional training
Entry	Receptionist	Professional training
Entry	Travel Counselor	Professional training
2	Travel Specialist	1–3 years
3	Travel Director	3–5 years
3	Corporate Travel Manager	3–5 years

Salaries in Corporate Travel

Entry	$25,000 to $28,000
Entry	$28,000 to $30,000
2	$30,000 to $35,000
2	$35,000 to $45,000
3	$45,000 to $55,000
3	$55,000 to $65,000+

Qualifications

Personal   Good communication skills. Effective interpersonal skills. Professional appearance. Positive attitude. Enthusiasm. Ability to articulate ideas. Initiative. Flexibility.

Professional   Awareness of product knowledge. Strong sales and marketing skills.

Where the Jobs Are

    Corporate travel firms

    Private industry

    Government

Tourist Bureaus and Offices

Level	Job Title	Experience Needed
Entry	Information Coordinator	Professional training
2	Attractions Specialist	Professional training
2	Research Analyst	1–3 years
2	Surveyor	1–3 years
2	Assistant Marketing Director	3–5 years
2	Interpreter	3–5 years
3	Director of Marketing and Sales	5–8 years
3	State Travel Director	5–8 years
3	Chief Tourism Officer	8–10 years
3	Deputy Commissioner of Tourism Development	8–10 years
3	Commissioner of Tourism	8–10 years

Salaries in Tourist Bureaus and Offices

Entry	$25,000 to $28,000
2	$28,000 to $32,000
2	$32,000 to $45,000
2	$45,000 to $50,000
3	$50,000 to $60,000
3	$60,000 to $70,000
3	$70,000 to $80,000+

Qualifications

Personal   Positive attitude. Enthusiasm. Resourcefulness. Ability to communicate well. Effective interpersonal skills. Flexibility. Detail oriented. Well-groomed appearance.

Professional   Ability to interpret, predict, and organize. Knowledge of area lodging, restaurants, attractions. Strong marketing and sales skills. Familiarity with computers. Attention to national trends.

Where the Jobs Are

    Research division

    Promotion division

    Information division

    News division

    Public affairs division

Convention and Visitors Bureaus

Level	Job Title	Experience Needed
Entry	Coordinator/Travel Information Center	Professional training
Entry	Coordinator of Membership Sales	Professional training

Level	Job Title	Experience Needed
2	Destinations Promoter	1–3 years
2	Public Relations Specialist	1–3 years
2	Convention Sales Manager	3–5 years
2	Convention Center Manager	3–5 years
2	Finance Manager	3–5 years
2	Director of Transportation	3–5 years
3	Executive Director	5–7 years
3	Vice President of Sales and Marketing	7–10 years

Salaries in Convention and Visitors' Bureaus
See Salaries in Tourist Bureaus and Offices.

Qualifications

Personal   Positive attitude. Enthusiasm. Accurate writing skills. Detail oriented. Flexibility. Good communication skills. Effective interpersonal skills. Well-groomed appearance. Resourcefulness.

Professional   Ability to conceptualize. Strong marketing and sales skills. Good organizational skills. Knowledge of area attractions, services, lodging, and restaurants.

Where the Jobs Are

  Convention and visitors' bureaus

Chambers of Commerce

Level	Job Title	Experience Needed
Entry	Membership Coordinator	Professional training
2	Sales Manager	3–5 years
2	Research Analyst	1–3 years
2	Program Coordinator	1–3 years
3	Executive Director	5–7 years
3	Vice President of Marketing and Sales	7–10 years

Salaries with Chambers of Commerce
See careers in Tourist Bureaus and Offices.

Qualifications

Personal   Positive attitude. Enthusiasm. Resourcefulness. Ability to communicate well. Flexibility. Detail oriented. Well-groomed appearance.

Professional   Awareness of area businesses. Ability to coordinate and plan. Strong marketing and sales skills.

Where the Jobs Are

  Sales

  Research

  Promotion

Department of Economic Development

Level	Job Title	Experience Needed
Entry	Information Coordinator	Professional training
2	Economic Development Coordinator	1–3 years
2	Demographer	2–4 years
2	Urban Planner	2–4 years
2	Director of Public Safety	3–5 years
3	Executive Director	5–7 years

Salaries with Departments of Economic Development
See Salaries in Tourist Bureaus and Offices.

Qualifications

Personal   Detail oriented. Ability to work independently. Accurate writing skills. Resourcefulness.

Professional   Familiarity with computers. Ability to evaluate, plan, coordinate, and interpret data. Awareness of local and national economic trends.

Where the Jobs Are
  Promotion
  Research

Education

Level	Job Title	Experience Needed
Entry	Instructor	Professional training and/or college degree
2	Academic Department Head	4–5 years
3	School Director/Administrator	6–8 years
3	Education Consultant	8–10 years

Salaries in Education
See Salaries in Healthcare—Education.

Qualifications

Personal   Listening skills. Patience. Enthusiasm. Positive attitude. Detail oriented. Flexibility. High energy level. Good communication skills.

Professional   Familiarity with computers. Broad knowledge of travel/tourism industry. Good organizational skills.

Where the Jobs Are
  Schools
  Consulting firms
  Travel companies

Tour Operations

Level	Job Title	Experience Needed
Entry	Tour Guide	Professional training
Entry	Tour Escort	Professional training

Level	Job Title	Experience Needed
Entry	Tourist Information Assistant	Professional training
2	Tour Operator	1–2 years
2	Director of Escort Services	3–5 years
2	Director of Tour Guides	3–5 years
2	Tour Director	3–5 years
3	Manager of Tour Operations	5+ years

Salaries in Tour Operations
See Salaries in Travel Agencies.

Qualifications

Personal   High energy level. Enthusiasm. Positive attitude. Effective interpersonal skills.

Professional   Problem-solving ability. Leadership skills. Ability to settle complaints and give advice. Background in geography.

Where the Jobs Are
- Tour operators
- Attractions
- Government
- Private industry

Associations

Level	Job Title	Experience Needed
Entry	Sales Representative	Professional training
Entry	Coordinator of Membership Sales	Professional training
2	Public Relations Specialist	1–3 years
2	Research Analyst	1–3 years
2	Meeting Planner	1–3 years
2	Special Events Coordinator	1–3 years
2	Sales Manager	3–5 years
3	Director of Sales and Marketing	5–7 years
3	Executive Director	5–7 years
3	Vice President of Marketing and Sales	7–10 years

Salaries in Associations
See Salaries in Tourist Bureaus and Offices.

Qualifications

Personal   Good communication skills. Enthusiasm. Positive attitude. Initiative. Detail oriented. Accurate writing skills.

Professional   Strong marketing and sales skills. Familiarity with computers. Awareness of local and national business interests. Ability to supervise.

Where the Jobs Are
- Professional associations
- Chambers of commerce

Conference and Meeting Planning

Level	Job Title	Experience Needed
Entry	Assistant Meeting Planner	Professional training
Entry	Assistant Conference Planner	Professional training
Entry	Assistant Convention Planner	Professional training
Entry	Assistant Front Office Manager	Professional training
Entry	Assistant Special Events Coordinator	
Entry	Assistant Conference Services Coordinator	
Entry	Assistant Sales Manager	Professional training
2	Meeting Planner	1–2 years
2	Conference Planner	1–2 years
2	Convention Planner	1–2 years
2	Front Office Manager	1–2 years
2	Mail and Information Coordinator	1–2 years
2	Special Events Coordinator	3–5 years
2	Conference Service Coordinator	3–5 years
3	Group Sales Manager	5+ years
3	Convention Sales Manager	5+ years

Salaries in Conference and Meeting Planning

Entry	$32,000 to $35,000
2	$35,000 to $45,000
2	$45,000 to $50,000
3	$50,000 to $60,000
3	$60,000 to $70,000+

Qualifications

Personal   Positive attitude. High energy level. Patience. Confidence. Good grooming. Professional appearance. Flexibility. Excellent interpersonal skills.

Professional   Negotiation skills. Sales and marketing skills. Ability to supervise.

Where the Jobs Are

    Company or corporate meeting planners

    Associations (or similar, usually not-for-profit, organizations)

    Independent meeting planners

Hotels, Motels, and Resorts

See careers in Hotels, Motels, and Resorts.

Where the Jobs Are

    Hotels

    Motels

    Resorts

Public Relations

Level	Job Title	Experience Needed
Entry	Account Representative	Professional training
2	Account Manager	1–3 years
2	Speaker	2–4 years

Level	Job Title	Experience Needed
2	Informer	2–4 years
2	Researcher and Evaluator	2–4 years
2	Special Events Coordinator	2–4 years
2	Press Coordinator	3–6 years
2	Communications Technician	3–6 years
3	Account Executive	6–8 years
3	Director of Public Relations	6–8 years
3	Vice President of Communications	8–10 years

Salaries in Public Relations

See Salaries in Hospitality Management—Sports and Entertainment/Marketing, Media, and Public Relations

Qualifications

Personal   Excellent written and oral communication skills. Effective interpersonal skills. Detail oriented. Positive attitude. Enthusiasm. High energy level. Flexibility. Ability to work under pressure.

Professional   Ability to meet deadlines. Strong sales and marketing skills. Ability to supervise.

Where the Jobs Are

Convention and visitors' bureaus

Hotels, motels, and resorts

Civic centers

Tourist bureaus and offices

Chambers of commerce

Conference and meeting planning

Departments of economic development

Travel Writing

Level	Job Title	Experience Needed
Entry	Travel Writer	Professional training
2	Proofreader	1–2 years
2	Coder	1–2 years
2	Freelancer	2–4 years
3	Travel Editor	5–8 years

Salaries in Travel Writing

Positions can pay well but will vary. Many publications feel that travel is a perk and pay less—even one-third—for travel stories than for other features.

Qualifications

Personal   Excellent writing skills. Detail oriented. High energy level.

Professional   Ability to conceptualize. Knowledge of subject matter. Ability to meet deadlines.

Where the Jobs Are

Travel journals

Publishing houses

Magazines
Public relations departments
Advertising agencies
Research organizations

Airlines and Airports

Level	Job Title	Experience Needed
Entry	Reservationist	Professional training
Entry	Customer Service Representative	Professional training
Entry	Flight Attendant	Professional training
Entry	Ticket Agent	Professional training
Entry	Sales Representative	Professional training
2	Airport Operations Agent	1–3 years
2	Passenger Service Agent	1–2 years
2	Ramp Agent	1–2 years
2	Customs Inspector	1–3 years
3	Supervisor of Gate Services	3–5 years
3	Airline Schedule Analyst	3–5 years
3	Airport Manager	5–8 years
3	Airport Security Officer	3–5 years
3	Schedule Planning Manager	5–7 years

Salaries in Airlines and Airports

Level	Salary
Entry	$28,000 to $33,000
2	$33,000 to $38,000
2	$38,000 to $45,000
3	$45,000 to $50,000
3	$50,000 to $60,000
3	$60,000 to $75,000

Qualifications

Personal   Positive attitude. Enthusiasm. Good communication skills. Effective interpersonal skills. Well-groomed appearance. Willingness to work nights, holidays, and weekends. Flexibility.

Professional   Awareness of airline and airport policies and procedures. Familiarity with computers. Supervisory skills. Planning skills.

Where the Jobs Are

Airlines
Airports

Car Rental Agencies

Level	Job Title	Experience Needed
Entry	Customer Service Agent	Professional training
Entry	Rental Sales Representative	Professional training
2	Station Manager	1–3 years
2	Lead Agent	1–3 years
3	City Manager	3–5 years

Salaries with Car Rental Agencies

Entry	$25,000 to $30,000
2	$30,000 to $40,000
3	$40,000 to $50,000
3	$50,000 to $70,000+

Qualifications

Personal   Positive attitude. Enthusiasm. High energy level. Good communication skills. Effective interpersonal skills.

Professional   Ability to work with figures. Negotiation skills. Knowledge of geographic areas. Resourcefulness.

Where the Jobs Are

Car rental agencies

Airports

Hotels

Major shopping malls

Cruise Lines

Level	Job Title	Experience Needed
Entry	Sales Representative	Professional training
Entry	Reservationist	Professional training
2	Activities Coordinator	1–3 years
2	Health Club Director	2–4 years
2	Recreation Director	2–4 years
3	Cruise Director	5–8 years
3	Director of Sales and Marketing	7–9 years

Salaries with Cruise Lines

Entry	$25,000 to $28,000
Entry	$28,000 to $32,000
2	$32,000 to $40,000
2	$40,000 to $45,000
3	$45,000 to $70,000

Most sales positions pay 25% in incentive pay and bonuses.

Qualifications

Personal   Positive attitude. High energy level. Enthusiasm. Good communication skills. Effective interpersonal skills. Flexibility.

Professional   Knowledge of safety policies and procedures. Strong marketing and sales skills.

Where the Jobs Are

Cruise Lines (on board)

Cruise Lines (on land)

Trade Publications

International Travel News
2120 28th Street
Sacramento, CA 95818

Meeting News
770 Broadway
New York, NY 10003

Travel Host, Inc.
10701 Stemmons Freeway
Dallas, TX 75220

Travel Weekly
Northstar Travel Media
One Park Avenue
New York, NY 10016

Professional Associations

American Association of Travel Agents
1101 King Street
Suite 200
Alexandria, VA 22314-2963

American Spa and Health Resort Association
P.O. Box 585
Lake Forest, IL 60045-0585

Association of Corporate Travel Executives
515 King Street
Suite 440
Alexandria, VA 22314-3137

National Association of Business Travel Agents
3699 Wilshire Boulevard
Suite 700
Los Angeles, CA 90010-2719

National Tour Association
546 East Main Street
Lexington, KY 40508-2342

Travel Industry Association of America
1100 New York Avenue
Suite 450
Washington, DC 20005-3934

National Association of Career Travel Agents
1101 King Street
Suite 200
Alexandria, VA 22314

International Business

Level	Accounting	Advertising	Banking	Customhouse Brokerages	Distribution
1. Entry ($30,000– $40,000)	Bookkeeper	Translator Photographer Graphic Artist Copywriter	Wire Transfer Specialist	Customs Entry Processor	Warehousing Agent

International Business (continued)

Level	Accounting	Advertising	Banking	Customhouse Brokerages	Distribution
2. Mid-management/ specialists ($40,000–$65,000)	Financial Auditor Regulatory Auditor Internal Auditor	Production Coordinator Market Analyst	Foreign Currency Investment Advisor/ Analyst Foreign Exchange Representative Finance/Business Loan Officer	Duty Drawback Specialist Customer Service Specialist Product Specialist	Transportation Analyst Marketing Representative Distributor
3. Management ($65,000–$90,000)	Tax Accountant Cost Analysis Accountant Reserves Accountant	Trade Account Executive	International Security/ Trade Officer	Compliance Manager Account Executive	Foreign Sales Agent

Level	Exporting	Importing	Marketing	Public Relations/ Public Affairs
1. Entry ($30,000–$40,000)	Traffic Coordinator Product Classifier	Traffic Coordinator Product Classifier	Export Marketing Representative	Publications Editor Special Events Coordinator
2. Mid-management/ specialists ($40,000–$65,000)	Documentation Specialist Licensing Agent Manufacturer's Representative Seller's Agent	Documentation Specialist Distribution Agent U.S. Customhouse Broker Buying/Purchasing Agent Retailer/Wholesaler	Advertising Specialist Public Relations Specialist	Media Relations Director Public Relations Director
3. Management ($65,000–$90,000)	Research Analyst of Foreign Trade Legislation	Auditor of Regulatory Compliance Research Analyst of Domestic and International Trade Legislation	Foreign Market Research Analyst	Community Relations Director Government Relations Director Policy Director

Level	Relief Organizations	Trade Show Management	Trading	Translator and Interpreter Services
1. Entry ($30,000–$40,000)	Transportation Specialist Volunteer Coordinator	Special Events Coordinator	Sales Representative	Marketing Representative
2. Mid-management/ specialists ($40,000–$65,000)	Program Coordinator	International Exhibit Coordinator	Documentation Specialist Marketing Director	Translator
3. Management ($65,000–$90,000)	Program Director Finance Director	Foreign Marketing Agent International Exhibit Coordinator	Goods and Commodities Trader Countertrade Specialist	Interpreter

Accounting

Level	Job Title	Experience Needed
Entry	Bookkeeper	Professional training
2	Financial Auditor	2–4 years
2	Regulatory Auditor	4–6 years
2	Internal Auditor	4–6 years
3	Tax Accountant	6–8 years
3	Cost Analysis Accountant	6–8 years
3	Reserves Accountant	8–10 years

Salaries in Accounting

Level	Salary
Entry	$30,000 to $40,000
2	$40,000 to $45,000
2	$45,000 to $50,000
2	$50,000 to $65,000
3	$65,000 to $75,000
3	$75,000 to $90,000

Qualifications

Personal   Multilingual skills. Flexibility. Critical-thinking skills. Decision-making skills. Problem-solving skills.

Professional   Marketing, management, or financial skills. Computer literacy. Interpretation and translation skills.

Where the Jobs Are

- Multilingual corporations
- Joint ventures
- Financial institutions
- Law firms
- Consulting firms
- Manufacturing

Advertising

Level	Job Title	Experience Needed
Entry	Translator	Professional training
Entry	Photographer	Professional training
Entry	Graphic Artist	Professional training
Entry	Copywriter	Professional training
2	Production Coordinator	2–4 years
2	Marketing Analyst	4–6 years
3	Trade Account Executive	6–8 years

Salaries in Advertising

Entry	$30,000 to $32,000
Entry	$32,000 to $35,000
Entry	$35,000 to $40,000
2	$40,000 to $55,000
2	$55,000 to $65,000
3	$65,000 to $90,000

Qualifications

Personal   Strong oral and written skills. Ability to conceptualize. Planning and organizational skills. Problem-solving skills. Ability to persuade and influence.

Professional   Product knowledge. Negotiation skills. Knowledge of media. Knowledge of industry standards and practices.

Where the Jobs Are

- Advertising firms
- Private business firms
- Consulting firms
- Marketing firms
- Hotels
- Restaurants
- Nonprofit organizations

Banking

Level	Job Title	Experience Needed
Entry	Wire Transfer Specialist	Professional training
2	Foreign Currency Investment Advisor/Analyst	2–4 years
2	Foreign Exchange Representative	4–7 years
2	Finance/Business Loan Officer	7–10 years
3	International/Security Trade Officer	7–10 years

Salaries in Banking

Entry	$35,000 to $40,000
2	$40,000 to $50,000
2	$50,000 to $60,000
2	$50,000 to $65,000
3	$65,000 to $80,000+

Qualifications

Personal   Strong written and oral skills. Ethical behavior. Analytical-thinking skills. Problem-solving skills. Attention to accuracy and detail. Multilingual skills.

Professional   Strong financial and accounting skills. Computer skills. Product knowledge. Knowledge of global currency. Awareness of global economics.

Where the Jobs Are
> Bank headquarters and branches
> Credit unions
> Financial services firms

Customhouse Brokerages

Level	Job Title	Experience Needed
Entry	Customs Entry Processor	Professional training
2	Duty Drawback Specialist	2–4 years
2	Customer Service Specialist	2–4 years
2	Product Specialist	3–5 years
3	Compliance Manager	5–7 years
3	Account Executive	8–10 years

Salaries in Customhouse Brokerages

Level	Salary
Entry	$30,000 to $40,000
2	$40,000 to $50,000
2	$50,000 to $65,000
3	$65,000 to $75,000
3	$75,000 to $90,000

Qualifications

Personal   Multilingual skills. Attention to detail and accuracy. Analytical-thinking skills. Ability to meet deadlines. Ability to work under pressure.

Professional   Knowledge of international trade regulations. Knowledge of global currency and tax structures. Ethical behavior. Computer skills.

Where the Jobs Are
> Government agencies
> Private businesses
> Trade centers
> Transportation, distribution, and logistics firms

Distribution

Level	Job Title	Experience Needed
Entry	Warehouse Agent	Professional training
2	Transportation Analyst	2–4 years
2	Marketing Representative	2–4 years
2	Distribution Agent	4–6 years
3	Foreign Sales Agent	6–8 years

Salaries in Distribution

Level	Salary
Entry	$30,000 to $40,000
2	$40,000 to $50,000
2	$50,000 to $65,000
3	$65,000 to $75,000
3	$75,000 to $90,000

Qualifications

Personal   Attention to detail. Planning and organizational skills. Quantitative skills.

Professional   Systems knowledge. Computer skills. Translation skills. Knowledge of monetary systems.

Where the Jobs Are

Manufacturing firms

Import–export businesses

Retail firms

Wholesalers

Exporting

Level	Job Title	Experience Needed
Entry	Traffic Coordinator	Professional training
Entry	Product Classifier	Professional training
2	Documentation Specialist	2–4 years
2	Licensing Agent	2–4 years
2	Manufacturer's Representative	4–6 years
2	Seller's Agent	6–8 years
3	Research Analyst of Foreign Trade Legislation	8–10 years

Salaries in Exporting

Entry	$30,000 to $34,000
Entry	$34,000 to $38,000
2	$38,000 to $55,000
2	$55,000 to $65,000
3	$65,000 to $70,000
3	$70,000 to $80,000

Qualifications

Personal   Multilingual skills. Strong written and oral skills. Detail oriented. Organizational skills.

Professional   Knowledge of regulations. Familiarity with international law. Product knowledge.

Where the Jobs Are

Distribution, export, and manufacturing firms

Trade centers

Importing

Level	Job Title	Experience Needed
Entry	Traffic Coordinator	Professional training
Entry	Product Classifier	Professional training
2	Documentation Specialist	2–3 years
2	Distribution Agent	2–4 years

Level	Job Title	Experience Needed
2	U.S. Customhouse Broker	2–4 years
2	Buying/Purchasing Agent	2–4 years
2	Retailer/Wholesaler	4–6 years
3	Auditor of Regulatory Compliance	4–6 years
3	Research Analyst of Domestic and International Trade Legislation	6–10 years

Salaries in Importing

Entry	$30,000 to $33,000
Entry	$33,000 to $38,000
2	$38,000 to $43,000
2	$43,000 to $48,000
2	$48,000 to $58,000
3	$58,000 to $70,000
3	$70,000 to $80,000

Qualifications

Personal   Multilingual skills. Strong written and oral skills. Detail oriented. Organizational skills.

Professional   Knowledge of regulations. Knowledge of international law. Product knowledge.

Where the Jobs Are

Distribution, import, and manufacturing firms

Trade centers

Marketing

Level	Job Title	Experience Needed
Entry	Export Marketing Representative	Professional training
2	Advertising Specialist	2–4 years
2	Public Relations Specialist	4–7 years
3	Foreign Market Research Analyst	7–10 years

Salaries in Marketing

Entry	$35,000 to $40,000
2	$40,000 to $55,000
2	$55,000 to $65,000
3	$65,000 to $90,000

Qualifications

Personal   Positive attitude. Ability to conceptualize. Strong written and oral communication skills. Planning and organizational skills. Multilingual skills.

Professional   Product knowledge. Computer skills. Perception of customer needs.

Where the Jobs Are

Private businesses

Nonprofit organizations

Banks

Manufacturing, retail, and financial firms

Hotels

Professional and trade associations

Public Relations/Public Affairs

Level	Job Title	Experience Needed
Entry	Publication Editor	Professional training
Entry	Special Events Coordinator	Professional training
2	Media Relations Director	2–5 years
2	Public Relations Director	2–5 years
3	Community Relations Director	4–7 years
3	Government Relations Director	7–10 years
3	Policy Director	7–10 years

Salaries in Public Relations/Public Affairs

Entry	$30,000 to $35,000
Entry	$35,000 to $40,000
2	$40,000 to $46,000
2	$46,000 to $60,000
3	$60,000 to $70,000
3	$70,000 to $80,000
3	$80,000 to $90,000+

Qualifications

Personal Positive attitude. Self-motivation. Strong written and oral skills. Strong presentation skills. Ability to persuade and influence.

Professional Cultural awareness. Knowledge of current issues. Knowledge of professional practices and policies.

Where the Jobs Are

Government agencies

Nonprofit agencies

Hospitals

Schools

Private businesses

Hotels

Banks

Manufacturing firms

Relief Organizations

Level	Job Title	Experience Needed
Entry	Transportation Specialist	Professional training
Entry	Volunteer Coordinator	Professional training
2	Program Coordinator	2–4 years
3	Program Director	3–6 years
3	Finance Director	4–7 years

Salaries in Relief Organizations

Entry	$30,000 to $33,000
Entry	$33,000 to $38,000
2	$38,000 to $45,000
3	$45,000 to $60,000
3	$60,000 to $70,000

Qualifications

Personal   Positive attitude. Self-motivation. Empathy. Flexibility. Initiative. Problem-solving skills. Persuasion skills.

Professional   Budget skills. Computer skills. Negotiation skills.

Where the Jobs Are

- Nonprofit agencies
- Government agencies
- Community organizations

Trade Show Management

Level	Job Title	Experience Needed
Entry	Special Events Coordinator	Professional training
2	International Exhibit Coordinator	2–4 years
3	Foreign Market Agent	5–7 years
3	International Exhibit Coordinator	5–7 years

Salaries in Trade Show Management

Entry	$30,000 to $40,000
2	$40,000 to $65,000
3	$65,000 to $70,000
3	$70,000 to $80,000

Qualifications

Personal   Positive attitude. Strong written and oral skills. Planning and organizational skills. Negotiation skills. Multilingual skills.

Professional   Sales and marketing skills. Product knowledge. Awareness of customer needs.

Where the Jobs Are

- Professional and trade associations
- Convention centers
- Private business firms
- Import–export firms

Trading

Level	Job Title	Experience Needed
Entry	Sales Representative	Professional training
2	Documentation Specialist	2–4 years
2	Marketing Director	2–4 years

Level	Job Title	Experience Needed
3	Goods and Commodities Trader	5–7 years
3	Countertrade Specialist	5–7 years

Salaries in Trading

Entry	$30,000 to $40,000
2	$40,000 to $50,000
2	$50,000 to $60,000
3	$60,000 to $75,000
3	$75,000 to $90,000

Qualifications

Personal   Strong decision-making skills. Analytical skills. Strong written and oral skills.

Professional   Knowledge of regulations. Product knowledge. Knowledge of international law.

Where the Jobs Are

Distribution, import, and export firms

Manufacturers

Trade centers

Translator and Interpreter Services

Level	Job Title	Experience Needed
Entry	Marketing Representative	Professional training
2	Translator	2–4 years
3	Interpreter	4–6 years

Salaries in Translator and Interpreter Services

Entry	$28,000 to $35,000
2	$35,000 to $55,000
3	$55,000 to $70,000

Qualifications

Personal   Multilingual skills. Strong oral and written communication skills. Cultural awareness.

Professional   Computer skills. Knowledge of world events. Familiarity with world geography and monetary systems.

Where the Jobs Are

Private businesses	Convention and visitors bureaus
Transportation firms	Private families
Chambers of commerce	Hospitals
Trade and professional associations	Schools
Hotels	Nonprofit organizations

Trade Publications

International Journal of Training and Development
Wiley-Blackwell
111 River Street
Hoboken, NJ 07030-5774

International Trade Reporter
BNA, Inc.
1801 S. Bell Street
Arlington, VA 22202

The International Trade Journal
Wiley-Blackwell
111 River Street
Hoboken, NJ 07030-5774

The Journal of Commerce
33 Washington Street
13th Floor
Newark, NJ 07102-3107

Professional Associations

Association of Career Professionals
World Headquarters
204 East Street NE
Washington, DC 20002

Association of Women in International Trade
204 E. Street, NE
Washington, DC 20002

Global Careers
One Dock Street
Suite 309
Stamford, CT 06902

International Chamber of Commerce
1212 Avenue of the Americas
New York, NY 10036

World Trade Organization
Rue de Lausanne 154
CH-1211
Geneva 21 Switzerland

Marketing

Level	Sales/Management	Market Research	Telemarketing	Retailing
1. Entry ($30,000–$40,000)	Sales Representative Customer Service Representative	Coder–Editor Junior Analyst Associate Analyst	Telemarketing Representative Junior Account Executive	Buyer Trainee Sales Representative

Marketing (continued)

Level	Sales/Management	Market Research	Telemarketing	Retailing
2. Mid-management/ specialists ($40,000–$65,000)	Sales Supervisor Branch Sales Manager District Sales Manager Regional Sales Manager Central Region Sales Manager Advertising Manager	Analyst Senior Analyst Research Manager Product Manager	Telemarketing Trainer Account Executive Telemarketing Communicator Script Writer Supervisor Telemarketing Center Manager	Assistant Buyer Sales Manager Buyer Merchandise Manager
3. Management ($65,000– $100,000+)	National Sales Manager Vice President of Marketing and Sales President	Market Research Director Vice President of Market Research President	Executive Administrator	Executive

Sales/Management

Level	Job Title	Experience Needed
Entry	Sales Representative	Professional training
Entry	Customer Service Representative	Professional training
2	Sales Supervisor	1–2 years
2	Branch Sales Manager	2–4 years
2	District Sales Manager	3–5 years
2	Regional Sales Manager	5+ years
2	Central Region Sales Manager	6–8 years
2	Advertising Manager	6–8 years
3	National Sales Manager	7–9 years
3	Vice President of Marketing and Sales	7–9 years
3	President	8–10 years

Salaries in Sales/Management

Entry	$35,000 to $40,000
2	$40,000 to $50,000
2	$50,000 to $65,000
3	$65,000 to $80,000
3	$80,000 to $100,000+

Qualifications

Personal   Positive attitude. Enthusiasm. Flexibility. High energy level. Good listening skills. Ability to speak and write effectively. Tolerance for rejection. Initiative. Self-motivation. Resourcefulness. Goal orientation.

Professional   Logic. Product knowledge. Perception of customer needs. Time management skills. Commitment. Good grooming. Professional social skills.

Where the Jobs Are
  Private industry
  Advertising
  Insurance
  Financial services
  Retailing
  Computer services
  Publishing houses
  Equipment suppliers
  Product manufacturers

Market Research

Level	Job Title	Experience Needed
Entry	Coder–Editor	Professional training
Entry	Junior Analyst	Professional training
Entry	Associate Analyst	Professional training
2	Analyst	2–4 years
2	Senior Analyst	4–6 years
2	Research Manager	4–6 years
2	Product Manager	6–8 years
3	Market Research Director	7–9 years
3	Vice President of Market Research	7–9 years
3	President	10 years+

Salaries in Market Research

Entry	$35,000 to $40,000
2	$40,000 to $45,000
2	$45,000 to $50,000
2	$50,000 to $55,000
2	$55,000 to $65,000
3	$65,000 to $80,000
3	$80,000 to $100,000+

Qualifications

Personal   Detail oriented. Good communication skills. Good organizational skills. Initiative. Patience. Resourcefulness. Ability to handle confidential information.

Professional   Familiarity with computers. Aptitude for figures. Analytical-thinking skills. Problem-solving skills. Ability to conceptualize. Ability to evaluate and predict.

Where the Jobs Are
  Private industry
  Government

Telemarketing

Level	Job Title	Experience Needed
Entry	Telemarketing Representative	Professional training
Entry	Junior Account Executive	Professional training
2	Telemarketing Trainer	2–4 years
2	Account Executive	2–4 years
2	Telemarketing Communicator	2–4 years
2	Script Writer	2–4 years
2	Supervisor	5–7 years
2	Telemarketing Center Manager	5–7 years
3	Executive/Administrator	7–10 years

Salaries in Telemarketing

Entry	$30,000 to $40,000
2	$40,000 to $50,000
2	$50,000 to $65,000
3	$65,000 to $90,000

Qualifications

Personal   Positive attitude. Good listening skills. Enthusiasm. Goal orientation. Self-motivation. Tolerance for rejection.

Professional   Product knowledge. Perception of customers' needs.

Where the Jobs Are

   Private industry

   Education

   Government

   Telemarketing

   Consulting

   Advertising agencies

   Computer service organizations

   Publishing houses

Retailing

See careers in Fashion and Retail Management.

Trade Publications

DM News
Editorial and Advertising Office
100 Avenue of the Americas
New York, NY 10013

Journal of Marketing
American Marketing Association
311 South Wacker Drive
Suite 5800
Chicago, IL 60606

Marketing News
American Marketing Association
311 South Wacker Drive
Suite 5800
Chicago, IL 60606

Market Research Magazine
American Marketing Association
311 South Wacker Drive
Suite 5800
Chicago, IL 60606

Marketing Today
7205 Exner Road
Darien, IL 60561

Professional Associations

American Marketing Association
311 South Wacker Drive
Suite 5800
Chicago, IL 60606

Business Marketing Association
400 North Michigan Avenue
15th Floor
Chicago, IL 60611

Hispanic Business Inc.
425 Pine Avenue
Santa Barbara, CA 93117-3709

Inc.com
Gruner + Jahr USA Publishing
375 Lexington Avenue
New York, NY 10017

Society for Marketing Professionals
99 Canal Center Plaza
Suite 444
Alexandria, VA 22314

Office Management and Support

Level	Administration	Information Processing	Paralegal
1. Entry ($30,000–$40,000)	Receptionist	Word Processor	Legal Assistant
	Secretary	Page Creator	Legal Technician
	Administrative Secretary	Editor	Paralegal Assistant
	Executive Secretary	Coder	Paralegal Instructor
	Customer Service Representative	Proofreader	Sales Representative

Office Management and Support (continued)

Level	Administration	Information Processing	Paralegal
2. Mid-management/ specialists ($40,000–$60,000)	Administrative Assistant Department Manager Human Resources Assistant Marketing Assistant Sales Associate	Information Packager Systems Administrator Information Broker Information Manager Coding Clerk Supervisor Production Planner Financial Analyst Marketing Director Research Analyst	Corporate Paralegal Information Specialist Legal Assistant Manager Litigation Support Consultant Litigation Real Estate Litigation Support Manager Paralegal Paralegal Coordinator Paralegal Supervisor Probate Paralegal Recruiting Coordinator/ Administrator Senior Legal Assistant
3. Management ($60,000–$100,000)	Executive Assistant Private Secretary Office Manager	Production Planner Financial Analyst Marketing Director Research Analyst	Case Manager Consultant/ Adviser Law Library Manager Law Librarian Law Office Administrator Lawyer (with further education) Paralegal Manager Program Director

Level	Specialization	Word Processing
1. Entry ($27,000–$35,000)	Legal Secretary Medical Secretary Technical Secretary School Secretary Membership Secretary Sales Secretary Travel Secretary Social Secretary International Group Secretary Statistical Typist City Mortgage and Real Estate Secretary	Word Processor Lead Word Processor
2. Mid-management/ specialists ($35,000–$50,000)	Human Resources Assistant Medical Records Technician Customer Service Representative Sales Assistant	Coordinator/Scheduler Records Manager Proofreader Trainer
3. Management ($50,000–$100,000)	Manager Trainee Office Manager	Administrative Support Manager Night Shift Supervisor Word Processing Manager

Administration

Level	Job Title	Experience Needed
Entry	Receptionist	Professional training
Entry	Secretary	Professional training
Entry	Administrative Secretary	Professional training
Entry	Executive Secretary	Professional training
Entry	Customer Service Representative	Professional training
2	Administrative Assistant	2–4 years
2	Department Manager	2–5 years
2	Human Resources Assistant	2–4 years
2	Marketing Assistant	2–4 years
2	Sales Associate	2–4 years
3	Executive Assistant	5–7 years
3	Private Secretary	5–7 years
3	Office Manager	5–7 years

Salaries in Administration

Entry	$30,000 to $33,000
Entry	$33,000 to $35,000
Entry	$35,000 to $40,000
2	$40,000 to $45,000
2	$45,000 to $50,000
2	$50,000 to $60,000
3	$60,000 to $75,000
3	$75,000 to $100,000+

Qualifications

Personal   Positive attitude. Enthusiasm. Detail oriented. Excellent communication skills. Flexibility. Ability to work under pressure. Self-starter. Dependability. Ethical behavior.

Professional   Strong computer skills. Strong spelling and grammar skills. Decision-making skills. Professional appearance. Responsibility. Team Worker. Resourcefulness. Ability to work independently.

Where the Jobs Are

Insurance offices

Banks

Hotels

Travel corporations

Education

Law offices

Medical offices

State and local government

Federal government

Manufacturing

Private corporations

Information Processing

Level	Job Title	Experience Needed
Entry	Word Processor	Professional training
Entry	Page Creator	Professional training
Entry	Editor	Professional training
Entry	Coder	Professional training
Entry	Proofreader	Professional training
2	Information Packager	2–4 years
2	Systems Administrator	2–4 years
2	Information Broker	2–4 years
2	Information Manager	2–4 years
2	Coding Clerk Supervisor	2–4 years
3	Production Planner	5–7 years
3	Financial Analyst	5–7 years
3	Marketing Director	7–10 years
3	Research Analyst	7–10 years

Salaries in Information Processing

Level	Salary
Entry	$30,000 to $40,000
2	$40,000 to $50,000
2	$50,000 to $60,000
3	$60,000 to $65,000
3	$65,000 to $70,000

Qualifications

Personal   Positive attitude. Enthusiasm. Detail oriented. Excellent written communication skills. Ability to work well under pressure. Ability to meet deadlines.

Professional   Proofreading skills. Ability to edit texts effectively. Good computer skills. Good spelling and grammar skills. Ability to work independently. Team worker. Professional appearance.

Where the Jobs Are

- Insurance offices
- Banks
- Education
- Publishing houses
- Advertising agencies
- Media
- Law offices
- State and local government
- Federal government
- Private corporations

Paralegal

Level	Job Title	Experience Needed
Entry	Legal Assistant	Professional training
Entry	Legal Technician	Professional training

Level	Job Title	Experience Needed
Entry	Paralegal Assistant	Professional training
Entry	Paralegal Instructor	Professional training
Entry	Sales Representative	Professional training
2	Corporate Paralegal	2–4 years
2	Information Specialist	2–4 years
2	Legal Assistant Manager	2–4 years
2	Litigation Support Consultant	2–4 years
2	Litigation Real Estate	2–4 years
2	Litigation Support Manager	3–5 years
2	Paralegal	3–5 years
2	Paralegal Coordinator	3–5 years
2	Paralegal Supervisor	3–5 years
2	Probate Paralegal	3–5 years
2	Research Coordinator/Administrator	3–5 years
2	Senior Legal Assistant	3–5 years
3	Case Manager	5–7 years
3	Consultant/Adviser	5–7 years
3	Law Library Manager	5–7 years
3	Law Librarian	5–7 years
3	Law Office Administrator	7–10 years
3	Lawyer	7–10 years
3	Paralegal Manager	7–10 years
3	Program Director	7–10 years

Salaries in Paralegal

Entry	$30,000 to $33,000
Entry	$33,000 to $35,000
Entry	$35,000 to $40,000
2	$40,000 to $43,000
2	$43,000 to $45,000
2	$45,000 to $50,000
2	$50,000 to $55,000
2	$55,000 to $60,000
3	$60,000 to $65,000
3	$65,000 to $70,000
3	$70,000 to $100,000

Qualifications

Personal   Proven written and oral communication skills. Interest in current events and history. Detail oriented. Patience. Ethical behavior.

Professional   Technical knowledge. Computer skills. Familiarity with legal terminology. Confidentiality. Logical-thinking skills. Analytical skills.

Where the Jobs Are

> Private corporations
>
> Government agencies

Community legal services

Education

Consulting

Law firms

Legal publishing houses

Specialization

Level	Job Title	Experience Needed
Entry	Legal Secretary	Professional training
Entry	Medical Secretary	Professional training
Entry	Technical Secretary	Professional training
Entry	School Secretary	Professional training
Entry	Membership Secretary	Professional training
Entry	Sales Secretary	Professional training
Entry	Travel Secretary	Professional training
Entry	Social Secretary	Professional training
Entry	International Group Secretary	Professional training
Entry	Statistical Typist	Professional training
Entry	City Mortgage and Real Estate Secretary	Professional training
2	Human Resources Assistant	1–3 years
2	Medical Records Technician	1–3 years
2	Customer Service Representative	1–3 years
2	Sales Assistant	2–4 years
3	Manager Trainee	2–4 years
3	Office Manager	3–5 years

Salaries in Specialization

Entry	$30,000 to $33,000
Entry	$33,000 to $35,000
2	$35,000 to $40,000
2	$40,000 to $45,000
2	$45,000 to $50,000
3	$50,000 to $65,000

Qualifications

Personal   Positive attitude. Enthusiasm. Excellent oral and written communication skills. Flexibility. Ability to work well under pressure. Dependability. Ethical behavior.

Professional   Excellent computer skills. Strong spelling and grammar skills. Decision-making skills. Professional appearance. Team worker. Resourcefulness. Ability to work independently. Knowledge of specialized terminology.

Where the Jobs Are

Law offices

Hospitals

Medical offices

Travel corporations

Hotels

Real estate companies

Insurance companies

Banks

Education

State and local government

Federal government

Word Processing

Level	Job Title	Experience Needed
Entry	Word Processor	Professional training
Entry	Lead Word Processor	Professional training
2	Coordinator/Scheduler	2–4 years
2	Records Manager	2–4 years
2	Proofreader	2–4 years
2	Trainer	4–6 years
3	Administrative Support Manager	4–6 years
3	Night Shift Supervisor	4–6 years
3	Word Processing Center Manager	5–10 years

Salaries in Word Processing

Entry	$30,000 to $40,000
2	$40,000 to $50,000
3	$50,000 to $65,000

Qualifications

Personal   Positive attitude. Detail oriented. Ability to work independently. Ability to make accurate decisions. Confidence. Enthusiasm. Ethical behavior.

Professional   Strong computer skills. Strong grammar, punctuation, and spelling skills. Supervisory skills. Team worker.

Where the Jobs Are

Law departments

Human resources

Claims area

Records departments

Medical departments

Information processing centers

Trade Publications

CRM Magazine
Information Today, Inc.
237 West 35th Street
14th Floor
New York, NY 10001-2509

National Paralegal Reporter
National Federation of Paralegal Associations
2517 Eastlake Avenue East
Suite 200
Seattle, WA 98102

OfficeOurs Magazine
Association of Professional Office Managers
1 Research Court
Suite 450
Rockville, MD 20850

Office Pro Magazine
International Association of Administrative Professionals (IAAP)
10502 NW Ambassador Drive
P.O. Box 20404
Kansas City, MO 64195-0404

Information Management Journal
ARMA International
13725 West 109th Street
Suite 101
Lenexa, KS 66215

Professional Associations

Association for Information and Image Management
11 Wayne Avenue
Suite 1100
Silver Spring, MD 20910

Association of Professional Office Managers
1 Research Court
Suite 450
Rockville, MD 20850

International Association of Administrative Professionals
10502 NW Ambassador Drive
P.O. Box 20404
Kansas City, MO 64195-0404

KM Pro—The Knowledge and Innovation Management Professional Society
P.O. Box 846
Severn, MD 21144-0846

National Court Reporters Association
8224 Old Courthouse Road
Vienna, VA 22182-3808

Project Management Institute (PMI)
4 Campus Boulevard
Newtown Square, PA 19073-3099

Technology

Level	Computer Applications and Networks	Computer Business Applications	Computer Drafting	Computer Graphics
1. Entry ($35,000–$50,000)	Field Technician LAN Technician PC Technician Help Desk Technician Network Technician Software Support Technician	Computer Programmer COBOL Programmer	Junior Drafter Computer-Aided Drafting and Design (CADD) Operator	Desktop Publisher Digital Publisher
2. Mid-management/ specialists ($50,000–$70,000)	Hardware Specialist Implementation Specialist Support Specialist LAN Specialist Network Security Specialist Support Engineer Support Administrator Network Administrator	Office Manager	Senior Drafter Junior Consultant	Graphic Designer Digital Artist
3. Management ($70,000–$90,000)	Support Engineer System Administrator Network Administrator	Database Administrator	Architect Designer Engineer Senior Consultant	Interactive Graphic Designer Technical Graphic Designer Computer Graphics Production Artist

Level	Computer Information Systems	Computer Technology Services	Cyberterrorism/ Network Security	Education/Training
1. Entry ($30,000–$50,000)	Database Programmer Programmer Analyst Information Analyst	Call Center Assistant Help Desk Assistant	Information Security Technician Network Security Technician	Instructor
2. Mid-management/ specialists ($50,000–$70,000)	Applications Developer Software Developer Technical Support Specialist Information Security Technician	Call Center Specialist Computer User Support Specialist Help Desk Analyst Software Support Specialist Technical Support Specialist	Information Security Analyst Network Security Specialist Manager of Network Security Services Manager of Information Security Services	Academic Department Head Computer Training Specialist Information Technology (IT) Training Specialist Microsoft Training Specialist Network Administration Training Specialist Oracle Training Specialist

Technology (continued)

Level	Computer Information Systems	Computer Technology Services	Cyberterrorism/ Network Security	Education/Training
3. Management ($70,000–$90,000)	Systems Analyst Support Engineer Information Security Administrator	Network Administrator	Information Security Administrator Network Security Administrator Owner/Operator Network Security Services Owner/Operator Information Security Services (See also careers in Criminal Justice— Information Security.)	Program Director School Director Director of Training

Level	Electronics	Information Science	Robotics	Marketing and Sales
1. Entry ($40,000–$50,000)	Electronicss Technician	Library Assistant Information Assistant	Assembler, Machinist, and Systems Tester Clinical Prosthetist Field Installer	Field Sales Representative Customer Service Representative
2. Mid-management/ specialists ($50,000–$70,000)	Broadcast Technician Engineering Technician Communications Equipment Technician Computer Technician Digital Technician Office Machine Repairer Commercial/Industrial Technician Medical Technician Health Technician Service Technician	Information Analyst Information Broker Information Retrieval Specialist Database Developer Information Architect Library Technician	Automation Technologist Computer-Aided Designer Sensory System Development Specialist System Integration Specialist Technical Prosthetist	Account Manager Sales Manager
3. Management ($70,000–$100,000+)	Electronics Engineer	Information Technical Consultant Director of Information Services Information Consultant Teacher Librarian Librarian	Software Developer	Account Supervisor Director of Marketing Vice President of Sales

Level	Technology Project Management	Web Site Management and Development
1. Entry ($45,000–$50,000)	Technology Business Developer Technical Writer	Technical Analyst Web Designer/Developer Web Programmer
2. Mid-management/specialists ($50,000–$65,000)	Technology Project Manager Technology Financial Analyst Technology Account Consultant Web Site Manager	Web Site Manager Technical Manager Information Architect Internet Marketer E-Commerce Developer E-Commerce Network Designer E-Commerce Technical Consultant Web or Database Applications Developer
3. Management ($65,000–$85,000+)	Entrepreneur Small Business Manager	Webmaster Web Storefront Designer E-Commerce Administrator

Computer Applications and Networks

Level	Job Title	Experience Needed
Entry	Field Technician	Professional training
Entry	LAN Technician	Professional training
Entry	PC Technician	Professional training
Entry	Help Desk Technician	Professional training
Entry	Network Technician	Professional training
Entry	Software Support Technician	Professional training
2	Hardware Specialist	2–4 years
2	Implementation Specialist	2–4 years
2	Support Specialist	2–4 years
2	LAN Specialist	2–6 years
2	Network Security Specialist	4–7 years
3	Support Engineer	4–7 years
3	System Administrator	7–10 years
3	Network Administrator	7–10 years

Salaries in Computer Applications and Networks

Entry	$35,000 to $40,000
Entry	$40,000 to $45,000
Entry	$45,000 to $50,000
2	$50,000 to $60,000
2	$60,000 to $70,000
3	$70,000 to $80,000
3	$80,000 to $90,000+

Qualifications

Personal   Problem solver. Patience. Ethical behavior.

Professional   Product knowledge. Technical skills; understanding of technical jargon; ability to use technical manuals.

Where the Jobs Are

High-tech firms

Technical services firms

Education

Government

Private corporations

Computer Business Applications

Level	Job Title	Experience Needed
Entry	Computer Programmer	Professional training
Entry	COBOL Programmer	Professional training
2	Office Manager	2–4 years
3	Database Administrator	4–6 years

Salaries in Computer Business Applications

Entry	$35,000 to $40,000
2	$40,000 to $50,000
2	$50,000 to $65,000
3	$65,000 to $80,000
3	$80,000 to $100,000+

Qualifications

Personal Patience. Attention to detail. Strong written and oral skills. Problem-solving skills. Ethical behavior.

Professional Technical competence. Analytical-thinking skills.

Where the Jobs Are

High-tech companies

Technical services firms

Education

Government

Computer Drafting

Level	Job Title	Experience Needed
Entry	Junior Drafter	Professional training
Entry	Computer-Aided Drafting and Design (CADD) Operator	Professional training
2	Senior Drafter	3–5 years
2	Junior Consultant	3–5 years
3	Architect	5–7 years
3	Designer	5–7 years
3	Engineer	7–10 years
3	Senior Consultant	7–10 years

Salaries in Computer Drafting

Entry	$35,000 to $40,000
2	$40,000 to $50,000

2	$50,000 to $60,000
3	$60,000 to $75,000

Qualifications

Personal   Patience. Attention to detail. Ability to work independently. Creative skills. Ability to conceptualize. Ability to meet deadlines. Team worker. Ethical behavior.

Professional   Technical competence. Planning and organizational skills. Knowledge of and commitment to industry standards.

Where the Jobs Are
Construction

Transportation

Communications

Utilities industries

Government agencies

Computer Graphics

Level	Job Title	Experience Needed
Entry	Desktop Publisher	Professional training
Entry	Digital Publisher	Professional training
2	Graphic Designer	2–4 years
2	Digital Artist	2–4 years
3	Interactive Graphic Designer	5–7 years
3	Technical Graphic Designer	5–7 years
3	Computer Graphics Production Artist	7–10 years

Salaries in Computer Graphics

Entry	$35,000 to $50,000
2	$50,000 to $70,000
3	$70,000 to $90,000

Qualifications

Personal   High energy level. Detail orientation. Creative skills. Ability to conceptualize. Analytical and problem-solving skills. Strong written and oral skills. Ability to work in teams. Ethical behavior.

Professional   Product knowledge. Technical skills. Computer skills. Strong mathematical skills. Specialized certifications.

Where the Jobs Are

Multimedia service providers

Cable networks

Television networks

Web development firms

Manufacturing

Retail

Media firms

Publishing houses

Consulting

Contract work

Advertising agencies

Private corporations

Computer Information Systems

Level	Job Title	Experience Needed
Entry	Database Programmer	Professional training
Entry	Programmer Analyst	Professional training
Entry	Information Analyst	Professional training
2	Applications Developer	2–4 years
2	Software Developer	2–4 years
2	Technical Support Specialist	4–6 years
2	Information Security Technician	4–6 years
3	Systems Analyst	5–7 years
3	Support Engineer	5–7 years
3	Information Security Administrator	7–10 years

Salaries in Computer Information Systems

Entry	$40,000 to $50,000
Entry	$50,000 to $60,000
2	$60,000 to $65,000
2	$65,000 to $70,000
3	$70,000 to $75,000
3	$75,000 to $100,000+

Qualifications

Personal   Patience. Persistence. Ability to work with extreme accuracy. Ability to work under pressure and with deadlines. Strong written and oral skills.

Professional   Ability to think logically. Ability to perform highly analytical work. Problem-solving ability. Strong decision-making skills. Computer skills. Ethical behavior.

Where the Jobs Are

- Computer systems integration design services
- Computer facilities
- Management services
- Manufacturing
- Government agencies
- Financial services firms
- Insurance firms

Computer Technology Services

Level	Job Title	Experience Needed
Entry	Call Center Assistant	Professional training
Entry	Help Desk Assistant	Professional training
2	Call Center Specialist	1–3 years
2	Computer User Support Specialist	2–4 years
2	Help Desk Analyst	2–4 years
2	Software Support Specialist	3–5 years
2	Technical Support Specialist	3–5 years
3	Network Administrator	3–5 years

Salaries in Computer Technology Services

Entry	$30,000 to $35,000
2	$35,000 to $40,000
2	$40,000 to $50,000
3	$50,000 to $65,000

Qualifications

Personal   Patience. Logical thinking skills. Problem-solving skills. Strong written and oral skills. Analytical skills. Interpersonal skills. Ethical behavior.

Professional   Product knowledge. Technical knowledge. Computer skills. Knowledge of industry practices and standards. Knowledge of diagnostic systems and solutions.

Where the Jobs Are

Small start-up firms

Private corporations

Technology service providers

Technology manufacturers

Government agencies

Education

Libraries

Training firms

Corporate training departments

Cyberterrorism/Network Security

Level	Job Title	Experience Needed
Entry	Information Security Technician	Professional training
Entry	Network Security Technician	Professional training
2	Information Security Analyst	2–4 years
2	Network Security Specialist	2–4 years
2	Manager of Network Security Services	4–6 years
2	Manager of Information Security Services	4–6 years
3	Information Security Administrator	5–7 years
3	Network Security Administrator	5–7 years
3	Owner/Operator Network Security Services	7–10 years
3	Owner/Operator Information Security Services	7–10 years
	(See also careers in Criminal Justice— Information Security.)	

Salaries in Cyberterrorism/Network Security

Entry	$40,000 to $45,000
2	$45,000 to $55,000
2	$55,000 to $65,000
3	$65,000 to $80,000
3	$80,000 to $100,000+

Qualifications

Personal   Patience. Analytical-thinking skills. Problem-solving skills. Decision-making skills. Strong oral and written skills. Confidentiality. Ethical behavior.

Professional   Product knowledge. Knowledge of mathematics, programming, and networking.

Where the Jobs Are

Government agencies

Law enforcement

Military

Computer manufacturing firms

Computer security firms

Consulting

Private corporations

Education/Training

Level	Job Title	Experience Needed
Entry	Instructor	Professional training
2	Academic Department Head	3–5 years
2	Computer Training Specialist	3–5 years
2	Information Technology Training Specialist	3–5 years
2	Microsoft Training Specialist	3–5 years
2	Network Administration Training Specialist	5–7 years
2	Oracle Training Specialist	5–7 years
3	Program Director	5–7 years
3	School Director	7–10 years
3	Director of Training	7–10 years

Salaries in Education/Training

Entry	$35,000 to $40,000
2	$40,000 to $50,000
2	$50,000 to $60,000
2	$60,000 to $70,000
3	$70,000 to $80,000+

Qualifications

Personal   Strong oral and written skills. Strong interpersonal skills. Planning and organizational skills. Leadership skills. Teaching skills. Ethical behavior.

Professional   Product knowledge. Technical skills. Computer skills. Knowledge of industry practices and standards. Specialized certification.

Where the Jobs Are

Colleges and universities

Career schools

High schools

Corporate training departments

Consulting

Contract training

Electronics

Level	Job Title	Experience Needed
Entry	Electronics Technician	Professional training
2	Broadcast Technician	2–4 years
2	Engineering Technician	2–4 years
2	Communications Equipment Technician	2–4 years
2	Computer Technician	2–4 years
2	Digital Technician	2–4 years
2	Office Machine Repairer	2–4 years
2	Commercial/Industrial Technician	2–4 years
2	Medical Technician	2–4 years
2	Health Technician	2–4 years
2	Service Technician	2–4 years
3	Electronics Engineer	5–7 years

Salaries in Electronics

Level	Salary
Entry	$40,000 to $45,000
Entry	$45,000 to $50,000
2	$50,000 to $55,000
2	$55,000 to $60,000
2	$60,000 to $65,000
3	$65,000 to $80,000

Qualifications

Personal   Ability to perform detailed work. Ability to work independently. Accuracy. Manual dexterity.

Professional   Product knowledge. Technical knowledge. Aptitude for mathematics and science. Computer skills. Problem-solving skills.

Where the Jobs Are

- Defense contractors
- Private corporations
- Government
- Education
- Broadcasting
- Computer service organizations
- Research organizations
- Radio and television stations

Information Science

Level	Job Title	Experience Needed
Entry	Library Assistant	Professional training
Entry	Information Assistant	Professional training
2	Information Analyst	2–4 years
2	Information Broker	2–4 years
2	Information Retrieval Specialist	2–4 years
2	Database Developer	2–4 years
2	Information Architect	3–5 years

Level	Job Title	Experience Needed
2	Library Technician	3–5 years
3	Information Technical Consultant	5–7 years
3	Director of Information Services	5–7 years
3	Information Consultant	5–7 years
3	Teacher Librarian	5–7 years
3	Librarian	5–7 years

Salaries in Information Science

Entry	$45,000 to $50,000
Entry	$50,000 to $55,000
2	$55,000 to $60,000
2	$60,000 to $70,000
3	$70,000 to $80,000

Qualifications

Personal   Patience. Detail oriented. Strong written and oral skills. Strong interpersonal skills. Problem-solving skills. Analytical skills. Ethical behavior.

Professional   Knowledge of computer systems and technology. Product knowledge. Knowledge of industry practices and standards. Specialized certifications.

Where the Jobs Are

- Government agencies
- Education
- Research firms
- Marketing firms
- Private corporations
- Libraries

Robotics

Level	Job Title	Experience Needed
Entry	Assembler, Machinist, and Systems Tester	Professional training
Entry	Clinical Prosthetist	Professional training
Entry	Field Installer	Professional training
2	Automation Technologist	2–4 years
2	Computer-Aided Designer	2–4 years
2	Sensory System Development Specialist	4–7 years
2	System Integration Specialist	7–10 years
2	Technical Prosthetist	7–10 years
3	Software Developer	7–10 years

Salaries in Robotics

Entry	$40,000 to $45,000
Entry	$45,000 to $50,000
2	$50,000 to $55,000
3	$55,000 to $75,000

Qualifications

Personal   Patience. Persistence. Ability to work with extreme accuracy. Ability to work under pressure and meet deadlines. Strong written and oral skills.

Professional   Knowledge of biomechanics, electronics, and physiology. Computer skills. Creative and artistic ability. Ethical behavior.

Where the Jobs Are

Research laboratories

Government agencies

Engineering firms

Education

Machine and equipment manufacturers

Prosthetic product manufacturers

Marketing and Sales

Level	Job Title	Experience Needed
Entry	Field Sales Representative	Professional training
Entry	Customer Service Representative	Professional training
2	Account Manager	2–4 years
2	Sales Manager	2–4 years
3	Account Supervisor	5–7 years
3	Director of Marketing	5–7 years
3	Vice President of Sales	7–10 years

Salaries in Marketing and Sales

Level	Salary
Entry	$40,000 to $50,000
2	$50,000 to $60,000
2	$60,000 to $70,000
3	$70,000 to $80,000
3	$80,000 to $90,000+

Qualifications

Personal   Strong written and oral communication skills. Confidence. Self-motivation. Ethical behavior.

Professional   Product knowledge. Perception of customer needs. Time management skills. Computer skills. Strong follow-up skills. Ethical behavior.

Where the Jobs Are

Computer service firms

Consulting

Computer manufacturers

Government agencies

Technology Project Management

Level	Job Title	Experience Needed
Entry	Technology Business Developer	Professional training
Entry	Technical Writer	Professional training
2	Technology Project Manager	2–4 years

Level	Job Title	Experience Needed
2	Technology Financial Analyst	2–4 years
2	Technology Account Consultant	2–4 years
2	Web Site Manager	5–7 years
3	Entrepreneur	5–7 years
3	Small Business Manager	7–10 years

Salaries in Technology Project Management

Entry	$45,000 to $50,000
2	$50,000 to $55,000
3	$55,000 to $60,000
3	$60,000 to $85,000

Qualifications

Personal   Strong oral and written skills. Ability to manage multiple priorities. Strong leadership skills. Planning and organization skills. Problem-solving skills. Analytical skills. Time management skills. Ability to work under pressure and meet deadlines. Ethical behavior.

Professional   Product knowledge. Technical knowledge. Familiarity with relational databases and Internet applications. Familiarity with project management methodology and project life cycle processes.

Where the Jobs Are

- Education
- Government agencies
- Training organizations
- Contract work
- Consulting
- Private corporations

Web Site Management and Development

Level	Job Title	Experience Needed
Entry	Technical Analyst	Professional training
Entry	Web Designer/Developer	Professional training
Entry	Web Programmer	Professional training
2	Web Site Manager	2–4 years
2	Technical Manager	2–4 years
2	Information Architect	2–4 years
2	Internet Marketer	2–4 years
2	E-Commerce Developer	5–7 years
2	E-Commerce Network Designer	5–7 years
2	E-Commerce Technical Consultant	5–7 years
2	Web or Database Applications Developer	5–7 years
3	Webmaster	7–10 years
3	Web Storefront Designer	7–10 years
3	E-Commerce Administrator	7–10 years

Salaries in Web Site Management and Development

Entry	$45,000 to $50,000
2	$50,000 to $55,000
2	$55,000 to $60,000
3	$60,000 to $65,000
3	$65,000 to $80,000+

Qualifications

Personal   Strong written and oral skills. Detail oriented. Logical- and analytical-thinking skills. Problem-solving skills. Ability to work under pressure. Ethical behavior.

Professional   Product knowledge. Technical knowledge. Computer skills. Experience working with databases. Knowledge of various programming languages. Basic understanding of HTML. Knowledge of Photoshop, Flash, and llustrator.

Where the Jobs Are
- Design firms
- Internet marketing firms
- Contract firms
- Consulting
- Service providers
- Applications providers
- Private corporations
- Education
- Government agencies

Trade Publications

Byte
70 Main Street
Peterborough, NH 03458

CIO
CXO Media Inc.
492 Old Connecticut Path
Framingham, MA 01701-9208

Computer Times
3206 Kings Court
Bardstown, KY 40004

Computerworld
P.O. Box 3500
Northbrook, IL 60065-3500

eWeek
500 Unicorn Drive
Woburn, MA 01801

Information Week
600 Community Drive
Manhasset, NY 11030

InfoWorld
Information World Media Group, Inc.
501 Second Street
San Francisco, CA 94107

Internet World
221 East 29th Street
Loveland, CO 80537

Professional Associations

Association for Women in Computing
41 Sutter Street
Suite 1006
San Francisco, CA 94104

American Society for Science and Technology
1320 Fenwick Lane
Suite 510
Silver Spring, MD 20910

IEEE Computer Society
1730 Massachusetts Avenue NW
Washington, DC 20036-1992

Information Technology Association of America
1401 Wilson Boulevard
Suite 1100
Arlington, VA 22209

International Webmasters Association
119 East Union Street
Suite F
Pasadena, CA 91103

U.S. Internet Industry Association
815 Connecticut Avenue NW
Suite 620
Washington, DC 20006

World Organization of Webmasters
9580 Oak Avenue Parkway
Suite 7-177
Folsom, CA 95630

Telecommunications

Level	Equipment Manufacturing	Marketing and Customer Support	Network Operations	Systems Operations
1. Entry ($40,000–$55,000)	Systems Technician	Technical Writer Telecommunications Technician Customer Support Staff	Switch Technician Telecommunications Line and Cable Worker	Network Technician

Level	Equipment Manufacturing	Marketing and Customer Support	Network Operations	Systems Operations
2. Mid-management/ specialists ($55,000–$75,000)	Senior Systems Engineer Test Engineer Telecommunications Specialist	Customer Sales Engineer Technical Sales Representative	Network Engineer Software or Applications Engineer Test Engineer	Network Engineer Telecommunications Network Engineer/ Planner Telecommunications Facility Examiner
3. Management ($75,000– $100,000+)	Chip Architect Product Manager	Marketing Manager Sales Manager Customer Relations Manager Government Relations/ Regulator	System Designer Engineer	System Designer

Equipment Manufacturing

Level	Job Title	Experience Needed
Entry	Systems Technician	Professional training
2	Senior Systems Engineer	2–4 years
2	Test Engineer	5–7 years
2	Telecommunications Specialist	5–7 years
3	Chip Architect	6–8 years
3	Product Manager	6–8 years

Salaries in Equipment Manufacturing

Entry	$45,000 to $55,000
2	$55,000 to $65,000
2	$65,000 to $75,000
3	$75,000 to $95,000+

Qualifications

Personal   Patience. Persistence. Ability to work with extreme accuracy. Ability to work under pressure and meet deadlines. Strong written and oral skills. Ethical behavior. Problem-solving and analytical skills.

Professional   Strong computer skills. Product knowledge. Technical knowledge. Certification.

Where the Jobs Are

Equipment manufacturers

Service providers

Wireless and satellite communications

On-site equipment manufacturers

Customer-premises equipment manufacturing

Marketing and Customer Support

Level	Job Title	Experience Needed
Entry	Technical Writer	Professional training
Entry	Telecommunications Technician	Professional training

Level	Job Title	Experience Needed
Entry	Customer Support Staff	Professional training
2	Customer Sales Engineer	2–4 years
2	Technical Sales Representative	2–4 years
3	Marketing Manager	4–6 years
3	Sales Manager	6–10 years
3	Customer Relations Manager	6–10 years
3	Government Relations/Regulator	6–10 years

Salaries in Marketing and Customer Support

Entry	$40,000 to $50,000
Entry	$50,000 to $60,000
2	$60,000 to $65,000
3	$65,000 to $80,000
3	$80,000 to $90,000+

Qualifications

Personal   Strong written and oral communication skills. Confidence. Problem-solving and analytical skills. Ethical behavior.

Professional   Product knowledge. Perception of customers' needs. Technical knowledge. Strong follow-through skills.

Where the Jobs Are

Network service providers

Equipment manufacturers

Network Operations

Level	Job Title	Experience Needed
Entry	Switch Technician	Professional training
Entry	Telecommunications Line and Cable Worker	Professional training
2	Network Engineer	2–5 years
2	Software or Applications Engineer	2–5 years
2	Test Engineer	2–5 years
3	System Designer	6–10 years
3	Engineer	6–10 years

Salaries in Network Operations

Entry	$40,000 to $45,000
Entry	$45,000 to $50,000
2	$50,000 to $55,000
3	$55,000 to $70,000+

Qualifications

Personal   Strong written and oral skills. Problem-solving and analytical skills. Ability to work independently. Ability to conceptualize. Persistence. Patience. Ability to make complex decisions. Ethical behavior.

Professional   Product knowledge. Technical skills. Knowledge of and commitment to industry practices and standards. Computer skills. Certification. Knowledge of safety standards.

Where the Jobs Are

    Network and fiber optics manufacturers

Systems Operations

Level	Job Title	Experience Needed
Entry	Network Technician	Professional training
2	Network Engineer	2–4 years
2	Telecommunications Network Engineer/Planner	4–6 years
2	Telecommunications Facility Examiner	4–6 years
3	System Designer	6–10 years

Salaries in Systems Operations

Entry	$40,000 to $45,000
2	$45,000 to $50,000
2	$50,000 to $65,000
3	$65,000 to $80,000+

Qualifications

Personal   Patience. Persistence. Ability to work under pressure. Strong written and oral skills. Detail oriented. Strong analytical skills. Ethical behavior.

Professional   Ability to make complex decisions. Knowledge of industry safety standards. Technical skills. Strong planning and organizational skills.

Where the Jobs Are

    Wireless service

    Internet service

    Satellite telecommunications and high-speed data service providers

    Software development firms

    Hardware manufacturing firms

Trade Publications

Cable Digital News
(Kinetic Strategies, Inc.)
10020 S. 46th Place
Phoenix, AZ 85044

Cable World Magazine
Access Intelligence, LLC
4 Choke Cherry Road
2nd Floor
Rockville, MD 20850

CED Magazine
P.O. Box 266007
Highlands Ranch, CO 80163-6007

IGI Group, Inc.
The Information Gatekeepers Group
320 Washington Street
Suite 302
Boston, MA 02135

Information Week
600 Community Drive
Manhasset, NY 11030

IT Architect
Network Magazine
600 Harrison Street
San Francisco, CA 94107

Telecommunications Magazine On-Line
Telecommunications Americas
685 Canton Street
Norwood, MA 02062

Wireless Week
8878 South Barrons Boulevard
Highlands Ranch, CO 80163-6007

Professional Associations

Alliance for Telecommunications Industry Solutions
1200 G Street NW
Suite 500
Washington, DC 20005

International Communications Industries Association, Inc.
11242 Waples Mill Road
Suite 200
Fairfax, VA 22030

National Association of Black Telecom Professionals, Inc.
2020 Pennsylvania Avenue NW
Box 735
Washington, DC 20006

National Association of Minorities in Communications
336 West 37th Street
Suite 302
New York, NY 10018

National Cable and Telecommunications Association
25 Massachusetts Avenue NW
Washington, DC 20036

Telecommunications
685 Canton Street
Norwood, MA 02062

Telecommunications Industry Association
2500 Wilson Boulevard
Suite 300
Arlington, VA 22201

Veterinary Technology

Level	Animal Care Services
1. Entry ($20,000–$35,000)	Veterinary Assistant Veterinary Technician Animal Health Technician Veterinary Technologist Animal Health Technologist
2. Mid-management/specialists ($35,000–$50,000)	Licensed Veterinary Technologist Registered Veterinary Technologist Certified Veterinary Technologist Emergency Critical Care Technician Equine Veterinary Technician Equine Veterinary Nursing Technician Internal Medicine Veterinary Technician Internal Medicine Neurology Veterinary Technician Research Veterinary Technician Veterinary Anesthetist Veterinary Behavior Technician Veterinary Dental Technician Veterinary Surgery Technician
3. Management ($50,000–$65,000)	Veterinary Nurse Veterinary Hospital Manager

Level	Animal Care and Pet Grooming
1. Entry ($20,000–$25,000)	Animal Attendant Animal Care Worker Dog Handler Horse Hot Walker Kennel Attendant Lab Animal Attendant Pound Attendant Receiving Barn Custodian Zoo Animal Attendant
2. Mid-management/specialists ($25,000–$30,000)	Animal Groomer Animal Trainer Aquarist Groomer Kennel Keeper

Level	Education
1. Entry ($30,000–$35,000)	Instructor
2. Mid-management/specialist ($35,000–$45,000)	Academic Department Head
3. Management ($45,000–$60,000)	School Director Administrator/Educator

Level	Laboratory Animal Care
1. Entry ($25,000–$30,000)	Animal Care Provider Assistant Lab Animal Technician Kennel Attendant Kennel Worker
2. Mid-management/specialist ($30,000–$45,000)	Kennel Assistant Kennel Technician Lab Animal Technician Veterinary Assistant Veterinarian Assistant Veterinary Technician
3. Management ($45,000–$60,000)	Lab Animal Technologist Lab Supervisor Veterinary Assistant/Lab Tech Surgery

Level	Veterinary Medicine
1. Entry ($40,000–$45,000)	Veterinary Intern
2. Mid-management/specialist ($45,000–$60,000)	Emergency Veterinarian Large Animal Veterinarian Mixed Animal Veterinarian Small Animal Veterinarian Staff Veterinarian Veterinarian
3. Management ($60,000–$80,000)	Medical Director Veterinary Medicine Doctor

Animal Care Services

Level	Job Title	Experience Needed
Entry	Veterinary Assistant	Professional Training
Entry	Veterinary Technician	Professional Training
Entry	Animal Health Technician	Professional Training
Entry	Veterinary Technologist	Professional Training
Entry	Animal Health Technologist	Professional Training
2	Licensed Veterinary Technologist	Professional Training
2	Registered Veterinary Technologist	Professional Training
2	Certified Veterinary Technologist	Professional Training
2	Emergency Critical Care Technician	1–2 years
2	Equine Veterinary Technician	1–2 years
2	Equine Veterinary Nursing Technician	1–4 years
2	Internal Medicine Veterinary Technician	2–4 years
2	Internal Medicine Neurology Veterinary Technician	2–4 years
2	Research Veterinary Technician	3–5 years
2	Veterinary Anesthetist	3–5 years
2	Veterinary Behavior Technician	3–5 years
2	Veterinary Dental Technician	3–5 years
2	Veterinary Surgery Technician	4–6 years
3	Veterinary Nurse	4–6 years
3	Veterinary Hospital Manager	6–8 years

Salaries in Animal Care Services

Entry	$20,000 to $30,000
Entry	$30,000 to $35,000
2	$35,000 to $40,000
2	$40,000 to $45,000
3	$45,000 to $50,000
3	$50,000 to $60,000

Qualifications

Personal   Strong oral and written communication skills. Listening skills. Empathy. Sensitivity to others. Ability to take initiative. Stress tolerance. Dependability. Flexibility. Interpersonal skills. Patience. Cooperation.

Professional   Ability to make quick decisions. Ability to evaluate clients' needs. Technical report writing skills. Critical thinking. Time management. Problem solving. Technical knowledge.

Where the Jobs Are

- Animal control facilities
- Animal shelters
- Biomedical facilities
- Boarding kennels
- Drug or food manufacturers
- Federal executive branch
- Humane societies
- Laboratories
- Local, state, and federal agencies
- Private veterinarian practices
- Research facilities
- Scientific research and development services
- Veterinary clinics
- Veterinary educational facilities
- Veterinary emergency care facilities
- Veterinary hospitals
- Wildlife facilities

Animal Care and Pet Grooming

Level	Job Title	Experience Needed
Entry	Animal Attendant	Professional Training
Entry	Animal Care Worker	Professional Training
Entry	Dog Handler	Professional Training
Entry	Horse Hot Walker	Professional Training
Entry	Kennel Attendant	Professional Training
Entry	Lab Animal Attendant	Professional Training
Entry	Pound Attendant	Professional Training
Entry	Receiving Barn Custodian	Professional Training
Entry	Zoo Animal Attendant	Professional Training

Level	Job Title	Experience Needed
2	Animal Groom	1–2 years
2	Animal Trainer	1–2 years
2	Aquarist	1–2 years
2	Groomer	2–4 years
2	Kennel Keeper	2–4 years

Salaries in Animal Care and Pet Grooming

Entry	$20,000 to $22,000
Entry	$22,000 to $25,000
2	$25,000 to $28,000
2	$28,000 to $32,000
2	$32,000 to $40,000

Qualifications

Personal   Empathy. Patience. Ability to take initiative. Stress tolerance. Dependability. Flexibility.

Professional   Ability to make quick decisions. Ability to evaluate clients' needs. Technical report writing skills. Critical thinking. Time management. Problem-solving skills. Technical knowledge.

Where the Jobs Are

Animal shelters

Grooming salons

Kennels

Stables

Zoos

Education

Level	Job Title	Experience Needed
Entry	Instructor	Professional Training
2	Academic Department Head	3–7 years
3	School Director/Administrator	7–10 years

Salaries in Education

Entry	$30,000 to $35,000
2	$35,000 to $45,000
3	$45,000 to $60,000

Qualifications

Personal   Positive attitude. High energy level. Strong oral and written communication skills. Strong planning and organizational skills.

Professional   Mastery of subject matter. Strong presentation and facilitation skills. Ability to explain complex concepts. Ability to motivate others.

Where the Jobs Are

Colleges and Universities

Teaching veterinary clinics

Teaching veterinary hospitals

Laboratory Animal Care

Level	Job Title	Experience Needed
Entry	Animal Care Provider	Professional Training
Entry	Assistant Lab Animal	Professional Training
	Technician	Professional Training
Entry	Kennel Attendant	Professional Training
Entry	Kennel Worker	Professional Training
2	Kennel Assistant	1–2 years
2	Kennel Technician	1–2 years
2	Lab Animal Technician	1–4 years
2	Veterinary Assistant	1–4 years
2	Veterinarian Assistant	1–4 years
2	Veterinary Technician	1–4 years
3	Lab Animal Technologist	2–5 years
3	Lab Supervisor	5–7 years
3	Veterinary Assistant Lab/	5–7 years
	Tech Surgery	

Salaries in Laboratory Animal Care

Entry	$25,000 to $30,000
2	$30,000 to $35,000
2	$35,000 to $40,000
2	$40,000 to $45,000
3	$45,000 to $50,000
3	$50,000 to $60,000

Qualifications

Personal   Strong oral and written communication skills. Patience. Sensitivity to others. Integrity. Flexibility. Tolerance for stress. Interpersonal skills. Emotional stability. Good judgment.

Professional   Ability to follow and give instructions. Analytical skills. Critical thinking. Ability to make quick decisions. Time management. Technical knowledge. Knowledge of regulatory policies and procedures.

Where the Jobs Are

Federal government research facilities

Kennels

Laboratories

Research veterinary clinics

Research educational facilities

Research veterinary hospitals

State and local research facilities

Veterinary Medicine

Level	Job Title	Experience Needed
Entry	Veterinary Intern	Professional Training
2	Emergency Veterinarian	1–4 years

Level	Job Title	Experience Needed
2	Large Animal Veterinarian	2–5 years
2	Mixed Animal Veterinarian	2–5 years
2	Small Animal Veterinarian	2–5 years
2	Staff Veterinarian	5–7 years
2	Veterinarian	5–7 years
3	Medical Director	7–10 years
3	Veterinary Medicine Doctor	7–10 years

Salaries in Veterinarian Medicine

Entry	$40,000 to $45,000
2	$45,000 to $50,000
2	$50,000 to $55,000
2	$55,000 to $60,000
3	$60,000 to $70,000
3	$70,000 to $80,000

Qualifications

Personal Strong oral and written communication skills. Integrity. Interpersonal skills. Tolerance for stress. Good judgment. Empathy. Flexibility. Detail oriented.

Professional Administrative and supervisory skills. Ability to coordinate people and resources. Leadership skills. Technical knowledge. Knowledge of regulatory policies and procedures.

Where the Jobs Are

> Private veterinarian practices
>
> Veterinary clinics
>
> Veterinary hospitals

Statistics
Alphabetical List of SOC Occupations

Trade Publications

DVM-Dental Veterinary Magazine
Advanstar Communications Inc.
6200 Canoga Avenue, 2nd floor
Woodland Hills, CA 91367

JAVA-Journal of the American Veterinary Association
American Veterinary Medical Association
1931 North Meacham Road
Suite 100
Schaumburg, IL 60173

Journal of Veterinary Dentistry
AVDS-American Veterinary Dental Society
P.O. Box 803
Fayetteville, TN 37334

Veterinary Practice News Magazine
Bow Tie, Inc.
P.O. Box 6050
Mission Viejo, CA 92690

Professional Associations

American Association of Equine Veterinary Technicians
1708 Redwing Street
San Marcos, CA 92078

American Association for Laboratory Animal Science
9190 Crestwyn Hills Drive
Memphis, TN 38125

American Board of Veterinary Practitioners
618 Church Street
Suite 220
Nashville, TN 37219

American College of Laboratory Animal Medicine
96 Chester Street
Chester, NH 03036

American College of Veterinary Anesthesiologists
P.O. Box 1100
Middleburg, VA 20118

American College of Veterinary Behaviorists
Texas A&M University
Department of Small Animal Medicine and Surgery
4474 TAMU
College Station, TX 77843

American College of Veterinary Emergency and Critical Care
Tufts Cummings School of Veterinary Medicine
200 Westboro Road
North Grafton, MA 01536

Canadian Association of Animal Health Technologists and Technicians
Box 595
Langham, SK
S0K 2LO, Canada

National Association of Veterinary Technicians in America
50 S. Pickett, #110
Alexandria, VA 22304

Glossary of Terms Used in Job Descriptions

accept   To receive with consent; to take without protest.

accountability   The state of being subject to judgment for an action or result which a person has been given authority and responsibility to perform.

act   To exert one's power so as to bring about a result; to carry out a plan or purpose. (See **execute, implement,** and **perform.**)

add   To affix or attach; to find the sum of figures.

administer   To direct the application, execution, use, or general conduct of.

adopt   To take and apply or put into action.

advise   To give recommendations to. (See **propose** and **recommend.**) To offer an informed opinion based on specialized knowledge.

affirm   To confirm or ratify.

align   To arrange or form in a line.

amend   To change or modify.

analyze   To study the factors of a situation or problem in order to determine the outcome or solution; to separate or distinguish the parts of a process or situation so as to discover their true relationships.

anticipate   To foresee events, trends, consequences, or problems in order to deal with them in advance.

apply   To adjust or direct; to put in use.

appraise   To evaluate as to quality, status, or effectiveness of.

approve   To sanction officially; to accept as satisfactory; to ratify thereby assuming responsibility for. (*Used only in the situation where the individual has final authority.*)

arrange   To place in proper or desired order; to prepare for an event. (See **prepare.**)

ascertain   To find out or learn with certainty.

assemble   To collect or gather together in a predetermined order or pattern. (See **collect, compile,** and **coordinate.**)

assign   To give specific duties to others to perform. (See **delegate.**)

assist   To lend aid or support in some undertaking or effort. (*No authority over the activity is implied.*)

This glossary was developed in 1981 by Richard B. Shore and Patricia Alcibar for American Management Associations. Used by permission.

From: JoAnn Sperling, *Job Descriptions in Human Resources* (New York: Amacom [*A Division of American Management Association*], 1985).

assume   To take upon oneself; to undertake; to take for granted.

assure   To confirm; to make certain of. (See **ensure.**)

attach   To bind, fasten, tie, or connect.

attend   To be present for the purpose of listening or contributing.

audit   To examine and review a situation, condition, or practice, and conclude with a detailed report on the findings.

authority   The power to influence or command thought, opinion, or behavior.

authorize   To empower; to permit; to establish by authority.

balance   To arrange or prove so that the sum of one group equals the sum of another.

batch   To group into a quantity for one operation.

calculate   To ascertain by mathematical processes; to reckon by exercise of practical judgment.

cancel   To strike or cross out.

carry   To convey through the use of the hands.

center   To place or fix at or around the center; to collect to a point.

chart   To draw or exhibit in a graph.

check   To examine for a condition; to compare for verification. (See **control, examine, inspect, monitor,** and **verify.**)

circulate   To distribute in accordance with a plan. (See **disseminate.**)

classify   To separate into groups having systematic relations.

clear   To get the agreement or disagreement of others.

close   To terminate or shut down.

code   To transpose words or figures into symbols or characters. (Also **encode.**)

collaborate   To work or act jointly with others.

collate   To bring together in a predetermined order.

collect   To gather facts or data; to assemble; to accumulate. (See **assemble** and **compile.**)

compile   To collect into a volume; to compose out of materials from other documents.

compose   To make up, fashion, or arrange.

concur   To agree with a position, statement, act, or opinion.

conduct   To lead, guide, or command the efforts of others toward producing a chosen result.

confer   To converse with others to compare views. (See **consult, discuss,** and **negotiate.**)

consolidate   To combine separate items into a single whole.

construct   To set in order mentally; to arrange.

consult   To seek advice of others; to confer.

control   To exert power over in order to guide or restrain; to measure, interpret, and evaluate for conformance with plans or expected results.

cooperate   To work jointly with others. (See **collaborate.**)

coordinate   To bring into common action or condition so as to harmonize by regulating, changing, adjusting, or combining. (See **assemble.**)

copy   To transfer or reproduce information.

correct   To rectify; to make right.

correlate   To establish a mutual or reciprocal relationship; to put in relation to each other.

cross off   To line out, strike out.

cross out   To eliminate by lining out.

date-stamp   To affix or note a date by stamping.

decide   To choose from among alternatives or possibilities so as to end debate or uncertainty.

delegate   To entrust to the care or management of another; to authorize or empower another to act in one's place. (See **assign, authorize,** and **represent.**)

delegation   Assigning to a subordinate the responsibility and commensurate authority to accomplish an objective or specific result.

delete   To erase; to remove.

design   To conceive and plan in the mind for a specific use; to create, fashion, execute, or construct according to a plan. (See **develop, devise, formulate,** and **plan.**)

determine   To make a decision; to bring about; to cause; to decide and set limits to, thereby fixing definitely and unalterably. To find out something not before known as a result of an intent to find defined and precise truth.

develop   To conceive and create; to make active, available, or usable; to set forth or make clear, evident, or apparent.

development   The result of developing.

devise   To come up with something new, especially by combining known ideas or principles. (See **design, develop, formulate,** and **plan.**)

direct   To lead, guide, or command the efforts of others toward producing a chosen result. (See **conduct, manage,** and **supervise.**)

direction   Guidance or supervision of others.

disassemble   To take apart.

discover   To find out something not known before as a result of chance, exploration, or investigation. (See **ascertain** and **determine.**)

discuss   To exchange views for the purpose of convincing or reaching a conclusion.

disseminate   To spread information or ideas. (See **circulate, distribute, issue,** and **release.**)

distribute   To divide or separate into classes; to pass around; to allot; to deliver to named places or persons. (See **circulate, disseminate, issue,** and **release.**)

divide   To separate into classes or parts subject to mathematical division.

draft   To compose or write papers and documents in preliminary or final form, often for the approval or clearance of others.

duty   Assigned task.

edit   To revise and prepare for publication.

endorse   To express approval of; to countersign.

ensure   To make safe or certain. (See **assure.**)

establish   To set up or bring into existence on a firm basis.

evaluate   To ascertain or determine the value of.

examine   To investigate; to scrutinize; to subject to inquiry by inspection or test.

execute   To put into effect; to follow through to the end.

exercise   To employ actively, as in authority or influence.

expedite   To accelerate the movement or progress of; to remove obstacles.

facilitate   To make easy or less difficult.

feed   To supply material to a machine.

figure   To compute.

file   To lay away papers, etc., arranged in some methodical manner.

fill in   To enter information on a form.

find   To locate by search.

flag   To mark distinctively.

follow up   To check the progress of; to see if results are satisfactory.

formulate   To develop or devise a plan, policy, or procedure; to put into a systemized statement.

furnish   To give or supply. (See **provide.**)

goal   An objective.

guidance   Conducting or directing along a course of action.

implement   To carry out; to perform acts essential to the execution of a plan or program; to give effect to.

inform   To instruct; to communicate knowledge.

initiate   To originate; to introduce for the first time.

insert   To put or thrust in.

inspect   To examine carefully for suitability or conformance with standards. (See **check, control, examine, monitor,** and **verify.**)

instruct   To impart knowledge to; to give information or direction to; to show how to do.

instructions   To furnish with directions; to inform.

General: Directions that are merely outlined; hence they do not closely limit what can be done or how it can be done.

intensive   Exhaustive or concentrated.

interpret   To explain or clarify; to translate.

interview   To question in order to obtain facts or opinions.

inventory   A list of items; stock on hand.

investigate   To study closely and methodically.

issue   To distribute formally.

itemize   To set or note down in detail; to set by particulars.

line   To cover the inside surface of; to draw lines on.

list   To itemize.

locate   To search for and find; to position.

maintain   To keep up-to-date or current; to keep at a given level or in working condition.

manage   To control and direct; to guide; to command the efforts of others toward producing a chosen result. (See **supervise.**)

measure   To find the quality or amount of; to ascertain dimension, count, intensity, etc.

merge   To combine.

mix   To unite or blend into one group or mass.

monitor   To observe or check periodically for a specific purpose.

multiply   To perform the operation of multiplication.

negotiate   To exchange views and proposals with an eye to reaching agreement by sifting possibilities, proposals, and pros and cons.

nonroutine   Irregular or infrequent situations that arise relating to business or official duties. Characteristic of higher-level jobs.

note   To observe, notice.

notify   To give notice to; to inform.

objective   A desired result. (See **goal.**)

observe   To perceive, notice, watch.

obtain   To gain possession of; to acquire.

open   To enter upon; to spread out; to make accessible.

operate   To conduct or perform activity.

organization   Individuals working together in related ways within a specific structure toward a common end.

organize   To arrange in interdependent parts; to systematize.

originate   To produce as new; to invent.

outline   To make a summary of the significant features of a subject.

participate   To take part in.

perform   To carry out; to accomplish; to execute.

place   To locate an employee in a job.

plan   To devise or project a method or course of action.

policy   A definite course or method of action selected from among alternatives and in light of given conditions, to guide and determine present and future decisions.

position description   A document that describes the purpose, scope, duties, responsibilities, authorities, and working relationships associated with a position or entity to be occupied and performed by one person.

position specification   A document that describes the physical characteristics, knowledge, skill, experience, and education requirements of a person who would be ideally suited to perform a specific job.

post   To announce by public, written notice; to transfer or carry information from one record to another.

practice   To work repeatedly to gain skill.

prepare   To make ready for a special purpose.

principle   A governing law of conduct; a fundamental belief serving as a responsible guide to action; a basis for policy.

procedure   A particular way of accomplishing something or of acting; a series of steps followed in a regular, definite order; a standardized practice.

proceed   To begin or carry out.

process   To subject to some special treatment; to handle in accordance with prescribed procedures.

program   A series of planned steps toward an objective.

promote   To act so as to increase sales or patronage; to advance someone to a higher level or job.

propose   To offer for consideration or adoption; to declare an intention.

provide   To supply for use; to make available; to furnish.

purchase   To buy or procure.

purpose   Something set up as an objective or end to be attained; a reason.

rate   To appraise or assess; to give one's opinion of the rank or quality of.

receive   To take something that is offered or sent.

recommend   To advise or counsel a course of action or to suggest for adoption a course of action.

reconstruct   To restore; to construct again.

record   To register; to make a record of.

refer   To direct attention to.

register   To enter in a record or list.

release   To authorize the publication of, dissemination of.

remit   To transmit or send money as payment.

render   To furnish, contribute.

report   To supply or furnish organized information.

represent   To act for or in place of; to serve as a counterpart of; to substitute in some capacity for.

request   To ask for something.

require   To demand as necessary or essential.

requisition   A document making a request.

research   Inquiry into a specific subject from several sources.

responsibility   The quality or state of being accountable for.

responsible for   Having caused; accountable for.

review   To examine, usually with intent to approve or dissent; to analyze results in order to give an opinion.

revise   To change in order to make new, to correct, to improve, or to bring up-to-date.

route   To prearrange the sending of an item to the location to which it is to be sent.

routine   Regular procedure, or normal course of business or official duties.

scan   To examine point by point; to scrutinize.

schedule   To plan a timetable; to set specific times for.

screen   To examine so as to separate into two or more groups or classes, usually rejecting one or more.

search   To look over and through for the purpose of finding something.

secure   To get possession of; to obtain; to make safe.

select   Chosen from a number of others of a similar kind.

separate   To set apart from others for special use; to keep apart.

serve   To hold an office; to act in a capacity; to discharge a duty or function.

sign   To authorize by affixing one's signature.

sort   To put in a definite place or rank according to kind, class, etc.

Specific: Precise and detailed directions that closely limit what can be done or how it can be done.

stack   To pile up.

standard of performance   A statement of the conditions that will exist when a job is acceptably done. Whenever possible, the elements of the statement include specific reference to quantity, quality, cost, and time.

stimulate   To excite, rouse, or spur on.

study   To consider attentively; to ponder or fix the mind closely upon a subject.

submit   To present information for another's judgment or decision.

subtotal   An interim total.

subtract   To deduct one number from another.

summarize   To give only the main points.

supervise   To oversee a work group—leading, guiding, or commanding its efforts to produce a chosen result.

support   To provide service, assistance, or supplies to another person or department.

survey   To ascertain facts regarding conditions or the condition of a situation usually in connection with the gathering of information.

tabulate   To form into a table by listing; to make a listing.

trace   To record the transfer of an application or document; to copy as a drawing.

train   To increase skill or knowledge by capable instruction.

transcribe   To make a typed copy from shorthand notes or dictated record; to write a copy of.

transpose   To transfer; to change the usual place or order.

underline   To emphasize or identify by drawing a line under the characters or subject.

verify   To prove to be true or accurate; to confirm or substantiate; to test or check the accuracy of.

Index of Job Descriptions

Academic Department Head   Administers affairs of an academic department. May administer department's budget and recruit academic personnel. Conducts meetings to discuss current teaching strategies and obtains recommendations for changes within the department.

Account Executive   Responsible for the development and service of a customer account. Brings business to the firm. Consults with the client and collaborates with associates to find the best strategies for servicing clients.

Account Executive (Advertising)   Meets with clients. Participates in meetings with other departments on the ideas for a campaign. Plans overall strategy for clients. Keeps up-to-date on media rate changes and new media outlets: Serves as a link between the agency and the clients.

Account Executive (Food Service)   Initiates and signs new customers, which includes scouting new business, helping survey clients' needs, writing formal request letters, and making formal presentations, usually accompanied by management representative(s). Representative of the food service contractor who deals directly with the liaison designate of the client.

Account Executive (Public Relations)   Meets with clients to determine needs for public relations program. May review company strategies and goals, current customer base, and reputation with the public. Recommends public relations program. Keeps up-to-date on new and existing programs and policies. Serves as a link between the public relations firm and the clients.

Account Executive (Telemarketing)   Organizes and manages a program internally once it has been brought in by a tele-marketing representative. Coordinates script writing, script testing, list preparation, forms design (to record sales and customer data), and client reports. Monitors the project and provides regular reports for the client.

Account Executive Trainee (Advertising)   Fields material from other departments. Takes calls from clients. Keeps in touch with traffic department on schedules for ads and spots.

Account Manager   Develops an efficient coverage pattern for the territory. Decides on the call frequency for major accounts. Develops a sales plan for the territory. Promotes, sells, and services product line. Reviews customer-call reports. Coordinates activities at individual key customer locations.

Account Representative   (See **Account Executive**)

Account Supervisor   (See **Account Manager**)

Accounts Supervisor/Manager   (See **Account Manager**)

Accountant   Helps businesses and individuals set up financial recordkeeping. Examines, analyzes, and interprets accounting records for the purpose of giving advice or preparing statements. Estimates future revenues and expenditures to prepare budgets.

Accountant (Food Service)   Prepares and analyzes financial reports that furnish up-to-date financial information. Accountants employed by large restaurant firms may travel extensively to audit or work for clients or branches of the firm.

Activities Coordinator (Cruise Lines)   Plans and implements activities for passengers on cruise lines.

Actuarial Trainee   Works for insurance companies analyzing statistics to determine probabilities of accident, death, injury, earthquake, flood, fire, etc., so that the rates charged for insurance policies will bring in profits for the company while still being competitive with those of other insurance carriers.

Actuary   Uses mathematical skills to predict probabilities of events that will be used for insurance plans and pension programs.

Adjudication Officer   Determines eligibility for types of immigration benefits, including permission to import foreign workers, permission for relatives to immigrate, and permission to become a U.S. citizen. Reviews applications for benefits and often conducts interviews with applicants.

Adjuster   Investigates and settles claims of losses suffered by policyholders of all kinds of insurance.

Adjuster Trainee   Assists with investigations and settling claims of losses suffered by policyholders of all kinds of insurance.

Administrative Analyst/Planner   Responsibilities include developing new systems and setting up long-range planning systems. Responsible for the planning group, which actually plans each day's shipment to distribution centers. Works on product allocation and inventory control. Responsible for anything that might affect the distribution area.

Administrative Assistant   An administrative support job performed with little or no supervision that is a step higher than an executive secretary. Handles dissemination of contract information or works with a chief officer of a company in preparing corporate reports. Often involves supervision of others.

Administrative Dental Assistant   Checks office and laboratory supplies; maintains waiting, reception, and examination rooms in a neat and orderly condition; answers telephones; greets patients and other callers; records and files patient data and medical records; fills out medical reports and insurance forms; handles correspondence; schedules appointments; and arranges for hospital admission and laboratory services. May transcribe dictation and handle the bookkeeping and billing.

Administrative Dietitian   Responsible for training and supervision of food service supervisor and assistants in food preparation and in formulating policies and enforcing sanitary and safety regulations. Buys food, equipment, and other supplies; thus must understand purchasing and budgeting.

Administrative Manager   Provides maximum support to all divisions through the regional or district distribution centers and ensures that timely, cost-effective service is provided to those units and their customers. Supervises personnel, equipment, materials, facilities, product handling, inventory control, building services, customer relations, order processing, office services, and district operations.

Administrative Medical Office Assistant   (See **Administrative Dental Assistant**)

Administrative Secretary   Handles everything except dictation and typing. Duties range from filing and setting up filing systems, routing mail, and answering telephones to more complex work such as answering letters, doing research, and preparing statistical reports.

Administrative Support Manager (Word Processing)
Responsible for the operation of the entire word processing center.

Administrator (Education)   Directs the administration of an educational institution, or a division of it, within the authority of the governing board. Develops or expands programs or services. Administers fiscal operations such as budget planning, accounting, and establishing costs for the institution. Directs hiring and training of personnel. Develops policies and procedures for activities within area of responsibility. Involved with developing curriculum and programs and directing teaching personnel of the school system. Confers with teaching and administrative staff to plan and develop curriculum designed to meet needs of the students. Visits classrooms to observe effectiveness of instructional methods and materials. Evaluates teaching techniques and recommends changes for improving them. Conducts workshops and conferences for teachers to study new classroom procedures, new instructional materials, and other aids to teaching.

Administrator of Healthcare Services   (see Vice President of Healthcare Administration).

Advertising Manager   Plans and executes advertising policies of an organization. Confers with department heads to discuss possible new accounts and to outline new policies or sales promotion campaigns. Confers with officials of newspapers and of radio and television stations and then arranges billboard advertising contracts. Allocates advertising space to departments. May authorize information for publication.

Advertising Sales Representative   Responsible for growth of new business and for maintaining current customer base. May use Web conferencing to give demos to companies all over the country.

Advertising Specialist   Plans, develops, coordinates, and implements campaigns to inform the organization's target market of the merits of purchasing particular products and services and of buying from the organization in general.

Agent (Insurance)   Sells traditional life insurance to clients. May also sell mutual funds and other equity-based products. Many agents also qualify as financial planners after obtaining certification. Explains financial products in detail to prospective clients. Processes necessary paperwork when closing a sale.

Air Patrol Officer   Patrols areas, by air, where the military is located.

Air Safety Investigator   Investigates aircraft incidents, such as equipment malfunctions and air traffic violations, and prepares factual reports of findings.

Airline Schedule Analyst   Reviews schedules for all incoming and outgoing flights. Makes recommendations for changes in schedules to ensure maximum service while still maintaining strict procedures.

Airport Manager   Responsible for operating a safe facility and for fund-raising. Keeps the public informed on safety decisions affecting the area surrounding the airport.

Airport Operations Agent   Customer service agent responsible for assigning boarding times, collecting tickets. Coordinates baggage service. Announces flight arrivals to main desk.

Airport Security Officer   Notes suspicious persons and reports to superior officer. Reports hazards. Inspects baggage of passengers. Assists passengers with lost luggage claims. Directs passengers to appropriate boarding areas. Warns or arrests persons violating ordinances. Issues tickets to traffic violators. Maintains overall security of the airport.

Animal Attendant   Prepares and delivers food and water to animals. Grooms animals. Responsible for transporting animals between enclosures. Rescues injured and neglected animals. Treats minor injuries and reports serious health issues to veterinarians. Maintains animal records. Works with the public and other staff members.

Animal Care Provider   Plans the diets and prepares the food for animals. Monitors eating patterns or any change in behavior and records the observation. Answers questions and ensures the visiting public behaves responsibly toward exhibited animals.

Animal Care Worker   (See **Animal Care Provider**)

Animal Groomer   Grooms pets by taking service order requests from owners, assessing pet conditions, performing grooming services, and easing pet anxieties.

Animal Health Technician   Provides routine care, exercise, basic training, and medical treatment to animals; cares for animals and assesses them for adoptability; assists in the placement of, or provides for the humane euthanasia of, shelter animals; assists veterinarians in the medical treatment of or spay or neuter of animals; assists in developing protocols and implementing programs to maintain kennels in a sanitary and disease-free condition; and performs other duties as required. Writes reports, recommends and sells products to clinic standards, maintains research information.

Animal Health Technologist/Technician   Performs nursing, dental, pre- and post-operative, lab, and clinical work under the supervision of a licensed veterinarian. Assists veterinarians as needed in all aspects of work.

Animal Trainer   Trains animals for riding, security, performance, obedience, or assisting people with disabilities. Familiarizes animals to human voice and contact and conditions animals to respond to commands.

Aquarist   Feeds, monitors, and otherwise cares for aquatic animals. May keep records of feedings, treatments, and animals received or discharged. May clean, disinfect, monitor water quality, and design or build exhibits. May answer phones, schedule appointments, and collect patient information.

Assistant Lab Animal Technician   Assists with administering medications to lab animals, prepares samples for laboratory examinations, and records information about animals' genealogy, diet, weight, medications, food intake, and clinical signs of pain and distress. Assists with ordering supplies and instruments. May assist with preoperative and postoperative care, performing standardized laboratory tests on animal specimen and reporting findings.

Analyst (Marketing)   (See **Market Research Analyst**)

Appeals Officer   Conducts conferences to settle cases in which taxpayers have appealed IRS determinations on their case or filed a petition in the U.S. Tax Court and approves final settlement of the case.

Applications Developer   Designs, develops, maintains, and enhances existing information systems. Assists in developing client interfaces for various information systems. Backs up the database administrator.

Architect   Involved with all aspects of the planning, design, and construction of buildings. Prepares proposals that include illustrations and scale drawings. Draws the structural system as well as the other elements that go into the project. Provides advice about choosing contractors.

Area Manager (Retail)   Manages a selling center within a store. This would include a small group of departments carrying related merchandise.

Arson Specialist   Collects evidence to determine the origin and cause of fires. Reports findings to police and fire departments and insurance companies.

Assembler, Machinist, and Systems Tester   Assemblers put together electronics and hardware components. Machinists shape hardware components. Systems testers troubleshoot components by checking for faults and identifying problem areas that need to be fixed.

Asset Manager   Employed by businesses and corporations to assist in the protection of assets, from both internal and external forces.

Assistant Actuary   (See **Actuary**)

Assistant Buyer (Production)   (See **Buyer—Production**)

Assistant Catering Manager   Assists in overseeing and coordinating operation of all catering needs and events.

Assistant Chef   (See **Chef**)

Assistant Club Manager   (See **Club Manager**)

Assistant Coach   Assists the head coach in the activities of an athletic team for a major sport. Critiques player performance to determine the skills and abilities that need strengthening for overall team performance.

Assistant Concessions Manager   Supervises the concessions operations within a specified area at the stadium. Oversees staffing and equipment maintenance and rental.

Assistant Dean   Plans, organizes, and directs the day-to-day operations of a department under administrative direction. Typically, serves as a resource and referral source for students seeking various types of assistance.

Assistant Department Head   Provides support to a department head. Serves as a staff advisor and performs support tasks.

Assistant Food and Beverage Manager   (See **Food and Beverage Manager**)

Assistant Hotel Manager   Assists with supervising the operations of the different departments of a hotel: food service, housekeeping, front office, and maintenance. Ensures the smooth functioning and profitability of the hotel by maintaining the property and providing quality guest service.

Assistant Housekeeper   (See **Housekeeper**)

Assistant Loan Officer   (See **Loan Officer**)

Assistant Manager (Food Service)   Performs supervisory duties under the manager's direction. Must be capable of filling in when the manager is absent; thus, needs good management skills and knowledge of the operation.

Assistant Manager (Front Office)   (See **Front Office Manager**)

Assistant Manager of Membership Sales   Assists with sales calls, in person and on the phone. Maintains sales records. Prepares promotional materials. Prepares new-member records and may conduct first consultation with new members.

Assistant Manager Trainee (Recreation)   (See **Assistant Club Manager**)

Assistant Marketing Director (Travel)   Assists with the development of competitive strategies for clients. Reviews services and products being offered and evaluates client's market position. Assists companies with monitoring themselves to make sure they are delivering what is promised.

Assistant Media Planner   Learns to interpret rate cards of various media. Analyzes audience ratings. Writes letters and memos. Compares media alternatives. Prepares and delivers presentations to clients. Talks with sales representatives from various media. Evaluates media buying.

Assistant Pastry Chef   (See **Pastry Chef**)

Assistant Product Manager   Assists the senior product manager or product manager in the development and execution of marketing plans. Assists in the achievement of profit objectives and market share.

Assistant Professor   A designation of faculty rank used to refer to faculty members with some, but not extensive, teaching experience in their area of expertise.

Assistant Purchasing Agent   (See **Purchasing Agent**)

Assistant Quality Assurance Manager   (See **Quality Assurance Manager**)

Assistant Stadium Manager   Assists in the planning, organizing, coordinating, and directing of stadium events. Assists in management activities. Learns and applies applicable federal, state, and county laws and ordinances. Assists in scheduling and training employees.

Assistant Steward   Oversees stewarding operations and inventory. Attends department meetings. Provides support and training in stewarding. Follows standards and procedures. Assists in banquet and kitchen operations.

Assistant Store Manager   (See **Store Manager**)

Assistant Travel Editor   (See **Travel Editor**)

Assistant Underwriter   (See **Underwriter**)

Assistant Wine Steward   (See **Wine Steward**)

Assistant Winemaker Supports all aspects of the wine-making process. Provides technical support and ensures wine quality at all stages of wine production. Responsible for influencing the growing of grapes to ensure the quality of wine delivered to the customer.

Associate Analyst (Marketing) (See **Market Research Analyst**)

Associate Media Director Makes decisions on media buying. Reviews alternative selections and results of ratings to determine decision.

Associate Product Manager—Sports Apparel Oversees and maintains brand integrity of product development in a region, from concept through production. Initiates and executes product development with vendors by region.

Associate Professor A higher designation of faculty rank than assistant professor; used to refer to faculty members with more extensive teaching experience in their area of expertise. Often this ranking is also marked by research work, publications, or industry experience.

Associate Research Director (Advertising) Evaluates information published by government, trade, or other groups as it relates to individual ad campaigns. Evaluates suggestions and findings of the research account executive to determine the best approach to each ad campaign. Keeps campaigns operating within specified guidelines.

Association Account Executive (Hospitality) Responsible for the development and service of professional or trade association business coming into a hotel or other related facility.

Athletic Director Provides leadership and serves as the primary spokesperson for athletic programs. Makes recommendations on goals, academics, capital needs, staff, budget, and other aspects of athletics. Establishes policies and procedures to ensure compliance with rules and regulations.

Attractions Specialist Has specific knowledge of local attractions and how to promote them. Provides input on target population for promotional effort.

Auditor of Regulatory Compliance Conducts compliance audits under a compliance audit plan. Creates and enhances audit programs, emphasizing regulatory and legal compliance and adherence to established procedures. Composes written reports summarizing compliance and audit findings.

Author The writer of a book, article, or other text. One who practices writing as a profession.

Automation Technician Installs, sets up, and operates programmable logic controllers, robots, and related electrical and automated equipment.

Automation Technologist Attends service calls as required by the plant supervisor. Works with and reports to the plant supervisor on all issues and projects. Takes an active part in maintenance programs.

Background Investigator A civilian employee who conducts and compiles personal and professional background investigations. May investigate credit history, previous criminal records, driving records, or history of drug or alcohol abuse or other areas of a person's background.

Baker Prepares all the baked items that are not desserts, such as breads, rolls, muffins, danish, and croissants, for use in dining rooms of hotels and restaurants and related facilities. Depending on the size of the staff and the operation, may also make pies, cakes, and some pastry items.

Ballistic Specialist Examines weapons used in the commission of crimes; conducts identification of guns used in crimes and conducts tests of firearms to determine potential match to weapons suspected if used in crime scenes.

Bank Officer Trainee Gains experience in the main functions of the banking business, including the trust department, where money is invested for families, institutions, or other businesses; the credit department, where decisions are made on lending money to customers; and operations in which all the normal business functions (data processing, personnel, public relations, and accounting) are monitored.

Banquet Manager Arranges banquet and food service functions. Arranges banquet details after they have been agreed upon by the catering manager and the customer. Prepares and updates banquet menus. Reports inventory needs to purchasing agent and storeroom. May supervise the scheduling of staff to work the functions.

Benefits Coordinator Administers various employee benefit programs such as group insurance—life, medical, and dental; accident and disability insurance; pensions; investment savings; and health maintenance organizations. Initiates medical and option forms and/or affidavits; arranges for their completion and submission within time limits. Implements new benefit programs; arranges and conducts employee information presentations and enrollments. Ensures program compliance with governmental regulations.

Beverage Manager Monitors and manages all beverage areas daily. Ensures that all accepted standards and policies are followed and enforced.

Bookkeeper Tracks all cash flows, billing, and lines of credit that affect the company.

Bookkeeping Manager Performs and manages all bookkeeping functions for a firm. Is responsible for the accuracy of all accounting records and compliance with GAAP (Generally Accepted Accounting Principles). Completes general ledger entries, account reconciliations, fixed asset management, financial statement preparation, and month-end closings. May supervise other staff.

Border Patrol Officer Responsible for guarding all U.S. points of entry to detect and prevent illegal entry into the United States. Inspects commercial carriers, terminals, and traffic checkpoints to stop those who attempt to enter the country without proper clearance. Also responsible for deportation actions.

Branch Manager Plans, coordinates, controls the work flow, updates systems, strives for administrative efficiency, and is responsible for all functions of a branch office.

Branch Sales Manager Makes a direct sales effort to the customers in the area to sell a product line. Provides management with sales and booking forecasts on monthly, quarterly, and annual bases. Keeps abreast of prices and performance of competitors' products in his or her territory. Handles service and related problems as they arise. Trains and supervises sales staff.

Brewer Oversees all aspects of the complex process that produces beer, from initial production through fermentation and on to packaging and quality assurance processes. Ensures that the quality of the product is consistent by testing ingredients and tasting the final product.

Broadcast Technician   Performs the work of an electronics technician, specifically on various types of broadcast equipment. (See **Electronics Technician**)

Broiler Cook   Prepares broiled meats, chicken, and seafood according to recipe requirements and adheres to product sensitivity and plate presentation guidelines.

Broker   A securities firm or an investment advisor associated with a firm. When acting as a broker for the purchase or sale of listed stock, the individual advisor does not own the securities but acts as an agent for the buyer and the seller.

Business Development Manager (Wine)   Proven wine professional with strong industry contacts to develop sales and marketing plans for wine products.

Business Director for Sports Performance Center   Prepares and maintains the daily schedule of clients and coaching staff. Stays current with training methods and equipment. Implements quality control program.

Business Event Planner   Offers a complete spectrum of corporate meetings and planning services. May provide services in conference management and keynote speaker sourcing. Plans meeting's food and beverage service. Handles guest registration and data tracking, audiovisual requests, on-site meeting coordination, and transportation and room arrangements. May provide invitations and program coordination.

Butcher   Responsible for cutting, boning, and otherwise caring for and preparing meats for cooking.

Buyer (Production)   Responsible for placing orders, expediting back orders, and processing paperwork for stock and nonstock supplies. Duties include processing requisitions, researching products, clarifying specifications, typing purchase orders, following up on back orders, selecting vendors, maintaining up-to-date product information files, and utilizing computer terminals and handheld order entry devices to place orders.

Buyer (Retail)   Selects the goods to be sold by retail stores or wholesale outlets. Helps plan the selling programs for the goods purchased. Normally specializes in one type of goods, such as men's clothing, housewares, or accessories.

Buyer Trainee (Retail)   Assists supervising buyer. Places orders and speaks with manufacturers by telephone. Supervises the inspection and unpacking of new merchandise and overseeing its distribution.

Buying/Purchasing Agent   Seeks to obtain the highest-quality merchandise at the lowest possible purchase cost for the firm. Purchasers buy goods and services for use by the firm; buyers buy items for resale.

Buy-side Research Analyst   An analyst, employed by an entity such as a mutual fund, that invests its own accounts and conducts market research available only to firms engaging its services.

Cafeteria Chef   Generally works in institutional kitchens in schools, cafeterias, businesses, and hospitals.

Cake Decorator   Decorates cakes and pastries of all shapes and sizes. May also bake cakes. Helps clients choose the type of cake suitable for various occasions.

Call Center Assistant   Facilitates internal and external customer requests, including transfer, escort, and/or fulfillment of inbound and outbound telephone, mail, or e-mail requests.

Call Center Specialist   Responsible for hands-on process design, process management, escalation management, capacity forecasting, training design, and implementation for all required call center transactions.

Computer-Aided Drafting and Design (CADD)   Operator Lays out and makes changes and corrections to detail and assembly drawings and three-dimensional solid models.

Captain (Police Department)   An officer ranking above a first lieutenant and below a major.

Cardiovascular Technician   Aids doctors in finding and caring for illnesses or injuries related to the heart or blood vessels. Specializes in invasive operations and procedures.

Cardiovascular Technologist   Tests and treats patients for heart, lung, and blood problems. Specializes in internal and external cardiovascular technology while working with catheters, pacemakers, and Holter monitors.

Case Manager   Organizes a case's pleadings, oversees the mechanics of producing documents and maintaining a documents library. Experience as a litigation paralegal is usually required.

Caseworker   Counsels and aids at-risk individuals and/or families requiring one or more forms of psychological services. Interviews clients experiencing problems with personal and family finances or employment. Refers clients to community resources and other organizations.

Catering Chef   Coordinates, plans, participates in, and supervises the production, preparation, and presentation of food for catering functions and additional food service production. Supervises catering production.

Catering Manager   Works with the Executive Chef on menus, food quality, or service problems. Responsible for arranging any catered functions held at the establishment, from weddings to conventions, banquets to dances. Draws up necessary contracts. Helps customers select menu, decorations, and room arrangement and transmits these requirements to various departments for execution.

Celebrity Chef   A chef who has become well-known for her or his culinary skills and participates in a wide range of media promotions.

Cellar Hand   Conducts lab tests to monitor the progress of grapes to ensure their quality and to determine correct time for harvesting with viticulturists, who may manage planting programs, harvest, cultivation, and production of grapes.

Cellar Master   A wine cellar manager responsible for the annual budget for purchasing inventory, and staffing day-to-day operations. Oversees crushing, pressing filtration, bottling, safety, sanitation, and other cellar-related activities. Works closely with the Enologist.

Central Region Sales Manager   Responsible for sales function in the central region. (See **Regional Sales Manager**)

Certified Culinarian   An entry-level culinary professional within a commercial food service operation responsible for preparing and cooking sauces, cold foods, fish, soups and stocks, meats, vegetables, eggs, and other food items. Possesses a basic knowledge of food safety and sanitation, culinary nutrition, and supervisory management.

Certified Culinary Educator   A culinary professional with an advanced culinary degree who is working as an educator in an accredited postsecondary institution or military training facility responsible for the development, implementation, administration, evaluation, and maintenance of a culinary arts or food service management curriculum.

Certified Executive Chef   A person who has been the department head responsible for all culinary units in a restaurant, hotel, club, hospital, cruise ship, or other food service establishment and has supervised more than five full-time people in food production for a minimum of five years and has four to five years' additional experience.

Certified Executive Pastry Chef   A pastry chef who is a department head and usually reports to the Executive Chef of a food operation or to the management of a research or pastry specialty firm. Maintains a safe and sanitary work environment for all employees and ensures that all bakery and pastry kitchens provide a nutritious, safe, eye-appealing, and properly flavored food.

Certified Information Systems Security Professional   An individual who has been awarded a certificate for achieving a prescribed level of information service experience, complying with a professional code of ethics, and passing a rigorous examination on the Common Body of Knowledge of Information Security.

Certified Master Chef   Possesses the highest degree of professional cooking and baking knowledge and skill, and demonstrates that mastery by successfully completing a series of written and practical exams covering subjects from menu development and nutritional cooking to international, classical, and American cuisines, and has had working experience equal to or greater than that of a certified chef.

Certified Master Pastry Chef   The consummate pastry chef. Possesses the highest degree of professional culinary knowledge and skill. Teaches and supervises an entire crew. Provides leadership and serves as a role model for the American Culinary Federation apprentices.

Certified Pastry Chef   Teaches and supervises an entire crew. Provides leadership and serves as a role model for American Culinary Federation apprentices.

Certified Registered Nurse   Develops and manages nursing care plans. Instructs patients and their families in proper care and helps individuals and groups take steps to improve or maintain their health.

Certified Sous-Chef   A chef who supervises a shift, station, or stations in a food service operation. A sous-chef must supervise a minimum of two full-time people in the preparation of food.

Certified Veterinary Technologist   Persons acknowledged by an educational institution or professional organization as qualified to perform the duties of a veterinary technologist. The certification does not imply a legal right to perform certain duties and is a voluntary achievement.

Chef   Supervises, coordinates, and participates in activities of cooks and other kitchen personnel engaged in preparing foods for a hotel, restaurant, cafeteria, or other establishment. Estimates food consumption and requisitions or purchases foodstuffs. Receives and checks recipes. Supervises personnel engaged in preparing, cooking, and serving meats, sauces, vegetables, soups, and other foods. May employ, train, and discharge workers. In small establishments, may maintain time and payroll records.

Chef de Cuisine (Maitre de Cuisine)   Is in complete charge of food services. Reports to the Food and Beverage Director in large operations or to the owner or manager in smaller operations. May assume duties of the Food and Beverage Director as well when needed.

Chef Instructor   Brings a chef's perspective to the lab/classroom and teaches hands-on cooking techniques. (See **Instructor**)

Chef Manager   Responsible for all back-of-the-house operations and food production. Oversees staffing, scheduling, training, and development of hourly staff. Handles food production, purchasing processes, and daily food service operations.

Chief Accountant   Responsible for the supervision and control of the general accounting functions, including general ledger, payables, payroll, property, budget reporting, and statistical accumulation. Responsible for financial statement and report preparation and budget reviews. Supervises and trains employees in accounting, payroll, and accounts payable.

Chief Accountant (Hospitality)   Responsible for the supervision and control of the general accounting functions of the hotel, including night audit functions, general ledger, payables, payroll, property, budget reporting, and statistical accumulation. Responsible for financial statement and report preparation and budget reviews. Supervises and trains hotel employees in accounting, payroll, and accounts payable.

Chief Actuary   Oversees the calculation of probabilities of death, sickness disability, injury, property loss, fire, and other hazards. Evaluates and analyzes relevant statistics. Determines the rate of expected losses due to the issuance of various types of policies. Determines the various provisions contained in insurance policies.

Chief Financial Officer   Develops corporate financial objectives. Establishes policies and procedures for the effective recording, analyzing, and reporting of all financial matters. Directs the controller, treasury, and corporate financial services activities to ensure that each of these functions meets established goals and provides effective service to the corporation as a whole.

Chief Internal Auditor   (See **Internal Auditor**)

Chief of Police   Serves as the chief officer of the police department and is the final authority in all matters of policy, operations, and discipline. Exercises all lawful powers of the office; issues such lawful orders as are necessary to assure the effective performance of the department. Plans, directs, coordinates, controls, and staffs activities of the department.

Chief Tourism Officer   Oversees the staff engaged in tourism development for a particular area. Works within established budgets. Approves promotional campaigns.

Chip Architect   Acts as a technical visionary to work with marketing and to research and propose future generations of products, as well as doing architecture and design for the current generation. Must be familiar with architecture performance modeling specification documentation and external vendor's evaluations; manages external design services.

City Manager   Responsible for managing inbound business for a car rental company.

City Mortgage and Real Estate Secretary   Works with real estate investment officers and provides secretarial support for an investment team. Prepares commitment letters and various reports, maintains files, and handles telephone communications.

Claims Examiner   Analyzes insurance claims to determine extent of insurance carrier's liability and settles claims with claimants in accordance with policy provisions. Investigates questionable inquiries.

Claims Representative   Reviews insurance claim forms for completeness, secures and adds missing data, and transmits claims for payment or for further investigation.

Clerical/Office Embezzlement Investigator   Is in charge of investigating potential fraudulent appropriation of property by a person to whom the property has been entrusted.

Clinical Dental Assistant   Reviews patients' records and presents them to the dentist. Obtains information needed to update medical histories. Takes patient X rays. Assists the dentist in examining patients. Instructs patients about medications.

Clinical Dietitian   Identifies nutritional problems and evaluates nutrition status of clients individually or in group sessions; principal role is providing appropriate nutrition plans. Promotes general health through food and nutrition.

Clinical Medical Assistant   Obtains patients' height, weight, temperature, and blood pressure; obtains medical histories; performs basic laboratory tests. Prepares patients for examination or treatment; assists the physician in examining patients. Instructs patients about medication and self-treatment, draws blood, prepares patients for X rays, takes EKGs, and applies dressings.

Clinical Nutrition Manager   Directs the function of clinical nutrition services in acute care settings. Directs nutrition assessment, nutrition counseling and consulting, and performance improvement to provide high-quality nutrition care to patients and/or residents.

Clinical Prosthetist   Designs, builds, and fits artificial limbs and braces.

Clinical Psychologist   Works closely with inmates as a member of an interdisciplinary health care team.

Club Manager   Estimates and orders food products and coordinates activity of workers engaged in selling alcoholic and nonalcoholic beverages for consumption on the premises. May manage staff involved in operating club with recreational facilities for private groups or the general public. Responsible for grounds and buildings, payroll, and promotion.

Coach   Develops athletic talent. Teaches sports techniques, playing rules, strategies, and playing tactics. Conditions athletes appropriately for sports activities; supervises and conducts practice and contests safety.

COBOL Programmer   Writes, tests, and maintains COBOL programs and/or software that tell the computer what to do.

Converts project specifications and statements of problems and procedures to detailed, logical flow charts for coding into computer languages. Develops coding into computer languages; develops and writes COBOL computer programs to store, locate, and retrieve specific documents, data, and information.

Coder   Converts routine items of information obtained from records and reports into codes for processing by data typing using predetermined coding systems.

Coder–Editor   Synthesizes the results of questionnaires or mail or telephone surveys. The results are then reviewed by the research analyst.

Coding Clerk Supervisor   Supervises and coordinates activities of workers engaged in converting routine items of information from source documents into codes to prepare records for data processing. Modifies, revises, or designs forms and initiates procedures to develop more efficient methods of data input.

Coffee Technologist   Performs sensory evaluation and classification testing of coffee. Identifies and audits strategic sourcing partners. Maintains consistent cup profile through the manufacturing process.

College Recruiter   Interviews college graduates on campus. Works in conjunction with the policies and standards approved by the Employment Manager.

Colonel   A military officer ranking above a lieutenant colonel and below a brigadier general.

Commercial/Industrial Technician   Specializes in either installation or maintenance and repair of a variety of equipment in residential, commercial, industrial, and other buildings.

Commercial Security Specialist   Assesses risk and threats to business property and employee safety and makes recommendations on security system products and services.

Commis Chef   A professional assistant in the kitchen or dining room.

Commissioner of Tourism   Promotes overall tourism efforts. Generates new sources for funding. Interfaces with businesses in the community to gain support for tourism development.

Communications Equipment Technician   Performs the work of an electronics technician specifically on various types of communications equipment. (See **Electronics Technician**)

Communications Technician   Directs activities of production, circulation, or promotional personnel. Prepares news or public relations releases, special brochures, and similar materials. Personally interviews individuals and attends gatherings to obtain items for publication, verify facts, and clarify information. May assign staff members to handle above-mentioned tasks.

Community Dietitian   Counsels individual and groups on nutrition practices designed to prevent disease and promote health. Working in places such as public health clinics, home health agencies, and health maintenance organizations, a community dietitian evaluates individual needs, develops nutritional care plans, and instructs individuals and their families. Provides instruction on grocery shopping and food preparation to the elderly, individuals with special needs, and children.

Community Relations Director   Implements community and professional outreach programs, plans events, and generates and closes program leads.

Compliance Manager   Plans, directs, or coordinates compliance activities and staff of an organization. Collaborates with state and federal officials on program, operations, facility, or safety compliance.

Computer-Aided Designer   Uses computer programs to design, analyze, simulate, and test a system before assembly begins.

Computer Graphics Production Artist   Responsibilities include layout and production of advertisements, brochures, billboards, logos, point-of-purchase displays, catalogs, stationery, flyers, packaging, and television storyboards.

Computer Operator   Operates computer equipment to ensure that tasks are processed in accordance with a schedule of operations. Maintains and completes daily logs. Maintains an accurate report of equipment and/or software malfunctions.

Computer Programmer   Writes programs creating a logical series of instructions the computer can follow, applying knowledge of computer capabilities, subject matter, and symbolic logic. Codes instructions into programming languages and tests and debugs programs.

Computer Security Specialist   Plans, coordinates, and implements the organization's information security. May educate users on computer security, install security software, monitor the network for security breaches, respond to cyberattacks, and in some cases, gather data and evidence to be used in prosecuting cybercrime.

Computer Specialist   Responsible for analyzing, managing, supervising, or performing work necessary to plan, design, develop, acquire, document, test, implement, integrate, maintain, or modify systems for solving problems or accomplishing work processes by using computers.

Computer Specialist Information Technology Specialist
Works with complex projects for the Modernization and Information Technology Services (MITS) Division of the Treasury Department. Assignments may include projects in operating systems, systems integration, customer support, Internet services, and security systems. Ensures all operations are conducted without information security breaches.

Computer Technician   Installs, maintains, troubleshoots, and upgrades computer hardware, software, personal computer network, peripheral equipment, and electronic mail systems.

Computer Training Specialist   Assesses user training needs, develops training programs, and conducts training.

Computer User Support Specialist   Provides technical assistance, support, and advice to customers and other users.

Concessions Manager   Manages concession programs; develops and implements menus, pricing and operating policies, and procedures for concessions. Coordinates and oversees cash management, operations, staffing, facilities, and equipment.

Concierge   Handles guests' problems in a hotel, makes reservation requests with restaurants and transportation facilities, arranges tours, procures theater tickets, and handles a host of other activities.

Conference and Meeting Coordinator   Coordinates the planning and execution of conferences and meetings on- and off-site. Notifies attendees of details. Makes necessary facilities arrangements. Makes travel arrangements if required. Oversees the function and conducts postmeeting evaluation.

Conference Planner   Compiles list of individuals or groups requesting space for activities and schedules needed facilities. Notifies program participants of locations assigned. Maintains schedules and records of available space, space used, and cancelations. Requisitions needed equipment. Arranges for services during the conference. Follows up with client after the conference for evaluation of services provided.

Conference Reporter   Attends conferences at the request of the conference coordinator. Records minutes of the meetings and activities that occur during the conference. Types up summaries and distributes to requesting parties.

Conference Service Coordinator   Books meetings, services them, and follows up with postmeeting evaluations.

Consultant   Consults with client to determine need or problem, conducts studies and surveys to obtain data, and analyzes data to advise on or recommend a solution. Advises client on alternate methods of solving a problem or recommends a specific solution. May negotiate contract for consulting service.

Consultant/Advisor (Paralegal)   Assists the legal publisher in planning new kinds of books to be written either about the paralegal profession or the procedures utilized by paralegals in law offices.

Consultant Dietitian   Works under contract with health care facilities or in own private practice. Helps prevent and treat illnesses by promoting healthy eating habits and suggesting diet modifications.

Consultant/Internet Security Systems   Conducts network risk assessments, audits, and vulnerability scans. Recommends standards and policies governing the security of firewall deployment and operations. Recommends security incident response plans and products.

Consumer Product Safety Commission Investigator
Responsible for enforcing all regulations that protect the consumer against unsafe products.

Consumer Product Sales Representative   Maintains and develops sales volume with a variety of existing and new customers with the objective of increasing overall business for the company. Sales increases are achieved by adding new and existing products into distribution.

Contact Representative   Provides information and assistance to taxpayers either over the phone or in person. Takes action where needed to resolve tax issues, often involving delinquent situations. May initiate liens or installment payment agreements or research taxpayer's ability to pay outstanding taxes. May conduct background investigation of the taxpayer if needed.

Controller   Directs financial affairs of an organization. Prepares financial analyses of operations for guidance of management. Establishes major economic objectives and policies for the company. Prepares reports that outline company's financial position in areas of income, expenses, and earnings based on past, present, and future operations. Directs preparation of budgets and financial forecasts.

Convention Center Manager   Manages the building and does marketing and public relations for events at the center. Responsible for entire budget for the center. Supervises personnel.

Convention Planner   Arranges space and facilities for conventions. Keeps exhibitors and attendees informed of procedures and policies for participation. Assigns troubleshooters to be available to provide needed services during the convention. Minimizes situations that may result in safety, legal, or logistical problems.

Convention Sales Manager   Responsible for generating convention business at hotel, civic center, or other appropriate facility. Oversees sales staff. Approves advertising and rate packages. Handles projections on business and expected income. Works within established budgets.

Cook   Prepares, seasons, and cooks soups, meats, vegetables, desserts, and other foodstuffs for consumption in hotels and restaurants. Reads menu to estimate food requirements and orders food from supplier or procures it from storage. Adjusts thermostat controls to regulate temperature of ovens, broilers, grills, and roasters. Measures and mixes ingredients according to recipe, using a variety of kitchen utensils and equipment, such as blenders, mixers, grinders, slicers, and tenderizers to prepare soups, salads, gravies, desserts, sauces, and casseroles. Bakes, roasts, broils, and steams meat, fish, vegetables, and other foods. Observes and tests foods being cooked by tasting, smelling, and piercing with fork. Carves meats, portions food on serving plates, adds gravies or sauces, and garnishes servings to fill orders.

Coordinator of Membership Sales   Maintains prospect lists for membership in travel clubs or travel associations. Coordinates marketing programs to solicit new members. Explains membership policies and benefits and receives payment of membership dues. Makes decisions on appropriateness of membership.

Coordinator of Scheduling (Retail)   Prepares production schedules. Determines type and quantity of material needed to process orders. Issues work orders. Calculates costs for manufacturing.

Coordinator/Scheduler (Word Processing)   Sees that there is an even flow of work to the word processor.

Coordinator of Travel Information Center   Supervises and coordinates activities of workers engaged in greeting and welcoming motorists at a state highway information center. Provides information, such as directions, road conditions, and vehicular travel regulations. Provides maps, brochures, and pamphlets to assist motorists in locating points of interest or in reaching destinations. May direct tourists to rest areas, camps, resorts, historical points, or other tourist attractions.

Copy Chief   Supervises one or more copywriters in an advertising agency, department, or service, whose function it is to assign the work of preparing the textual matter for advertisements. Supervises the actual writing and transmits the completed work in accordance with the existing traffic arrangement in the firm. Coordinates copywriting activities with the layout, art, and production departments of the organization.

Copywriter   Writes original advertising material about products or services for newspapers, magazines, radio and television, posters, or other media.

Corporal   The lowest-ranking noncommissioned military officer, just below a sergeant.

Corporate Account Executive (Hospitality)   Responsible for the development and service of corporate (business and industry) business coming into the hotel.

Corporate Event Planner   Develops and executes successful events, meetings, and training opportunities in a firm. Manages projects. Creates and negotiates contracts. Negotiates, plans, and executes internal and external meetings and events.

Corporate Finance Manager   Assists a firm in generating funds necessary to support and expand business operations. Puts together acquisitions. Manages cash resources and ensures future economic stability.

Corporate Nurse   Provides nursing care at work sites to employees, customers, and others with injuries and illness. Provides emergency care and prepares accident reports. Arranges for further care if necessary.

Corporate Paralegal   Drafts minutes, forms and dissolves corporations, works with the Securities and Exchange Commission (SEC), reviews Blue Sky laws, oversees mergers and acquisitions, assists with leveraged buyouts.

Corporate Recruiter   Recruits corporate-level staff for the organization. Works in conjunction with the policies and standards approved by the Employment Manager.

Corporate Research Chef   Responsibilities focus on new products for a branded line and custom products for a national accounts line. Is involved in all aspects of product development, including formulation, benchwork, spreadsheets, and costing and sales at the plant level. May establish a database of standard culinary recipes as benchmarks for commercialized products.

Corporate Ticket Sales Representative   Responsible for sales and service of all corporate ticket accounts.

Corporate Travel Manager   Sets up travel budget, establishing policies for employees to follow; acts as a liaison with an outside travel agency that actually handles the arrangements. Handles personnel relocation as well as meetings and convention planning. May administer use of corporate aircraft, transportation to training programs, car pools, and possibly, group recreational trips or vacations for employees. May also negotiate discounts with travel suppliers.

Correctional Officer   Responsible for maintaining security in prison facilities and overseeing the safety of the inmate population.

Corrections Treatment Specialist   Provides guidance and support to an inmate population.

Cost Analysis Accountant   An accountant with specific focus on breaking down the cost of some operation and reporting on each factor separately.

Court Reporter   Makes accurate records of what is said during proceedings of all types. Memorizes and then reproduces the appropriate symbols involved in shorthand and machine reporting. All types of recordings—manual, machine, and tape—are transcribed accurately and typed in the required format.

Creative Director   Develops basic presentation approaches and directs layout design and copywriting for promotional material. Reviews materials and information presented by client and discusses various production factors to determine most desirable presentation concept. Confers with heads of art, copywriting, and production departments to discuss client requirements and scheduling, outlines basic presentation concepts, and coordinates creative activities.

Credit Analyst   Monitors a company's operating performance in order to anticipate and/or respond to changes that affect the company's creditworthiness.

Credit Manager   Responsible for the collection of accounts deemed to be delinquent and for determining when the accounts should be referred to an outside agency for further collection efforts. Generates reports on a daily and monthly basis. Posts cash on a daily basis.

Crime Lab Technician   Collects and examines evidence from crime scenes and submits results to be used as evidence in criminal cases.

Criminal and Drug Investigator   Plans and conducts investigations, often undercover, concerning possible violations of criminal and administrative provisions of the Immigration and Nationality Act and other statutes under the U.S. jurisdiction. These officers carry firearms, make arrests, prepare investigative reports, present cases to the U.S. Attorneys for prosecution, and give testimony in judicial and administrative proceedings.

Criminal Investigator   Conducts investigations of collusion, bribery, conflicts of interest, thefts from government jurisdictions, and offenses specified in the acts protecting government personnel and procedures.

Cruise Director   Supervises all activity on board a cruise ship. Responsible for overall safety of passengers and for quality of service. Oversees staff on board.

Cryptographer   Engages in research, writes papers, breaks algorithms and protocols, and sometimes writes his or her own algorithms and protocols.

Culinary Event Demonstrator   Demonstrates food items or kitchen equipment at trade shows, community events, educational programs, or media events.

Culinary Nutrition Assistant   Helps plan food and nutrition programs. Assists in the supervision and preparation and serving of meals. Helps prevent and treat illnesses by promoting healthy habits and recommending dietary modifications.

Culinary Nutrition Manager   Plans food and nutrition programs. Supervises the preparation and serving of meals. Helps prevent and treat illnesses by promoting healthy eating habits and recommending dietary modifications.

Culinary Nutrition Specialist   Culinary professional specializing in the research or practice of integration of nutrition standards and trends into food product development, menu development, or personal and group health planning.

Culinologist   A food service industry professional whose job integrates the application of culinary arts and food technology.

Customer Sales Engineer   Uses technical skills to demonstrate to potential customers how and why the products or services he or she is selling would suit the customer better than the competitors' products. Provides customer input to production, engineering, or research and development departments of the company to determine how products and services can be designed to best meet customer needs.

Customer Service Agent (Travel)   Arranges for car rental on-site at rental company by phone with travel agent or in person with individual customer. Processes contracts and arranges billing upon return of the rental vehicle.

Customer Service Investigator   Investigates customer claims about unsatisfactory customer service. Negotiates settlements and recommends solutions to resolve complaints.

Customer Service Manager (Retail)   Makes certain that shipments take place as scheduled. Acts as a liaison between customers and the sales force. Spends most of the time on administrative duties, including reviewing performance standards. Also trains personnel.

Customer Service Representative   Responds to customer inquiries and performs a variety of duties related to customer service. Works with customers to offer alternatives to unresolvable problems. Receives, researches, and answers customer inquiries and requests regarding accounts, products, rates, and services. Develops and maintains company's image and corporate philosophy in the community.

Customer Service Representative (Airlines)   Duties include booking onward flight reservations, securing hotel and car rental reservations, and ticketing passengers in flight.

Customer Service Representative (Retail)   Resolves customer complaints and requests for refunds, exchanges, and adjustments. Provides customers with catalogs and information concerning prices, shipping time, and costs. Approves customers' checks and provides check-cashing service according to exchange policy. Issues temporary charges. Keeps records of items in layaway, receives and posts customer payments, and prepares and forwards delinquent notices.

Customer Service Specialist   Responds to customer requests and questions regarding a specialized or technical, large or complex product, service, or account.

Customer Support Staff   Oversees activities of the support desk group, including assignment of duties and schedules. Maintains PC equipment and coordinates hardware and software installation.

Customs Agent   Examines incoming travelers' luggage, registers weights of incoming vessels, and enforces approximately 400 laws and regulations for the federal government. Ensures that revenue is paid for incoming goods and prevents prohibited goods from entering or leaving the country.

Customs Aide   Assists with responsibilities of other customs service positions.

Customs Canine Enforcement Officer   Trains and uses dogs to help her or him enforce rules and regulations pertaining to smuggling of controlled substances.

Customs Entry Processor   Processes a record entry for every shipment being imported into a zone.

Customs Import Specialist   Determines values of incoming merchandise and classifies these goods under tariff. Uses schedules to determine correct duty and taxes required. Can be assigned to seaport, airport, or land post.

Customs Inspector   Ensures compliance with tariff laws and prevents smuggling, fraud, and cargo theft. Detects illegal importation and exportation of narcotics and other contraband. Can search holds of ship.

Customs Pilot   Performs flight duties involving air surveillance of illegal activities. Can apprehend, arrest, and search violators.

Customs Special Agent   Investigates criminal fraud against the revenue, countervaluing, and major cargo thefts. Investigates illegal importation and exportation of contraband.

Database Administrator   Manages the design and development of information system databases and related master files. Oversees contributions by systems, operations, and tech support to develop and improve databases and master files. Guarantees the performance integrity and quality of the databases. Controls system capacity for existing requirements and plans for future needs.

Database Developer   Evaluates, designs, implements, and maintains database and data warehouse applications. Performs, designs, implements, and maintains databases. Performs design reviews and system testing.

Database Programmer   Maintains and develops functionality for existing information management systems. Imports data from multiple disparate sources into databases; develops ad hoc database queries and export procedures to extract data. Develops forms to enable users to enter and manipulate data.

Deadbeat Spouse Collections Investigator   Investigates allegations of mothers or fathers who do not pay child support obligations.

Dean   Develops academic policies and programs for a college or university. Directs and coordinates activities of academic department heads within the college. Participates in activities of faculty committees and in the development of academic budgets. Serves as a liaison with accrediting agencies that evaluate academic programs.

Demographer   Plans and conducts demographic research and surveys to study the population of a given area and how it affects trends.

Dental Assistant   Helps dentist during the examination and treatment of patients. Sets up and maintains instruments, arranges appointments, and keeps records of patients.

Dental Hygienist   Licensed to clean teeth under the supervision of a dentist. Instructs patients in dental care, diet, and nutrition for proper mouth care.

Dental Lab Assistant   Assists dental lab technicians, who make and repair artificial replacements for natural teeth and make corrective devices.

Dental Lab Technician: Fills prescriptions for dentists; constructs and repairs dentures, bridges, crowns and other artificial tooth replacement devices.

Dentist   Helps patients take care of their teeth and gums, either to correct dental problems or to advise patients on ways to prevent future cavities and gum problems.

Department Head   Supervises faculty and staff. Manages resources and coordinates facility use and program development.

Department Manager (Office)   Directs and coordinates departmental activities and functions using knowledge of department functions and company policies, standards, and practices. Gives work directions, resolves problems, prepares work schedules, and sets deadlines to ensure completion of operational functions. Evaluates procedures and makes recommendations for improvements. Assigns or delegates responsibility for specific work.

Department Manager (Retail)   Supervises and coordinates activities of personnel in one department of a retail store. Assigns duties to workers and schedules lunch, breaks, work hours, and vacations. Trains staff in store policies, department procedures, and job duties. Evaluates staff. Handles customer complaints. Ensures that merchandise is correctly priced and displayed. Prepares sales and inventory reports. Plans department layout. Approves checks for payment and issues credit and cash refunds.

Deportation Officer   Controls or removes persons who have been ordered deported or otherwise required to depart from the United States. Close liaison work with foreign consulates and embassies is required to facilitate the timely issuance of passports and travel documents required for deportation.

Deputy Commissioner of Tourism Development   Establishes goals, policies, and procedures of tourism development for a given area.

Design Assistant   Researches colors by contacting color forecasting services. Visits color forecasters to see presentations. Finds new garments on the market and in stores. Contacts fabric salespeople by phone for fabric samples. Keeps records, designs patterns, and design room organized.

Designer (Drafting)   Makes design drawings, using specifications and sketches, to assist in developing experimental ideas created by research engineers. Employs knowledge of engineering theory and its applications to solve mechanical and fabrication problems.

Desk Trader   Specialty trader who works with the Foreign Exchange Desk. Buys and sells securities.

Desktop Publisher   Uses computer software to format and combine text, numerical data, photographs, charts, and other graphic elements to produce publication-ready materials.

Destination Promoter   Sells meeting and convention planners, tour operators, and wholesalers on the idea of choosing a destination for their program. Services individual travelers with information and products that will make their business or pleasure trips more satisfying.

Detention Enforcement Officer   Locates, apprehends, arrests, transports, safeguards, and supervises aliens being detained and/or deported for violations of immigration laws.

Diagnostic Technologist   Helps scientists, doctors, and pathologists with tests and other duties involved in the operation of a diagnostic medical lab.

Dietetic Technician   Helps dietitians provide nutrition care. Assists in developing nutrition care plans. Gathers information about patients' dietary needs. Educates people about nutrition.

Dietitian   Assesses a person's nutritional state and needs. Develops and implements an appropriate dietary plan. Evaluates and records results. Coordinates with food services to ensure that dietary plans are implemented.

Digital Artist   Creates art for digital environments, such as CD-ROMs, video games, Web sites, or compact disks.

Digital Publisher   Creates, processes, produces, protects, and preserves content in digital form. Content is ultimately delivered as print, as an e-book, or on the Web.

Digital Technician   Captures and digitizes images from books, microfilm, photographs. Performs preservation microfilming of rare and valuable materials by operating a micrographic camera.

Dining Room Captain   Works under the general supervision of the dining room manager; is in charge of one section of the dining room. Instructs, supervises, and gives help to the staff working the area when needed. Watches all the tables in a given jurisdiction to detect any dissatisfaction; may make adjustments in response to complaints.

Dining Room Manager   Supervises all dining room staff and activities, including staff training, scheduling of staff working hours, keeping time records, and assigning work-stations. Should be capable of working in a formal public atmosphere.

Director of Escort Services   Responsible for the hiring, training, and assignment of tour escorts. Trains the escorts in the areas for which they will be responsible.

Director of Human Resources   Oversees the day-to-day activities of the human resources staff. Ensures that staff members comply with policies set and approved by the Vice President of Human Resources and senior management. (See **Vice President of Human Resources**)

Director of Information Services   Plans, establishes goals and objectives, directs, reviews, and approves procedures, programs, and services of the information services department. Initiates and executes department policies, rules, and regulations. Directs the purchase, requisition, and maintenance of hardware and software.

Director of Marketing and Sales   Supervises sales department. Coordinates sales and marketing departments to develop and implement an effective marketing effort. Responsible for increasing sales volume through direct sales efforts and by assisting sales representatives in the field. Coordinates future market growth plans with regard to products, services, and markets. May plan and implement advertising and promotion activities.

Director of Marketing and Advertising (Food Service)   Plans and carries out advertising and promotional programs. Works with company's top-level management to prepare an overall marketing plan. Arranges with various suppliers regarding schedule and cost of brochures, menus, advertisements, etc. Responsible for the advertising budget.

Director of Marketing/Sales (Cruise Lines)   Develops pricing strategies for packages sold to groups and individuals. Establishes advertising and promotion programs. Reviews competition's strategies for attracting clients and implements competitive strategies.

Director of Media Advertising   Defines corporate media objectives. Provides media information and advice to the company. Measures media costs against industry standards. Searches for new, creative ways to use media. Reports on controls, quality, and cost of media purchases.

Director of Nutrition Services   Plans, directs, and coordinates activities of nutrition services departments. Determines resource needs and prepares and manages budgets. Develops and implements new program services.

Director of Operations   Manages and coordinates the operational and systems infrastructure of a major operating unit. Develops and implements policies and procedures. Prepares financial and other management reports.

Director of Public Affairs   Directs a firm's efforts with regard to media relations, public affairs, publications, and community relations.

Director of Public Relations   Plans, directs, and conducts public relations programs designed to keep the public informed of employer's programs, accomplishments, and point of view.

Director of Public Safety   Responsible for the safety of the people and equipment in a city, town, or state. Evaluates, approves, and implements emergency plans in response to safety-threatening incidents resulting from crimes, natural disasters, or neglect of care of city, towns, or state property and assets.

Director of Recipe Development   Creates new recipes for the menus of larger restaurants or restaurant chains. Requires thorough knowledge of food preparation and the ability to apply this knowledge creatively.

Director of Research and Development   Directs and coordinates activities concerned with research and development of new concepts, ideas, basic data on, and applications for organization's products, services, or ideologies. Reviews and analyzes proposals submitted to determine if benefits derived and possible applications justify expenditures. Develops and implements methods and procedures for monitoring projects. May negotiate contracts with consulting firms to perform research studies.

Director of Sales and Marketing   (See **Director of Marketing and Sales**)

Director of Special Events   Generates ideas to increase participation in major events. Recruits and manages event committee and works with event volunteers. Creates corporate sponsorship strategy, and coordinates venue, entertainment, and all event logistics. Manages event budgets.

Director of Tour Guides   Responsible for the hiring, training, and assignment of tour guides.

Director of Training   Oversees training function for an entire company at all locations. Responsible for approval of recommended programs and proposed budgets. (See **Training Manager**)

Director of Transportation   Responsible for getting convention goers from their hotels to and from the center and for trafficking trucks in and out of the building. Works with the city to make sure streetlights are working. Deals with city's Taxi and Limousine Commission to ensure there are adequate services for the center.

Display Coordinator   Designs and implements the window decorations and interior displays that are so important in promoting sales. Must work well within limitations of time, space, and money.

Display Director   Supervises the display of merchandise in windows, in showcases, and on the sales floor of retail stores. Schedules plans for displays and ensures that staff follow store plans. Often responsible for several stores within a designated division.

Distribution Agent   Implements distribution channels as required by wholesale dealers. Negotiates service levels and pricing with distribution companies on a global basis while developing existing services to ensure that maximum consolidation, service, and profitability are maintained.

Distribution Manager (Retail)   Oversees the routing of merchandise from one branch store to another on the basis of sales. Analyzes reports of stock on hand and kind and amount sold.

Distributor   Intermediary between the wineries on one end and wine shops, grocery stores, restaurants, and hotels on the other. Distributors purchase the wine from multiple producers, warehouse it, and then ship it to the end users.

District Manager   Manages personnel for an assigned district, ensuring the development and accomplishment of established objectives. Trains, develops, and motivates staff. Recruits new hires. Maintains good business relationships with customers through periodic contacts and proper handling of administrative functions.

District Manager (Food Service)   Supervises smaller facilities in certain areas. Purchasing, negotiation, and supervision of area personnel are main responsibilities.

District Sales Manager   Carries out cold calls. Maintains reporting forms and business files. Holds periodic meetings with sales staff.

Divisional Manager (Banking)   Responsible for the activities of a related group of departments in a bank, such as all departments involved with customer service versus operations or systems.

Divisional Manager (Retail)   Retail executive responsible for the activities of a related group of selling departments or divisions.

Document Specialist   Determines whether or not handwriting is forged by comparing questioned handwriting with known handwriting.

Documentation Specialist   Specializes in writing, producing, and maintaining manuals.

Dog Handler   Works with dogs who are trained to locate missing persons or perform searches for illegal substances. Ensures the dog's navigation, survival, and man-tracking skills are adequate for assignment. May groom the dog and administer first aid when necessary.

Drafter   Develops detailed design drawings and related specifications of mechanical equipment according to engineering sketches and design-proposal specifications. Often calculates the strength, quality, quantity, and cost of materials. Usually specializes in a particular field of work, such as mechanical, electrical, electronic, aeronautical, structural, or architectural drafting.

Drafter (Computer Assisted Drafting and Design—CADD)   Drafts layouts, drawings, and designs for applications in such fields as aeronautics, architecture, or electronics, according to engineering specifications, using the computer. Locates file relating to projection database library and loads program into computer. Retrieves information from file and displays information on cathode-ray tube (CRT) screen using required computer languages. Displays final drawing on-screen to verify completeness, after typing in commands to rotate or zoom in on display to redesign, modify, or otherwise edit existing design. Types command to transfer drawing dimensions from computer onto hard copy.

Duty Drawback Specialist   Coordinates a refund of duty paid on imported merchandise when it is exported later, whether in the same or a different form.

E-Commerce Administrator   Evaluates, implements, and administers e-commerce-based software solutions. Analyzes, designs, and develops the systems for e-commerce solutions.

E-Commerce Developer   Develops e-commerce components. Implements new design features and product enhancements to meet market needs of a packaged software product. Serves as primary interface between development, quality assurance, and support functions. Develops software integration and system test plans.

E-Commerce Network Designer   Plans the network to support e-commerce communications.

E-Commerce Technical Consultant   Responsible for developing and maintaining e-commerce applications for a company's public Web site.

Economic Development Coordinator   Directs economic development planning activities for city, state, or region. Negotiates with industry representatives to encourage location in an area. Directs activities, such as research, analysis, and evaluation of technical information, to determine feasibility and economic impact of proposed expansions and developments.

Economist   Provides support to revenue agents and tax lawyers as an economic advisor and consultant on a wide range of economic issues and tax cases. Serves as a financial expert in the valuation of products, services, and assets.

Editor   Reads the rough drafts and manuscripts of regular contributors and other writers that are to be published in a magazine, book, or newspaper. Corrects grammatical errors and makes suggestions for improving readability and consistency of style.

Editor (Word Processing)   Helps design the overall package and rough out the information to be contained on each page of a videotext display. Once the information is set up, the page creator takes over.

Education Consultant   Develops programs for in-service education of teaching personnel. Reviews and evaluates curricula used in schools and assists in adaptation to local needs. Prepares or approves manuals, guidelines, and reports on educational policies. Conducts research into areas such as teaching methods and strategies.

Education Event Planner   Plans, organizes, and implements all aspects of events for schools, colleges and universities, and/or industry training programs.

Educator/Administrator (Food Service)   Designs and teaches courses tailored to students of food service, such as sanitation, food service management, and nutrition. Develops curriculum and hires staff. Works within designated budget to purchase equipment and materials needed to operate the school. Seeks support from industry with instruction and funding.

Electronics Engineer   Works on research and development, production, and quality control problems. Highly specialized; may work in a specific area such as the design and implementation of solid-state circuitry in radar, computers, or calculators.

Electronics Technician   Repairs and maintains machines and equipment used in processing and assembly of electronic components. Starts equipment or machine. Reads blueprints and schematic drawings to determine repair procedures. Dismantles machine. Removes and sets aside defective units for repair or replacement. Starts repaired or newly installed machines and verifies readiness for operation.

Emergency Critical Care Technician   Assists veterinarian with providing prompt emergency care to pets who suddenly become injured or develop an acute life-threatening disease. Monitors progress of recovery, diagnoses, and treats threatening disease in an emergency.

Emergency Medical Technician (EMT):   A certified healthcare provider who is trained to treat and transport victims of medical emergencies and provide emergency life support to victims.

Emergency Room Nurse   Cares for patients in the emergency or critical phase of their illness or injury. Is skilled at determining life-threatening problems and urgency of care needed. Works mostly within hospital or walk-in clinic emergency rooms.

Emergency Veterinarian   Responsible for administering and overseeing critical emergency care and specialty veterinarian services for wounded or ill animals. Is trained to use diagnostic, therapeutic, and monitoring equipment to provide medical and surgical care. Prescribes and administers medication, treats wounds, and provides advice and instruction to pet owner about follow-up care.

Employment Interviewer   (See **Interviewer**)

Employment Manager   Oversees the recruiting function, including soliciting qualified applicants through various sources, such as advertising and college recruiting. Oversees screening, interviewing, and selection procedures. Responsible for overseeing the hiring of all personnel.

Employment Recruiter   Matches job seekers with job openings that employers have listed with placement firms, employment agencies, or governmental employment offices.

Engineer   Applies the theories and principles of science and mathematics to practical technical problems. Designs and develops consumer products. Determines the general way the device will work, designs and tests all components, and fits them together in an integrated plan. Evaluates overall effectiveness of the new device, as well as its cost and reliability.

Engineer (Internal Revenue Service)   Combines engineering skills with a broad knowledge of tax law to provide high-level technical advice and input to field investigations involving valuations of real estate and personal property using generally accepted appraisal principles.

Engineering Technician   Develops and tests machinery and equipment, applying knowledge of mechanical engineering technology, under direction of engineering and scientific staff.

Enologist   A specialist in wine making.

Equal Employment Opportunity Coordinator   Monitors and enforces governmental regulations concerning equal employment practices in all levels of the organization. Maintains required records to verify adherence to approved affirmative action plan.

Equine Veterinary Nursing Technician   Assists equine veterinarians with providing medical services to sick or injured horses. Prepares horses for examination by the veterinarian. Obtains medical history, performs simple lab tests, orders supplies, and administers medicines and vaccinations with the approval of the veterinarian. Provides assistance to the veterinarian performing the examination. May advise the owner about exercise, diet, and medication important to maintaining proper health of the horse after the visit.

Equine Veterinary Technician   Veterinary technician specializing in care of horses. Typical duties include wound management, bandaging, and pain management. Performs grooming functions and is knowledgeable and able to monitor horse nutrition by providing proper meals that meet dietary guidelines. Can assist veterinarians with establishing and managing herds or work for government agencies to help maintain the quality of the feedstock.

Equipment Sales Representative   Responsible for equipment sales development in a particular territory. Establishes new customer accounts and services existing clients.

E-Reporter   Uses audio recording equipment to register court proceedings and produces the subsequent transcripts.

Event Coordinator   Coordinates and manages events. Selects sites, oversees event logistics, including food and beverage service, room blocks, technical provisions, vendor coordination and management, pre-event logistics, operational details, and on-site management.

Events Consultant   Consults with event chairpersons on their responsibilities for the event. Provides event calendar and vendor lists. Obtains permits and contracts, sponsorship and donations.

Executive Administrator (Education)   Oversees curriculum and policy decisions; makes projections for future needs. Hires and supervises personnel; prepares school budget. Works with local groups to ensure that the best interest of the community is being met.

Executive Chef   Coordinates activities of and directs indoctrination and training of chefs, cooks, and other kitchen personnel engaged in preparing and cooking food. Plans menus and utilization of food surpluses and leftovers, taking into account probable number of guests, marketing conditions, and population, and purchases or requisitions foodstuffs and kitchen supplies. Reviews menus; analyzes recipes; determines food, labor, and overhead costs; and assigns prices to the menu items. Observes methods of food preparation and cooking, sizes of portions, and garnishing of foods to ensure food is prepared in the prescribed manner. Develops exclusive recipes and varied menus.

Executive Director   Develops and coordinates an administrative organization plan and staff to carry out the plan. Delegates authority and responsibility for the execution of the organization's many departments and functions. Establishes operating policies and procedures and standards of service and performance. Is involved with fund-raising. Serves on various civic committees.

Executive/Administrator (Telemarketing)   Directs the planning and operations of telemarketing function. Sets goals and objectives for telemarketing programs and establishes budgets as well as sales goals. Guides development of telemarketing programs and evaluates available systems applications.

Executive Assistant   Member of the management team that is responsible for overseeing the overall administrative functions of an office. Ensures productivity of office staff. Makes recommendations for improved systems. Supervises staff. Handles special projects and confidential materials. Assists executive.

Represents the company at professional and community events on a regular basis. Often acts as a spokesperson for the executive.

Executive Director, Associations   Directs and coordinates activities of professional or trade associations in accordance with established policies to further the achievement of goals, objectives, and standards of the profession or association. Directs or participates in the preparation of educational and informative materials for presentation to membership or public in newsletters, magazines, and news releases, or on radio or television.

Executive Director, Chamber of Commerce   Directs activities to promote business, industrial, and job development, and civic improvements in the community. Administers programs of departments and committees that perform such functions as providing members with economic and marketing information, promoting economic growth and stability in the community, and counseling business organizations and industry on problems affecting local economy, Coordinates work with that of other community agencies to provide public services. Prepares and submits annual budgets to elected officials for approval. Studies governmental legislation, taxation, and other fiscal matters to determine effect on community interests, and makes recommendations based on organizational policy.

Executive Director, Convention Bureau   Directs activities of convention bureau to promote convention business in the area. Administers promotional programs. Coordinates efforts with local hotels, restaurants, transportation companies, exhibit centers, and other related facilities. Works within specified budgets. Serves on various civic and community boards to enhance the position of the bureau.

Executive Director, Department of Economic Development   Directs activities of the department. Ensures that demographic and economic information is maintained. Decides on research projects to be conducted. Directs publications prepared for public information. Works in conjunction with local and national agencies.

Executive Housekeeper   Supervises housekeeping staff. May hire and train new employees. Orders supplies, takes inventories and keeps records, prepares budgets, sees to needed repairs, draws up work schedules, inspects rooms. May be in charge of interior decoration.

Executive Pastry Chef   Oversees the operations of the pastry function of the kitchen. Develops and prepares dessert menus and recipes for baked goods.

Executive Secretary   Schedules meetings, takes minutes at meetings, and transcribes and types them; composes letters; evaluates priority of incoming mail and telephone calls. Organizes and executes special projects and reports. May prepare budget reports. Works with a minimum of supervision; initiates much of his or her own work according to office priorities.

Expeditor   Ensures that merchandise and supplies that have been ordered are shipped and received when and where needed.

Export Marketing Representative   Represents firms interested in selling goods oversees.

Facilities Designer   Plans and designs utilization of space and facilities for hotels, food service operations, and other related properties. Draws design layout, showing location of equipment, furniture, work spaces, doorways, electrical outlets, and other related facilities. May review real estate contracts for compliance with regulations and suitability for occupancy. Suggests decor that is both practical and attractive to suit the purpose of the facility as well as maximize client business.

Facilities Manager   Manages maintenance activities relating to organization's physical property. Directs provision of building maintenance and operation or custodial function. Arranges lease agreements and renovation of new construction projects. Ensures that work done adheres to zoning, hazardous waste, and traffic regulations.

Fashion Coordinator   Offers advice to the buying staff in large department stores on changing tastes, trends, and styles. Works with buying staff to be sure that the store's merchandise is completely up-to-date.

Fashion Designer   Creative specialist responsible for designing coats, suits, dresses, as well as other lines of apparel. Adapts higher-priced merchandise to meet the price range of the customers.

Fashion Display Specialist   Responsible for designing display windows and display units within department or clothing stores. May have supervisory responsibilities as a coordinator for a chain of stores.

Fashion Writer   Writes articles on the subject of fashion. Writes press releases and complete public relations projects. Writes about projected fashion trends, designers, new store openings. Writes newsletters for stores and buying offices. Covers fashion shows and does research.

FBI Special Agent   Federal agent with a mandate to investigate kidnapping, bank robbery, organized crime, civil rights violations, fraud, spying, and other criminal activities.

Federal Aviation Administrator   Responsible for the advancement, safety, and regulation of civic aviation, as well as overseeing air traffic pattern development.

Field Installer   Sets up, maintains, and repairs systems on customer sites.

Field Operations Manager   Responsible for daily management of field technicians.

Field Technician   Installs, operates, and maintains on-site equipment. Troubleshoots customer and equipment issues. Assists with new-site turnup development, design, and maintenance of access points.

Finance Business Loan Officer   Approves loans within specified limits and refers loan applications outside those limits to management for approval. Analyzes applicants' financial status, credit, and property evaluations to determine feasibility of grants and loans.

Finance Director   Responsible for implementing cost savings, business improvements, and efficiencies to include development of a profitable top-line growth.

Finance Manager   Directs activities of workers engaged in performing such financial functions as accounting and recording financial transactions. Establishes procedures for control of assets, records, loan collateral, and securities.

Financial Advisor   Provides advice to customers on personal investment product purchases. Determines specific customer needs and ensures that appropriate market transactions are executed.

Financial Analyst   Performs the quantitative analysis required for strategic planning and investments. Evaluates the financing and refinancing of certain projects and lines of credit. Prepares various reports for management. Collects data for financial comparisons with similar companies and securities.

Financial Auditor   Collects and analyzes financial data to detect deficient controls, duplicate efforts, extravagance, fraud, or noncompliance with laws, regulations, and management policies. Prepares detailed reports on audit findings.

Fingerprint Specialist   Responsible for collecting, classifying, analyzing, and identifying fingerprint impressions.

Finisher   Pastry cook or chef expert at finishing desserts, including cakes and pastries, with glazes, icings, or other creative toppings and/or by plating the desserts using a variety of creative presentation techniques.

Fitness Center Sales Representative   Responsible for increasing club membership; plans membership drives. Develops sales plans and makes sales calls. Responds to customer requests and inquiries. Processes new membership orders and ensures they are properly filled.

Fitness Consultant   Keeps updated with relevant information regarding exercise, fitness, health, and health behavior change. Provides consultation for new and current clients and conducts activity programs.

Fitness Instructor   Involved in the assessment, teaching, training, and supervision of a variety of people in health and fitness clubs, gymnasiums, sports centers, and community recreation organizations.

Flight Attendant   Directly responsible for making passengers' flight comfortable, enjoyable, and safe. Ensures that cabin is in order and supplies and equipment are on board. Greets passengers as they board the plane. Helps passengers with carry-on luggage and with finding their seats. Instructs passengers before take-off in the location and proper usage of oxygen masks and other emergency equipment and exits. Serves meals and beverages.

Floor Trader   An exchange member who executes transactions from the floor of the exchange.

Food and Beverage Manager   Responsible for compiling statistics of food and liquor costs, sales, and profits and losses. May also develop the procedures of portion control and item usage. May inventory bars as needed and prepare daily consumption reports that are forwarded to the auditing office. Takes inventory of foodstuffs with the chef and works closely with the chef on matters of buying and producing.

Food Director (Recreation)   Responsible for all food service areas at a particular theme park, amusement park, arcade, or other type of recreational facility. Supervises the procurement and preparation of food and drinks for concession stands, snack bars, dining halls, and rooms. Hires and trains staff. Maintains control of food costs and inventories. Deals directly with

suppliers in ordering and paying for all food products. Enforces sanitation policies and health department codes throughout all food service facilities.

Food Photographer   Specializes in photography marketed toward food companies, corporate test kitchens, advertising creatives, food promotion agencies, and photo studios.

Food Production Manager   Responsible for all food preparation and supervision of kitchen staff. Must possess leadership skills and have knowledge of food preparation techniques, food quality, sanitation standards, and cost control methods.

Food Research Scientist   Usually works in the food processing industry. Combines knowledge of chemistry, microbiology, and other sciences to develop new or better ways of preserving, processing, packaging, storing, and delivering foods.

Food Service Consultant   Advises clients on site selection for food service operation, menu design and selection, interior decor, equipment, and overall design and layout of dining facility. Advises owner/operator of expected food and beverage costs and helps develop an effective pricing strategy for all menu items.

Food Service Director   Exercises general supervision over all production areas in one or more kitchens. Also responsible for all the service that may be needed on counters and in the dining rooms. Responsible for the buying of food, its storage, its preparation, and the service necessary to handle large groups.

Food Service Engineer   Analyzes and creates efficient and cost-effective food production processes, designs food manufacturing equipment, or operates a food plant's physical systems.

Food Service Manager   Responsible for the operation's accounts and records and compliance with all laws and regulations, especially those concerning licensing, health, and sanitation.

Food Service Publisher   Publishing house that is a leading information provider for the food industries, with a portfolio that includes online communities, print images, newsletters, directories, reference books, and industry conferences.

Food Service Regulator   Responsible for identifying what types of food processes are at a facility and evaluating what type of food safety hazards might exist.

Food Service Salesperson   Tells customers how a given item performs against the competition, how it will benefit the buyer, and ultimately, how it can increase profits and encourage repeat business. Demonstrates new products, gives customers actual product samplings, advises on menu ideas and serving suggestions, and even helps work out portion costs.

Food Technologist   Provides project leadership for newproduct development and for providing improvements to existing products and processes.

Food Writer   Writes restaurant reviews. May be a staff food writer, freelance writer, or food critic.

Foreign Currency Investment Advisor/Analyst   Evaluates risk and places foreign exchange investments accordingly in spots, forwards, and options.

Foreign Exchange Representative   Responsible for providing service in selling and/or buying foreign currencies, travelers cheques, and bank drafts, as well as cross-selling ancillary products.

Foreign Market Research Analyst   Analyzes the foreign exchange market events, such as interest rate decisions, interventions, and the impact of geopolitical events.

Foreign Marketing Agent   Hired to represent firms in overseas markets as their agent. Has knowledge of foreign business practices, languages, laws, and culture. Identifies customers for firms and products.

Foreign Sales Agent   Responsible for selling products to foreign investors and distributors.

Forensic Scientist   Responsible for determining facts surrounding a crime on the basis of physical evidence analysis.

Franchise Sales Manager   Identifies, develops, and maintains franchise sales and marketing objectives, plans, and programs.

Freelance Reporter (Court Reporting)   Self-employed reporter who develops her or his own contracts, follows up on recommendations of those for whom she or he may already have worked, and generally initiates own assignments.

Freelancer (Travel)   Submits articles to travel editor for publication. Works independently. Initiates own stories and also writes specific articles or stories for publications upon request.

Freelancer (Visual Merchandising)   Initiates own designs and plans and offers services to Designers and Display Directors.

Front Desk Clerk   Responsible for direct personal contact with the guests. Handles reservations, special needs, check-in, and checkout. Familiarizes guests with the facility as well as the surrounding area. Prepares status reports on available rooms for manager. Receives guests' complaints and makes appropriate decisions about how to resolve them.

Front Desk Supervisor (Hospitality)   Directs the front desk operations in the hotel. Oversees those responsible for guests' reservations, special needs, check-in, and checkout. Reviews status reports on available rooms. Ensures that guests' complaints are handled promptly and properly.

Front Office Manager (Hospitality)   Supervises front office operations of the rooms division of a hotel or motel.

Fund Accountant   Serves to facilitate expenditure control and stewardship reporting of funds managed for the public sector.

Garde-Manger (Cold Cook)   Prepares and works with all cold meat, fish, and poultry dishes. Prepares appetizers and hors d'oeuvres such as canapes. Makes all salad dressings and mayonnaise according to recipe. Works with leftover foods to make appetizing dishes. Prepares and serves pâté maison. Makes ice and vegetable carvings.

General Accountant   Handles daily business activities and reports, as payroll, budgeting, accounts receivable, accounts payable, general ledger, and financial statements. Must pay close attention to all laws and regulations affecting daily business operations. Is involved in sending out all payments, royalties, dividends, rents, and other necessary expenditures.

General Manager (Food Service)   Acts as overseer to all phases of a particular food service management group, working with the management team to plan future food service accounts and solve day-to-day problems.

General Manager (Hospitality)   Establishes standards for personnel administration and performance, service to patrons, room rates, advertising, publicity, credit, food selection and service, and type of patronage to be solicited. Plans dining room, bar, and banquet operations. Allocates funds, authorizes expenditures, and assists in planning budgets for departments.

Goods and Commodities Trader and Countertrader Specialist   Is actively engaged in trading contracts, such as regulated futures contracts, foreign currency contracts, non-equity options, dealer equity options, or dealer securities future contracts. Countertrades by bartering, the direct exchange of goods or services of approximate value; and buybacks, in which the exporter takes back output from the equipment exported. Is registered with a domestic board of trade.

Government Relations Director   Plans, develops, and directs all aspects and phases of a firm's government relations operations to secure funding and legislative provisions and rules favorable to the firm. Plans and directs public policy development, review, analysis, and evaluation.

Government Relations Regulator   Establishes and maintains relationships with federal regulatory agencies on strategic public policy objectives. Monitors, tracks, and analyzes regulatory and judicial issues that have an impact on the firm's industry.

Graphic Artist   Creates technical illustrations, design, layouts, and electronic presentations. Exhibits knowledge of electronic file retrieval and archiving and of commercial art methods, techniques, prepress, and scanning.

Graphic Designer   Conceptualizes, designs, and produces curriculum, training, and/or promotional materials, such as flyers, ads, brochures, logos, office signage, exhibits and/or displays. Designs and produces camera-ready art.

Groomer   Grooms pets by taking service order requests from owners, assessing pet condition, performing grooming services, and easing pet anxieties.

Group Event Sales Specialist   Coordinates sales for group's travel accommodations, ticket packages, special event planning, and one-of-a-kind entertainment programs.

Group Exercise Manager   Responsible for overseeing a group exercise program. Recruits group exercise instructors for all corporate sites.

Group Manager (Retail)   Supervises many departments within a retail operation.

Group Sales Manager   Concentrates on managing group sales efforts, including planning and forecasting sales and supervising sales staff. Identifies target markets and assigns specific groups to specific sales personnel. Devises and implements promotions and training programs.

Group Sales Representative (Travel)   Promotes sale of group season tickets for sports or other entertainment events. Telephones, visits, or writes to organizations, such as chambers of commerce, corporate employee recreation clubs, social clubs, and professional groups, to persuade them to purchase group tickets or season tickets to sports or other entertainment events, such as baseball, horse racing, or stage plays. Quotes group ticket rates, arranges for sale of tickets and seating for groups on specific dates, and obtains payment. May arrange for club to sponsor a sports event, such as one of the races at a horse racing track.

Guest Services Agent (Hospitality)   Works as a liaison between hotel guests and party providing desired services. Informs guests on services available to them in the hotel facility and assists them with making the proper connections. Deals with any requests that guests may have and with providing answers to questions that concern guests.

Hardware Specialist   Computer professional prepared to assemble, upgrade, maintain, and repair personal computers and to work in the area of local area networks and Internet routing and switching.

Head Cashier (Hospitality)   Oversees the duties of the hotel's cashiers, which include receiving guests' payments when checking out of the hotel. Approves the cashing of guests' checks and the processing of certain loans. Responsible for security of the safe deposit box.

Head Chef   Responsible for all aspects of running the kitchen, including staff management, stock control, budgets, and sanitation.

Head Nurse   Supervises nurses' activities in a variety of settings. Sets up work schedules, assigns duties to nursing staff, and ensures that each member of the team is properly trained. Ensures that records are correctly maintained and that shift reports are completed. Ensures that necessary equipment and supplies are in stock as needed.

Health Care Administrator   Directs, supervises, and evaluates work activities of medical, nursing, technical, clerical, service, maintenance, and other personnel. Develops and implements organizational policy and procedures.

Health Club Director (Cruise Lines)   Oversees use of the health club on a cruise ship. Ensures passenger understanding of use of the equipment and of the exercise programs available. Ensures safety and cleanliness of equipment. Supervises staff and approves recommended programs.

Horse Hot Walker   Walks horses around the stable area after a race or exercise.

Health Technician (Electronics)   Performs the work of an electronics technician, specifically on various types of health equipment. (See **Electronics Technician**)

Hearing Reporter   Follows up and records all that is said during various types of proceedings, whether they be court trials or informal meetings. Hearings are presided over by a commissioner and there is no jury. Hearings may be conducted by various governmental agencies and departments with differing functions and responsibilities.

Help Desk Analyst   Supports the provision of a high-performance, highly productive desktop, applications, and communications infrastructure. Develops and revises IT strategy to offer excellent customer service to staff, both remotely and desk-side.

Help Desk Assistant   Point of contact for technology users seeking technical assistance. Provides technical support on the phone or in person. Screens calls and refers complex problems to help desk manager.

Help Desk Technician   Responds to inquiries and requests for assistance with the organizations computer system or PCs. Troubleshoots, identifies problems, and provides advice to assist users. Coordinates with other information service areas to resolve problems.

Home Economics Teacher   Teaches everything from healthful menus to hygiene to food journalism.

Homeland Security Specialist   Is an expert in domestic and international terrorism, communication, emergency planning, and immigration. Researches and analyzes situations presenting security threats and takes quick action to resolve issues.

Housekeeper   Ensures clean, orderly, attractive rooms in the hotel or related facility. Inventories stock to ensure adequate supplies. Issues supplies and equipment to workers. May record data and prepare reports concerning room occupancy, payroll expenses, and department expenses.

Human Resources Assistant   Executes human resources support activities that are fairly complicated in nature. Provides assistance in the areas of employment, affirmative action, salary and benefits administration, employee events, or communications.

Identity and Social Security Identity Theft Investigator   Investigates allegations of false identity resulting from illegally accessing a Social Security number on a public Internet Web site and using it and the victim's name to apply for credit cards, bank and corporate credit, passports, and/or a variety of other legal documents.

Immigration Information Officer   Provides information about immigration and nationality law and regulations. Assists with information necessary to complete required forms and explains the administrative procedures and normal processing times for each application for benefits available through the Immigration and Nationality Law.

Immigration Inspector   Inspects all applicants for admission into the United States and determines eligibility or ineligibility for entry. Inspectors must be guided in their work by a knowledge of controlling laws, regulations and policies, and court and administrative decisions.

Immigration Officer   Checks entry of visitors and immigrants from other countries according to U.S. immigration laws and policies.

Implementation Specialist   Manages a new-client orientation and onboarding process to ensure a zero-defect experience.

Industrial Security Specialist   Performs initial clearance and recurring reviews of facilities. Develops instructions and procedures needed to implement policies to create efficient clearance processing. Maintains communications strategies for hiring managers.

Incentive Travel Specialist   Travel specialist responsible for developing special packages for trips that have been won as a prize or premium.

Information Analyst   Develops information systems documentation; gathers, documents, confirms, and publishes the requirements for an information system. Ensures that test, design, and user documents conform to requirements.

Information Architect   Builds the blueprint of a Web site upon which all other aspects are built, such as forms, functions, navigations, and interface, interaction with other Web sites, and the sites' visual design.

Information Assistant   Performs a wide range of administrative tasks in support of the work of professional library staff. Handles inquiries, checks status of loans and reserves using control databases, and purchases new stock.

Information Broker (Word Processing)   Responsible for formulating specifications on the basis of which information is pulled from the database and then relayed to the client company.

Information Consultant   Identifies, researches, and reports information needed for decision making in a specialized field for a targeted client.

Information Coordinator (Travel)   Coordinates organization and communication of travel information as needed. Responsible for providing accurate information to telephone inquirers and visitors about a destination, attraction, activity, or program. Participates in and conducts surveys.

Information Manager   Involves specializing in database management. Besides a general knowledge of how organizations work and how information flows through them, knowledge of how to set up and improve information systems is important. Knowledge of library referencing and indexing systems is applied. Helps a technical expert set up an electronic filing system or corporate database. Sorts and updates database files, advises how to design the automated office system that would best fit with the organization's style, work flow, and procedures.

Information Packager   Edits word processing systems and their software, applies working knowledge of word processing and text, and finds imaginative opportunities in which to further apply that knowledge and those related skills.

Information Retrieval Specialist   Assists with the process of organizing, finding, and leveraging information for improved decision making. Is an expert at use of new information retrieval technologies.

Information Security Administrator   Responsible for all security of a system on a day-to-day basis. Holds the highest-power password in the system so that the most sensitive information transactions can be undertaken with a combination of both system administration and security administration top-level passwords.

Information Security Analyst   Designs, develops, and administers security systems and processes that will protect the integrity, confidentiality, and security of the company's information resources. Plans the security and provides input on selection of products and methods used to protect the company's data and information systems.

Information Security Engineer   Ensures that software and infrastructure are designed and implemented to security standards. Probes applications and reviews code for security holes. Performs security audits, application level vulnerability testing, and security code reviews.

Information Security Technician   Supports the information technology infrastructure. Maintains data communication networks and their end users.

Information Specialist (Hospitality)   Provides specific information on area attractions and services to guests staying at the hotel. May work in conjunction with the Concierge in providing guests with information on restaurants, shopping areas, museums, historical sites, theaters, and local entertainment. Is well informed on the history of the area. Is familiar with information available at the area's chamber of commerce and visitors and convention bureau.

Information Specialist (Paralegal)   After research, consolidates legal information for easy accessibility. Lists resources for future research by subject and sets up reference library to maintain information in sequential order. Advises users on how to extract the information they need quickly and efficiently.

Information Technical Consultant   Provides on-site and off-site IT services and one-on-one training to small and medium-sized businesses. Builds and evaluates wired and wireless networks, handles PC maintenance and troubleshooting. Recommends security programs, disaster recovery plans, digital media services, and Internet-based business solutions.

Informer   Person assigned by an organization as the contact person for the press or other media for obtaining desired information on an as-needed basis.

Inspector   Supervises cleaning staff and inspects hotel guest rooms, corridors, and lobbies. Assigns work to cleaning staff and trains personnel in housekeeping duties. Posts room occupancy records. Attends to guests' complaints regarding housekeeping service or equipment. Writes requisitions for room supplies and furniture renovation or replacements.

Institutional Researcher   Develops, implements, and manages information systems to provide data for institutional planning and assessment.

Institutional Security Specialist   Plans, directs, or coordinates security activities and security staff of an organization or institution.

Instructor (Education)   Instructs students in commercial subjects (typing, accounting, computer systems), communications courses (reading and writing), and personality development in business schools, community colleges, or training programs. Instructs students in subject matter, utilizing various methods, such as lecture and demonstration, and uses audiovisual aids and other materials to supplement presentation. Prepares or follows teaching outline. Administers tests. Maintains discipline.

Insurance Agent   (See **Agent**—Insurance)

Insurance Fraud Investigator   Works for an insurance company and handles investigation of suspected criminal activity.

Insurance Investigation Specialist   Examines insurance claims made by individuals and businesses to ensure that the claims being made are legitimate. Investigates false claims and determines appropriate course of action.

Integrity Shopping Service Investigator   Poses as shopper in retail establishments to detect thieves and help manage loss prevention.

Intelligence Support Analyst   Supports the development of various reports, presentations, and documentation. Duties include information gathering from various sources, report preparation, and interface with the government client in order to resolve issues.

Intelligence Support Clerk Provides support for and/or assists with the collection, analysis, evaluation, interpretation, and dissemination of information that directly or indirectly affects national security.

Interactive Graphic Designer Graphic designer incorporating such interactive media as action scripting, audio voiceovers, animation, or three-dimensional graphics.

Internal Auditor Examines, verifies, evaluates, and reports on financial, operational, and managerial processes, systems, and outcomes to ensure financial and operational integrity and compliance.

Internal Medicine Neurology Veterinary Technician Assists veterinarians whose focus is on the neurological wellness of animals. Assists with the treatment and diagnosis of neurological illnesses of both small to large animals.

Internal Medicine Veterinary Technician Assists veterinarians whose focus is on animal general wellness and preventive medicine. Assists with the treatment and diagnosis of illnesses related to anatomy, physiology and non-surgical pathology issues of small to large animals.

International Exhibit Coordinator Plans, coordinates, and implements exhibit programming at overseas trade shows and related events.

International Group Secretary Provides secretarial support for a team headed by an account executive. Duties include transcribing letters and memos from dictaphone tapes and typing comprehensive multicountry proposals for clients, preparing travel arrangements, and assisting with clients, brokers, and foreign visitors.

International Service Trade Officer Provides policy advice on foreign affairs and trade issues to government ministers. Keeps government informed about international strategic, political, economic, and trade issues.

International Trade Documentation Specialist Expedites import or export documents for transportation intermediary companies such as freight forwarders or customhouse brokers or for commercial banks.

Internet and Web Hacker Programmer Investigator Investigates network security violations caused by an intruder who tries to discover sensitive information by accessing secure systems. Investigates and prosecutes computer crimes that involve hacking.

Internet Marketer Oversees implementation of new corporate Web site and trains user groups on new interface. Develops and implements a search engine program with Internet agency to increase traffic to redesigned Web site. Updates Web site regularly and oversees content management systems.

Interpreter Translates spoken word from one language to another. Provides consecutive or simultaneous translation between languages. Usually receives briefing on subject area prior to interpreting session.

Interviewer Interviews job applicants to select persons meeting employers' qualifications. Searches files of job orders from employers and matches applicants' qualifications with job requirements and employer specifications.

Inventory Control Manager Ensures that all stock units, both components and finished goods, are in adequate supply. Responsible for overall quality of the product. Maximizes customer service levels, inventory investment, and manufacturing efficiencies.

Inventory Coordinator Prepares reports of inventory balance, prices, and shortages. Compiles information on receipt or disbursement of goods and computes inventory balance, price, and costs. Verifies clerical computations against physical count of stock and adjusts errors in computation or count. Investigates and reports reasons for discrepancies.

Inventory Manager Supervises compilation of records of amount, kind, and value of merchandise, material, or stock on hand in establishment or department of establishment. Compares inventories taken by workers with office records or computer figures from sales, equipment shipping, production, purchase, or stock records to obtain current theoretical inventory. Prepares inventory reports. Makes planning decisions.

Investment Banker Analyzes the needs of clients and makes recommendations to them on the best way to obtain the money they need. Obtains permission from each of the state governments to sell the issue in that state.

Investment Banking Analyst Provides analytical support by preparing financial models, doing analyses, and preparing presentations for various transactions.

Investment Banking Associate Works on a variety of transactions in all stages from initial client pitches to transaction closing.

Investment Banking Researcher Researches and manages all aspects of merger and acquisition assignments for clients, including solicitation and sales.

IRS Agent Responsible for examining taxpayers' records to determine tax liabilities and for investigating cases involving tax fraud or evasion of tax payments.

IRS Criminal Investigator Investigates charges of criminal and civil violations of Internal Revenue laws.

IRS Internal Security Inspector Performs investigations to ensure that honesty and integrity are maintained within all levels of the service.

IT Training Specialist Presents information, directs structured learning experiences, and manages group discussion and group services.

Job Analyst Reviews all job functions within the company to continuously maintain updated details on job requirements, specific functions, and qualifications needed.

Junior Accountant (See **Accountant**)

Junior Account Executive (Telemarketing) (See **Account Executive—Telemarketing**)

Junior Analyst (Marketing) (See **Market Research Analyst**)

Junior Buyer (Retail) Performs duties of buyer trainee and also becomes involved in deciding on products for purchase and evaluating the store's needs. Learns to study the competition on a regular basis so as to evaluate and predict decisions.

Junior Consultant (See **Consultant**)

Junior Copywriter   Studies clients from printed materials and past correspondence. May answer phone, type, file, or draft simple correspondence. May write some descriptive copy and come up with concepts for new ad campaigns. Works with the art department on presentations.

Junior Drafter   Copies plans and drawings prepared by drafters by tracing them with ink and pencil on transparent paper or cloth spread over drawings, using triangles, T-square, compass, pens, or other drafting instruments. Makes simple sketches or drawings under close supervision.

Juvenile Justice Counselor   Counsels juveniles assigned to state youth divisions. Works with juveniles from Persons in Need of Supervision (PINS) to hard-core adolescents.

Juvenile Probation Officer   Provides intake, investigation, and supervisory service to family court for juveniles.

Kennel Assistant   (See **Kennel Attendant**)

Kennel Attendant   Cares for pets while their owners are working or traveling out of town. Grooms animals. May assist with obedience training, help with breeding, or prepare animals for shipping or other mode of transportation.

Kennel Keeper   Maintains condition of the kennel by ensuring equipment functions properly, enclosures are properly fitted and registers of admitted and discharged animals are accurately maintained. May hire and supervise kennel staff.

Kennel Technician   Maintains kennel equipment. Ensures proper kennel temperature control. Works with cleaning services and design vendors and manufacturers. Ensures proper levels of animal food, medicine, and other supplies are properly maintained. Oversees routine kennel inspections and ensures the facility is in compliance with required standards.

Kennel Worker   Feeds, grooms, and exercises animals and cleans, disinfects, and repairs their cages. Plays with animals to provide companionship and observes behavioral changes that could indicate illness or injury.

Kitchen Manager   Supervises all the production personnel in the kitchen area. Oversees the buying, storing, and preparation of all food. Takes inventory and reorders when necessary. Usually employed in operations where chefs are not employed.

Lab Animal Attendant   Cares for small lab animals while veterinarian assistant or technician is performing administrative functions or working with other animals in the lab setting. May help prepare animals for lab procedure and may assist with maintaining updated client records.

Lab Animal Technician   Performs less complex tests and lab procedures than lab animal technologists. Technicians may prepare specimens and operate automated analyzers, for example, or they may perform manual tests in accordance with instruction. Works under the direct supervision of a lab supervisor.

Lab Animal Technologist   Works in research facilities and assists with the care of a wide variety of animals. Feeds lab animals. Examines animals for diseases, illness, or injury. May administer medication under the supervision of the lab manager or veterinarian. Prepares samples for lab exams, sterilizes lab equipment, and records information on animals.

Lab Manager   Directly supervises the technical and support personnel in the general laboratory, guiding and developing their performance.

Labor Relations Specialist   Responsible for being fully knowledgeable of current contracts or established policies affecting the working environment of all personnel, including such areas as hiring requirements, pay policies, performance standards, leave of absence authorizations, and disciplinary procedures. When dealing with bargaining units, negotiates contracts as needed.

Lab Supervisor   Plans and oversees the day-to-day function of the veterinary laboratory. Oversees clinical lab testing performed to diagnose, detect, and treat disease in animals.

LAN Specialist   Administers, installs, maintains, and troubleshoots data communication systems. Responsible for providing PC and network support to all computer users. Troubleshoots user hardware, software, and network problems on all systems; repairs hardware; rolls out software and hardware to employees.

LAN Technician   Provides technical support for computer hardware and software by answering incoming help desk phone calls. Provides personal service to computer users, installs PC hardware and software, configures PC workstations, and troubleshoots system failure.

Large Animal Veterinarian   Doctors trained to protect the health of both animals and people. Work with large animals to evaluate animals' health, diagnose and treat illnesses, provide routine preventive care (such as vaccines), prescribe medication, and perform surgery. May provide stallion services, ambulatory veterinarian services, and haul-in services. Large animals usually include horses, cattle, sheep, goats, and llamas.

Law Librarian   Ensures that books and other legal materials are updated periodically. Conducts legal research as needed, frequently accessing database information.

Law Library Manager   Manages the ordering and organizing of all materials to be housed in the law library. Responsible for keeping up-to-date on changes in the law and for obtaining new literature describing most current laws. Supervises staff. Trains staff and library users on how to use the library. Oversees telephone information service.

Law Office Administrator   Designs, develops, and plans new procedures, techniques, services, processes, and applications in the office. Plans, supervises, and assists in the installation and maintenance of relatively complex office equipment. Plans production, operations of service for the efficient use of personnel, materials, money, and equipment in the office.

Lawyer   Conducts civil and criminal lawsuits. Draws up legal documents, advises clients as to legal rights, and practices other phases of the law.

Lead Agent (Travel)   A car rental agent responsible for answering customers' questions.

Lead Word Processing Operator   Coordinates work priorities and assigns work to word processors. May train and supervise word processors. Ensures quality of work output.

Legal Assistant   Oversees the work of other paralegals in a firm. Delegates work, handles personnel-related problems, writes appraisals of other paralegals, and supervises the hiring of paralegals when needed. Works on special projects.

Legal Assistant Manager   Acts as a liaison between management and legal assistants. Responsible for hiring, supervision, review, and dismissals, if necessary, as well as budgetary responsibilities. Also assigns case work to ensure work distribution, quality, and timeliness.

Legal Secretary   Schedules appointments and court appearances. Prepares documents. Is responsible for billing, bookkeeping, and recordkeeping. Handles subpoenas, mortgages, deeds, closings, pleadings, briefs, wills, proxies, and abstracts. May also review law journals and assist in other ways with legal research.

Legal Technician   Initiates and composes standardized legal forms routinely as needed for specific legal actions. Accepts service of legal documents, reviews for correct form and timeliness, annotates case files and status records to reflect receipt and due dates for responses. Establishes, maintains, and closes out case files or systems of legal records. Maintains tickler system, coordinates schedules with court clerks, notifies witnesses of appearances, and reminds attorneys of court appearances and deadlines for submitting various actions or documents.

Legal Technology Specialist   Office technical professional familiar with legal proofreading and editing, records management, financial records, business communication database, presentation, and legal document production.

Legislative Reporter   Records events, speeches, and debates that take place in state legislatures. Records and reports on committee meetings.

Librarian   Professional person trained in library science and engaged in library services.

Library Assistant   Registers patrons so they can borrow materials from the library. Issues library cards. Maintains book inventory and patrons' databases.

Library Technician   Helps librarians acquire, prepare, and organize material. Assist users in finding information.

Licensed Practical Nurse (LPN)   Provides nursing care for ill, injured, convalescent, and disabled patients. Monitors and records patients' vital signs, dresses wounds, and provides assistance with satisfying needs. May assist high-level medical or nursing staff in providing patient care.

Licensed Veterinary Technologist   Person who has been granted the legal right to perform certain veterinary technology duties by a recognized governing body. Without having earned the license, it is illegal to perform those certain functions.

Licensed Vocational Nurse (LVN)   A person who is specifically prepared in the techniques of nursing, is a graduate of an accredited school of vocational nursing, and whose qualifications have been examined by a state board of nursing.

Licensing Agent   Provides licenses to business agents seeking approval to conduct business. Represents the business interests of a firm.

Lieutenant   A commissioned military officer, an officer in a police force, or an assistant with power to act when the supervisor is absent.

Line Cook   Responsible for any duties necessary to prepare and produce menu items efficiently. Duties may include cutting and portioning, cooking, and serving items.

Litigation Paralegal   Assists attorneys at trial, prepares for trial, digests or summarizes depositions, indexes or organizes documents, prepares simple pleadings and discoveries such as interrogatories.

Litigation Real Estate Manager   Manages litigation resulting from real estate transactions.

Litigation Support Consultant   Provides consulting services in litigation support. Consultation areas include analyzing the project, designing a database structure, developing a database building plan, creating coding sheets, and writing report programs.

Litigation Support Manager   Responsible for computerized litigation support. Consults with attorneys about whether a certain case will require automation and, if so, how to design the document retrieval database.

Loan Manager   Supervises loan personnel and approves recommendations of customer applications for lines of credit when loan officer is not able to do so. Communicates changes in policies and regulations regularly to loan personnel and customers.

Loan Officer   Interviews applicants applying for loans. Prepares loan request paper, obtains related documents from applicants. Investigates applicants' background and verifies credit and bank references. Informs applicants whether loan requests have been approved or rejected. Processes the loans.

Long-Term Care Nurse   Directs, initiates, and implements a patient care plan in a long-term care environment. Assists physicians during examinations and procedures. Prepares equipment, applies and changes dressings, and monitors patients.

Loss Prevention Specialist   Guards the internal security of a business to prevent employee thefts and inventory loss.

Mail and Information Coordinator   Coordinates the information and mail services, usually at the front desk. Responsible for ensuring that outgoing and incoming mail for the facility as well as for guests is properly routed. Advises guests on most efficient procedures for receiving or sending important mail. Ensures that messages get to hotel personnel and guests on a timely and accurate basis. May also provide guests with general information about the facility and the area.

Maître d'Hôtel   Is in charge of the dining room in a hotel or restaurant. Supervises a team of captains, servers, and junior servers.

Management Dietitian   Develops and directs the implementation of menus. Selects, trains, supervises, and evaluates food service personnel. Develops, implements, and evaluates food service policies, procedures, and standards.

Manager (Accounting)   Organizes and directs all general accounting activities. Maintains accounting systems that ensure the proper accounting and recording of company resources. Provides financial statements, analysis, and other key management reports.

Manager (Recreation)   Manages recreation facilities, such as tennis courts, golf courses, or arcades, and coordinates activities of workers engaged in providing services of the facility. Determines work activities necessary to operate facility, hires workers, and assigns tasks and work hours accordingly. Initiates promotion to acquaint public with activities of the facility. Maintains financial records.

Manager of Information Security Systems and Services
Supervises, directs, and leads the operations of a firm providing information security solutions. Oversees a team of engineers and/or information technicians responsible for safeguarding information systems and Web sites, or a sales team responsible for selling systems that provide technical security solutions.

Manager of Membership Sales   Plans and implements annual campaign sales. Creates and targets varied market segments for promotion. Establishes and implements annual sales goals and manages the membership budget.

Manager of Network Security   (See **Network Security Manager**)

Manager of Tour Operations   Supervises support functions related to the execution of a successful tour. Areas of responsibility include the bookkeeping, secretarial, and computer operations areas.

Manager Trainee   Performs assigned duties, under direction of experienced personnel, to gain knowledge and experience needed for management position. Receives training and performs duties in various departments to become familiar with personnel functions and operations and management viewpoints and policies that affect each phase of the business.

Manager Trainee (Finance)   Works with financial manager while gaining an overall exposure to all aspects of the finance function of the company. Assists with budgets, purchase options, and expenses. Helps review financial reports for different product lines and assists with consolidating financial data for updated reports. May interview other department heads, customers, vendors, and other key people dealing with the finance area.

Manager Trainee (Food Service)   Assists with all functions of the area assigned. Learns the overview of the entire operation before specializing. If in a large operation, may rotate within one area of the facility, such as the production or purchasing area, to learn all of its functions if that is the area of specialty. Usually trains by rotating among various stations in the kitchen itself and among related areas such as purchasing, the storeroom, front of the house, etc.

Manager Trainee (Retail)   Works with store manager organizing and managing the store on a daily basis. Spends time on the selling floor to learn customer service techniques and computerized systems. Assists with managing, merchandising, and analyzing stock. Directs and physically puts stock out on the floor and presents merchandise. May work with buyer to learn financial planning, vendor negotiations, and branch store communications.

Manufacturing Manager   Coordinates all manufacturing operations to produce products of high quality and reliability at optimum cost and in accordance with customer shipping schedules. Participates in the preparation of the manufacturing budget. Ensures safety of employees in their exposure to varied manufacturing process hazards. Resolves various manufacturing and production problems.

Manufacturing Representative   Self-employed sales worker or independent firm that contract its services to all types of manufacturing companies.

Market Analyst   Collects and analyzes data on customer demographics, preferences, needs, and buying habits to identify potential markets and factors affecting product demand. Conducts research on consumer opinions and marketing strategies. Forecasts and tracks marketing and sales trends.

Market Manager (Food Service)   Responsible for compiling information on the age, sex, and income level of restaurants' potential clientele and their dining habits and preferences. Marketing managers consider customer preferences in order to suggest appropriate sales advertising techniques. This information provides the basis for success/failure projections in certain demographic areas.

Market Research Analyst   Researches market conditions in local, regional, or national area to determine potential sales of product or service. Examines and analyzes statistical data to forecast future marketing trends. Gathers data on competitors and analyzes prices, sales, and methods of marketing and distribution. Formulates surveys, opinion polls, or questionnaires.

Market Research Director   Oversees market research for a company. Sets goals and objectives for projects. Sets timetables for completion and assigns personnel to projects. Keeps appropriate administrators informed on findings and makes recommendations and proposes marketing strategies based on results.

Marketing Analyst (Paralegal)   Examines and analyzes statistical data to forecast future marketing trends in the paralegal field. (See **Market Research Analyst**)

Marketing Art Director   Creates art copy to promote products or services; formulates basic layout design or presentation approach. Confers with creative, art, copywriting, or production department heads to discuss client needs and presentation concepts.

Marketing Assistant   Supports the development and distribution of marketing and sales materials, assists in production of advertising, marketing brochures, sales kits, or other promotional materials.

Marketing Director   Directs and coordinates the development of marketing programs assigned to attain maximum penetration in the required market segments. Directs the creation, writing, and publishing of market and product plans. Explores development of product line offerings.

Marketing and Promotion Manager (Food Service)
Supervises any advertising or sales promotion for the operation. Works with food production staff to create menus and promotions with customer appeal. Often coordinates these activities with an advertising agency.

Marketing Representative (Paralegal)   Promotes and sells law-related books. Works in the marketing division of legal publishing companies.

Marketing Support Representative   Backs up the sales force by demonstrating the equipment and working with the customers after the equipment is installed; teaches the customers' word processing specialists to use the equipment and helps them find the best methods of doing the company's particular tasks.

Massage Therapist   Performs physical evaluations and applies a range of treatments, to include massage therapy, to patients or clients. Develops and implements massage treatment and therapy plans.

Master Brewer   Ensures that an entire brewery operation is productive and that the product meets all industry standards.

Materials Manager   Studies receiving or shipping notices, requests for movement of raw materials and finished products, and reports of warehousing space available to develop schedules for material-handling activities. May confer with supervisors of other departments to coordinate flow of materials or products. Supervises activities of shipping and receiving personnel.

Media Director of Planning   Plans media relations in line with company goals. Reports and analyzes industry media trends. Communicates with product development to determine product market plans as they relate to media proposals and media scheduling. Oversees Media Planners.

Media Planner   Plans and administers media programs in advertising department. Confers with representatives of advertising agencies, product managers, and corporate advertising staff to establish media goals, objectives, and strategies within corporate advertising budget. Studies demographic data and consumer profiles to identify target audiences of media advertising.

Media Relations Director   Oversees planning groups that select the communication media—for example, radio, television, newspapers, magazines, Internet, or outdoor signs—to disseminate the advertising.

Medical Assistant   Works in hospitals or clinics cleaning and sterilizing equipment, performing various tests, and helping maintain records.

Medical Billing Clerk   Assists with compiling the fees that are owed to a medical facility or physician. Reviews and maintains orders, invoices, and records to ensure accuracy and maintain all patient payment records.

Medical Claims Examiner   Claims examiner for the medical field. (See **Claims Examiner**)

Medical Claims Representative   Claims representative for the medical field. (See **Claims Representative**)

Medical Coding Clerk   Analyzes medical records and assigns codes to classify diagnoses and procedures to support the reimbursement system, assessment of clinical care, and medical research activity.

Medical Director   Allocates resources, supervises and trains staff, oversees budgeting and marketing of medical services and facility. Ensures compliance with policies and regulatory issues.

Medical and Health Services Manager   Plans, directs, coordinates, and supervises the delivery of health care services. Generalists manage an entire facility, while specialists manage a department.

Medical Librarian   Records, arranges, and makes medical information available to people. Handles books, films, periodicals, documents, and other media related to the medical field.

Medical Negligence Investigator   Investigates allegations of medical fraud resulting from neglect of duty, misdiagnosis, or poor standards of care.

Medical Records Administrator   Plans, develops, and administers medical record systems for hospital, clinic, health center, or similar facility to meet standards of accrediting and regulatory agencies. Assists medical staff in evaluating quality of patient care and in developing criteria and methods for such evaluation. Develops and implements policies and procedures for documenting, storing, and retrieving information and for processing medical/legal documents.

Medical Records and Health Information Technician   Performs a variety of clerical duties to provide for the ongoing accuracy and completeness of all medical records in accordance with established policy, practice, and regulations.

Medical Records Technician   Gathers all information on patient's condition and records it on permanent files that become the history and progress of treatment of a patient's illness or injury. Accumulates the results of a physician's examinations, information on laboratory tests, and electrocardiograms, and records these results in the records. Accuracy is particularly important because much of this information is referred to during malpractice cases, and it is also vital when processing insurance claims.

Medical Secretary   Processes many kinds of complex health insurance forms. Responsible for patient billing, records management, medical and office supply organization, and appointments. Takes dictation and transcribes on dictaphone. Deals with medical supply vendors and pharmaceutical houses. Prepares correspondence and assists physicians with reports, speeches, articles, and conference proceedings.

Medical Technician (Electronics)   Performs the work of an electronics technician, specifically on various types of medical equipment. (See **Electronics Technician**)

Medical Transcriptionist   Transcribes medical records, operative reports, discharge summary, letters, examinations, and patient history, using word processing equipment.

Meeting Planner   Establishes objectives of the meeting, selects the hotel site and facilities, negotiates rates, sets budgets, makes air and hotel reservations, chooses speakers, plans food and beverages, arranges for all audiovisual equipment. Arranges meeting registration, exhibits, promotion and publicity scheduling, and room setup, and arranges postmeeting evaluation. Planners are involved with negotiations that save the organization money.

Membership Coordinator   Solicits membership for club or trade association. Visits or contacts prospective members to explain benefits and costs of membership and to describe organization of club or association. May collect dues and payments for publications from members.

Membership Sales Representative   Sells individual and group memberships for a variety of products, services, and organizations. Is usually rewarded through commission for hitting predetermined targets.

Membership Secretary   Compiles and maintains membership lists, records the receipt of dues and contributions, and gives out information to members of the organizations and associations. Sends out newsletters and other promotional materials on a regular basis. Answers telephone inquiries and coordinates mass mailings.

Menu Planner   Works with the Executive Chef to select all items offered on menus. Must know food service costs, preparation techniques and equipment, customer trends and preferences.

Merchandise Analyst   Evaluates available merchandise in different locations and identifies when transfers might be appropriate. With the buyer, evaluates quality of merchandise from the vendors for price paid.

Merchandise Manager   Takes charge of a group of departments, usually organized by merchandise. Coordinates and oversees the efforts of the buyers. Develops merchandise plans, divides up the buyers' merchandise assignments, and reviews their selections. Visits the manufacturers' showrooms and travels abroad.

Merchandise Planner   Allocates merchandise from distribution point to stores as requested by buyers and merchandise managers. Ensures that merchandise is shipped properly and on a timely basis from the distribution center.

Merchandising Supervisor (Food Service)   Plans and carries out promotional programs to increase sales. Works with printers, artists, writers, and other suppliers. Must know employer's food service operations thoroughly and be able to apply market research techniques as well as budgeting and planning skills.

Microsoft Training Specialist   Provides training on overall comprehension of Microsoft Office or Microsoft Project programs, including use of advanced features and integration with other software programs.

MIS Director   Recommends and initiates programs and/or systems that support the desired corporate profit objectives. Issues business data and management information that facilitate the businesses' planning and decision-making process at all levels. Responsible for total information service provided to user departments.

MIS Specialist   Has specific knowledge of and provides service to a specialized area in the company. May concentrate on such areas as accounting, sales, production, or any other function requiring the services of the MIS department to meet its particular need.

Missing Persons Research Investigator   Conducts investigations to locate, arrest, and return fugitives and persons wanted for nonpayment of support payments or unemployment insurance fraud, and to locate missing persons.

Mixed Animal Veterinarian   Doctors trained to protect the health of both animals and people. Provide services for both small companion animals and large non-domestic, animals. Evaluate animals' health, diagnose and treat illnesses, provide routine preventive care (such as vaccines), prescribe medication, and perform surgery.

Mixologist   Mixes and serves alcoholic drinks at drinking establishments, hotels, restaurants, and events. Is fully knowledgeable in all aspects of beverage management, and in the drinking laws and regulations for the state in which the establishment operates. May manage all bar operations, including staffing, budgeting, inventory control, and beverage menu development.

National Sales Manager (Marketing)   Devises and implements sales strategies, forecasts sales, supervises in-house salespeople; establishes and attains sales goals; trains and develops sales personnel. Develops and implements marketing and advertising strategy.

Network Administration Training Specialist   Provides training activities to software and high-end technical applications, and network administration operating systems.

Network Administrator   Designs, installs, and supports an organization's LAN (local area network), network segment, Internet or intranet system. Provides day-to-day onsite administrative support for software users in a variety of work environments, including professional offices, small businesses, government, and large corporations. Maintains network hardware and software, analyzes problems, and monitors the network to ensure its availability to system users. Administrators may plan, coordinate, and implement network security measures.

Network Defense Manager   Expert knowledgeable on sourcing and implementing security products and services to provide network security to a firm.

Network Engineer   Handles all inner workings of a company's computers, including connecting offices with specified computer lines, hooking them up to the Internet, and configuring all internal systems, such as net routers and firewalls.

Network Security Administrator   Troubleshoots network access problems and implements network security policies and procedures. Designs and manages an organization's LANs and WANs. Chooses a company's hardware and software to meet IT needs; rolls out new equipment and systems and ensures that corrective and preventive measures are performed on existing equipment and systems. Analyzes the organization's business needs and then the related design and implementation and management of the network infrastructure to support those business needs.

Network Security Manager   Implements and supports complex security systems, software programs, and hardware devices used to provide protection to corporate networks. Develops network security architecture, network security management investigations, crisis response, and intrusion detection system. Provides project security leadership.

Network Security Specialist   Applies computer networking concepts with emphasis on network administration with client server, network defense and countermeasures, basic security implementation, enterprise security solution and biometrics through the use of retinal scanners, thumbprint scanners, and other current service devices.

Network Security Technician   Responsible for incident response, intervention detection, firewall management, and programming.

Network Technician   Performs help desk, desktop, and network problem determinations and resolutions. Knowledge of multiple technologies is required. Defines problems, collects data, establishes facts, and draws conclusions.

Night Auditor (Hospitality)   Brings all the establishment's accounts up-to-date so that a day's revenue report can be made to upper management. (In a hotel, a revenue report includes such items as a detailed account of room revenues, number of rooms occupied, average room revenue, percentage of occupancy figures, and the like.) The night audit process is usually augmented by a computerized system. The night auditor often plays the role of the night manager.

Night Shift Supervisor (Word Processing)   Supervises work of word processing department during the night shift. Schedules the staff for the shift. Prioritizes work that must be completed. Responsible for maintaining the equipment and resolving routine problems that may occur in processing.

Nuclear Medicine Technologist   Uses radionuclides for diagnostic, therapeutic, and investigative purposes. Performs tests and examinations using radiation detectors, scanning apparatus, and related equipment in medical labs and clinics.

Nurse   Cares for ill, injured, convalescent, and handicapped persons in hospitals, clinics, private homes, sanitariums, and similar institutions. Observes patient and reports adverse reactions to medical personnel in charge. Administers specified medications, and notes time and amount on patient's chart. Performs routine laboratory work.

Nurse Anesthesiologist   Anesthesia professional who administers approximately 65 percent of all anesthetics given to patients.

Nurse's Assistant   Assists nursing staff in providing care to patients. Responds to basic patient requests and assists with feeding, clothing, and bathing patients.

Nursing Home Care Investigator   Investigates allegations of fraud or malpractice resulting from complaints about nursing home services provided.

Nutrition Consultant   Assists schools, health care professionals, and community groups in developing or maintaining nutrition and food service programs and in the development of policy pertaining to clinical nutrition.

Nutritionist   Identifies the kinds and amounts of nutrients in food, translates this knowledge for schools and health care menus and restaurants and hotels. Develops new foods and ingredients.

Occupational Physical Therapist   Helps people improve their ability to perform tasks in their daily living and working environments. Helps clients develop, recover, or maintain daily living and work skills.

Occupational Therapist Assistant   Assists with providing a variety of therapy activities designed to rehabilitate patients or allow them to adjust to their handicaps. Writes patient progress reports.

Office Machine Repairer   Installs, services, and repairs office machines, such as typewriters, calculators, cash registers, mail processing equipment, and copiers.

Office Manager   (See **Department Manager—Office**)

Operating Room Nurse   Registered professional nurse responsible for the direct and indirect nursing care of the patients assigned to the operating room.

Operations Manager (Retail)   Oversees all functions of store operations, which include personnel, credit, payroll, shipping and receiving, customer service, warehousing and distribution, security, and maintenance.

Operations Research Analyst   Conducts analyses of management and operational problems and formulates mathematical or simulation models of the problem. Analyzes problems in terms of management information and conceptualizes and defines problems. Studies information and selects plan from

competitive proposals that affords maximum profitability or effectiveness in relation to cost or risk.

Oracle Training Specialist   Provides general and technical training, custom training, or Oracle developer training.

Outside Sales Agent (Travel)   Brings new business to an agency on a referral basis.

Owner/Operator (Events Services Business)   Owns and/or operates a business providing event planning services.

Owner/Operator (Food Service)   Coordinates all employees; may be responsible for buying food and supplies; may help with menu planning; keeps the restaurant within health and sanitation guidelines; oversees payroll function. In small restaurants, may oversee marketing and promotion effort.

Owner/Operator (Information Security Services)   Owns and/or operates a business providing information security services.

Owner/Operator (Network Security Services)   Owns and/or operates a business providing network security services.

Owner/Operator (Travel Agency)   Delegates responsibilities to qualified managers. Encourages creative marketing and sales activities. Manages budget for the overall operation.

Owner/Operator (Wellness Center)   Owns and/or operates a business providing programs and services that enhance overall client wellness.

Packaging Specialist   Develops packaging to fit specific products for industry needs.

Page Creator (Word Processing)   Composes actual pages of catalogs relayed to home television or telephones. Involves word processing, text editing, and formatting, together with computer graphics. The system plus its computer graphics is called videotex.

Pantry Person   Draws from the storeroom all the raw materials needed to prepare all the fruit or vegetable salads, seafood cocktails, canapes, and other cold dishes. Serves these items to waiters and waitresses. May slice and portion cold meats and cheeses. Serves desserts and side dishes such as bread and butter. Makes sandwiches and prepares garnishes for other departments.

Paralegal   Assists a lawyer with routine legal assignments. Maintains legal volumes to make sure they are up-to-date; assists with legal research. Helps administer estates, draft wills and trusts, complete federal and state tax returns, prepare initial and amended articles of incorporation, stock certificates, and other securities. Helps prepare court-related forms. Performs a variety of related duties upon request of the attorney.

Paralegal (Publishing House)   Assists the general counsel in the company's legal department with the areas of law that affect publishing, such as contract law and copyright law. May assist the legal publisher in planning new books about the paralegal profession or the procedures utilized by paralegals in the office.

Paralegal Assistant   Assists paralegals in large-scale litigation with such duties as organizing and indexing documents, summarizing simple depositions, and performing assignments that enhance the overall organization of the case.

Paralegal Coordinator   Responsible for paralegal workload management, both as a resource for attorneys needing paralegal assistance and to ensure fairly divided workloads among paralegals on staff.

Paralegal Instructor   Teaches paralegal students the legal procedures used by paralegals in the law office.

Paralegal Manager   Responsible for hiring, performance reviews, salary administration, budgets, and work assignments.

Paralegal Supervisor   Oversees work of paralegal responsible for researching law, investigating facts, and preparing documents to assist lawyers.

Paramedic: A person who is trained to give emergency medical treatment or to assist physicians in providing medical care.

Park Ranger   Provides law enforcement services in national parks.

Parole Officer   Helps clients find a place to live or work after being conditionally released from prison; must enforce the specific conditions of the client's release at all times.

Partner (CPA Firm)   Responsible for major audit accounts. Solves complex accounting problems for clients, using standard accounting principles. Also responsible for quality of client service and volume of new business brought in to the firm. Achieves objectives through the effective management of the technicians and sales staff in the firm.

Passenger Service Agent   Provides passengers with information; assists passengers when boarding the plane.

Pastry Chef   Oversees the bread and pastry needs of all kitchens and departments in a large hotel, club, or restaurant. Supervises pastry cooks and bakers. Requires ability to coordinate the activity of others. Supervises the preparation of desserts, pastries, frozen desserts, fondants, fillings, and fancy sugar decorations. Creates new recipes and produces delicate items that require mastery of fine techniques.

Pastry Cook   Prepares desserts (both hot and cold), ices, and cakes for both daily use and for special occasions.

Pastry Production Manager   Provides training and guidance to bakers and pastry cooks. Analyzes food cost and determines cost-effective recipes. Supervises the production of baked goods in a large kitchen facility within a hotel, restaurant, or independent supplier of baked goods.

PC Technician   Installs PCs and related hardware. Investigates hardware problems and performs minor system hardware and communication connection repairs; performs basic diagnostic testing; refers major problems to outside vendors.

Personal Chef   Prepares meals off-premise in quantity and delivers to the client's home with instructions for use at a later time.

Personal Trainer   Plans and leads a range of individual exercises and activity sessions for clients in standard to advanced fitness specialty areas.

Personnel Assistant   Performs diversified duties in the processing and monitoring of employee benefits programs and maintenance of all employee personnel files. Sets up files on new employees. Records changes in employee status as necessary and forwards to payroll department.

Personnel Director   Supervises the hiring and firing of company employees. Prepares performance reports and sets

up personnel policies and regulations. In a large corporation, oversees the entire personnel function.

Personnel Manager   Responsible for developing, implementing, and coordinating policies and programs covering the following: employment, labor relations, wage and salary administration, fringe benefits administration, indoctrination and training, placement, safety, insurance, health benefits, and employee services.

Pharmaceutical Sales Representative   Actively promotes the sale of pharmaceutical products within a particular geographic region.

Pharmacist   Expert in drugs who advises doctors and patients on which prescription and over-the-counter drugs, medicines, and therapies are appropriate for treating certain health conditions.

Pharmacy Aide   Establishes and maintains patient profiles; prepares insurance claim forms. Inventories prescription and over-the-counter medication stock.

Pharmacy Technician   Works with a licensed pharmacist to provide medication and other health care products to patients; may prepare prescribed medicines for delivery directly to patients or to nurses. Measures appropriate quantity of medication, places in containers, and labels appropriately.

Phising Attack Security Officer   Prevents the use of Internet fraud resulting from fraudulent Internet sites geared to stealing personal information through false advertising.

Phlebotomist   Explains and performs a variety of routine blood-drawing procedures, including venipuncture, using standard equipment. Obtains patient information for lab records. Processes labels and stores blood for early analysis.

Photographer   Schedules, coordinates, and provides photographic services, including stills, motion pictures, and videotape. Performs related location, studio, and darkroom functions.

Physical Therapist   Provides services that help restore function, improve mobility, relieve pain, and prevent or limit permanent physical disabilities of patients suffering from injury or disease.

Physical Therapist Assistant   Under supervision of a physical therapist, provides a variety of treatments to patients, including exercises, massages, electrical stimulation, paraffin baths, traction, and ultrasounds. Records patient's progress.

Physician's Assistant   Provides health care services under supervision of a physician. Takes medical histories, examines and treats patients, orders and interprets lab tests, makes diagnoses, and prescribes medication.

Placement Director (Paralegal)   Responsible for employment orientation and job development, and may act as a liaison between the employer and the paralegal graduate seeking a position.

Plant Manager   Responsible for manufacturing of products in the required quantity and quality and for performing this function safely at a minimum cost. Recommends improvements in manufacturing methods. Sets up and approves production schedules. Regularly reviews inventories of required materials. Directs and approves all requisitions for maintenance and repair of building and equipment and for machine parts and manufacturing supplies.

Plant Safety Specialist   Coordinates safety programs. Communicates policies, programs, and regulations to appropriate personnel. Ensures compliance with governmental regulations. Enforces safety policies for chemical use, fire codes, equipment, and ventilation systems. Ensures proper guarding of machinery to avoid operator injury. Maintains records as well.

Police Patrol Officer   Responsible for the enforcement of laws and ordinances for the protection of life and property in an assigned area during a specific period. Conducts preliminary investigations; assists in the apprehension of criminals.

Policy Director   Researches, evaluates, and implements policy for a private firm or public institution in a wide range of areas, from accounting, safety, human resources, and legal to technology security.

Polygraph Operator   Tests victims, suspects, witnesses, and others through the use of a lie detector machine.

Polygraph Specialist   Conducts examinations of individuals to learn if responses are truthful.

Portfolio Banker   Provides financial advice to high–net worth customers on asset allocation and investment.

Portfolio Manager   Manages nontrust accounts, such as the pension fund of a corporation or a university endowment. Decides what stocks should be bought and sold within the portfolio.

Postal Inspector   Investigates losses and thefts of the mail or property owned by the post office. In addition, investigators and security force personnel protect postal buildings and installations.

Pound Attendant   Feeds and grooms or otherwise cares for pets and other nonfarm animals such as dogs, cats, ornamental fish or birds, and zoo animals. May keep records of feedings, treatments, and animals received or discharged. Typically works in kennels, animal shelters, zoos, circuses, and aquariums.

Preemployment Check Specialist   Conducts investigations into job applicants' employment history to verify statements on job applications and résumés prior to employment.

Prep Cook   Responsible for any duties necessary in order to prepare food items for production.

Prerelease Program Correctional Counselor   Counsels clients; helps transition clients from custody to society.

Prerelease Program Employment Counselor   Provides career guidance for those soon to be released from incarceration; work involves placement of difficult-to-employ clients.

Prerelease Program Halfway House Counselor   Guards, observes, and supervises inmates in halfway houses.

President   Plans, develops, and establishes policies and objectives of the business organization in accordance with the board of directors and corporate charter. Plans business objectives and develops policies to coordinate functions between departments. Reviews financial statements to determine progress and status in attaining objectives. Directs and coordinates formulation of financial programs to provide funding for new or continuing operations to maximize return on investments. May preside over board of directors. Evaluates performance of company executives.

President/Owner   Acts as president of a business and owns and operates it as well. (See **President**)

Press Coordinator   Arranges meetings and special events with the press. Contacts press either by phone or mail to detail upcoming events.

Private   An enlisted person of either of the two lowest ranks in the U.S. Marine Corps.

Private Asset Manager   Focuses exclusively on marketing investment management, financial, and advisory services to the high–net worth arena.

Private Banker   Manages private clients' money; specializes in clients with large accounts who want their money invested and managed for the long term.

Private Chef   May live in client's residence and prepare up to three meals per day; menu selection is based on client's dietary needs and cuisine preference. Does food shopping as needed; provides table service, and cleans up.

Private Client Services   Provides personal assistance with creating a personal investment management strategy.

Private First Class   An enlisted person ranking just below a corporal in the U.S. Army and just below a lance corporal in the U.S. Marine Corps.

Private Investigator   Obtains information for the legal profession, commerce, industry, and the general public in all areas of civil, criminal, and personal matters. May trace missing persons and conduct surveillance, background checks, or corporate investigations.

Private Nurse   Works in physician's office, clinic, nursing home, rehabilitation center, private corporation, school, or private residence to provide nursing care to patients.

Private Secretary   The executive's administrative partner. Duties vary according to the size of the organization and the executive's responsibilities. May outline day's work for the office, scheduling duties to be performed by all who work in the office; keeps everything on schedule despite interruptions. Greets callers, handles mail, keeps track of financial records, and processes data.

Probate Paralegal   Oversees probate proceedings from beginning to end, prepares federal tax forms, assists at the sales of assets, and drafts wills and trusts.

Probation Officer   Responsible for compiling the presentence investigation for the court. Makes formal court reports and recommendations to the judge for case deposition. Works with caseloads of individuals to assist them with counseling, job placement, and traditional social work–oriented functions while at the same time enforcing the rules imposed on the clients by the court.

Product Classifier   Codes products being imported or exported to determine duty rates.

Product Development Chef   Develops new recipes by experimenting with ingredients; develops new products and product lines. Evaluates ingredients and ensures current products meet company standards for flavor and quality.

Product Development Technologist   Technologist working in the food service industry conducting experiments to improve flavor, texture, shelf life, or other product characteristics. Develops new products or packaging materials. Compares competitive products. Ensures that every item meets quality standards. Interprets and solves the problems of the food service operator.

Product Manager   Oversees the research, development, and production of a particular product. Assesses need for modifications on the product based on input from market research. Estimates timely and cost-effective procedures for implementing periodic modifications. Ensures that quality of product is maintained.

Product Specialist   Assists customers with deciding which products best fit their needs, from standard product offerings to specialty products.

Production Coordinator   Coordinates flow of work within or between departments of manufacturer to expedite production. Reviews master production schedule and work orders, establishes priorities and availability or capability of workers, parts, or material. Confers with department supervisors to determine progress of work. Compiles reports on the progress of work.

Production Hand   Assists with the grape harvesting and performs other wine-making tasks at a winery.

Production Manager   Supervises and coordinates activities of those who expedite flow of materials, parts, and assemblies and processes within or between departments.

Production Manager (Food Service)   Takes leadership position in food service production operation areas such as engineering, scheduling, purchasing, quality control, inventory control, distribution, and human relations.

Production Planner   Ensures that inventories of stock items are maintained at reasonable levels and that orders for non-stock items are processed in a timely, effective manner. Works with plant supervisor to establish worker levels that are appropriate based on current and projected levels of activity. Requisitions all raw materials and supplies required to manufacture products.

Production Technician   Assists engineer in preparing layouts of machinery and equipment, work flow plans, time-and-motion studies, and analyses of production costs to produce the most efficient use of personnel, materials, and machines.

Program Coordinator   Oversees programs after the planning stage. Takes appropriate action to initiate planned programs, service them while in progress, and arrange for program evaluation. May assist with recommending speakers, agendas, room setup, and promotional efforts.

Program Director   Plans and develops methods and procedures for implementing programs; directs and coordinates program activities, and exercises control over personnel according to knowledge and experience in area with which the program is concerned. Prepares program reports. Controls expenditures.

Program Director (Education)   Supervises the development of a variety of academic programs or other programs related to an educational institution. Such programs might involve parents, student organizations, industry, or other special interest groups. (See **Program Director**)

Programmer Analyst   Analyzes user specifications and requirements. Encodes, tests, debugs, and documents programs on large-scale, complex projects and revises and updates programs and documentation.

Project Director   Plans, directs, and coordinates activities of designated project to ensure that aims, goals, or objectives specified for project are accomplished in accordance with set priorities, timetables, and funding. Develops staffing plan and establishes work schedules for each phase of the project. Prepares project status reports for management.

Promotions Manager   Supervises staff of promotion specialists; directs promotional programs that combine advertising with purchase incentives to increase sales.

Proofreader   Reads typeset (original copy) or proof of type setup to detect and mark for corrections and grammatical, typographical, or compositional errors. Reads proof against copy, marking by standardized codes errors that appear in proof. Returns marked proof for correction and later checks corrected proof against copy.

Proofreader (Paralegal)   Reviews the content of law-related manuscripts to verify facts needed in case preparation. Also can act as person who checks for improper usage or spelling or grammar errors in legal copy.

Proofreader (Word Processing)   Checks the work of the correspondence secretary and word processor for accuracy of copy.

Protective Specialist   Investigates and resolves allegations of personal neglect and/or abuse.

Public Relations Director   (See **Public Relations Manager**)

Public Relations Manager   Oversees the representation of a positive organizational image to the general public, clients, shareholders, and the community. Oversees preparation and dissemination of press releases and articles, and coordinates media events. Directs writing, editing, and publishing of organizational publications.

Public Relations Specialist   Writes news releases, directs advertising campaigns, or conducts public opinion polls. Tries to create favorable attitudes about a client or its products.

Publications Editor   Responsible for editing, layout, and production of the publications for a department or for a major specialized unit. Works with authors in determining best method of writing.

Purchasing Agent   Responsible for buying the raw materials, machinery, supplies, and services necessary to run a business.

Purchasing Agent (Food Service)   Purchases foodstuffs, kitchen supplies, and equipment. Makes large contracts for several products. Purchases all supplies with the exception of capital goods such as furniture and fixed equipment.

Purchasing Assistant   (See **Purchasing Agent**)

Purchasing Manager   Responsible for the management of the procurement functions of the company. Establishes practices and procedures to be followed by buyers and other department personnel. Negotiates price and delivery. Selects vendors, assesses vendor capabilities, develops alternate sources, and evaluates vendor performance. Ensures that department records are maintained.

Purchasing Manager (Food Service)   Responsible for the actual purchase of all supplies and equipment, usually coordinated through the Executive Chef or Cook. Required to monitor and control costs and to maintain accurate inventories. Supervises purchasing agents responsible for a particular product line.

Quality Assurance Manager   Develops and maintains a system to ensure that all products manufactured by the organization meet customer specifications and achieve superior quality and reliability levels. Revises and updates quality control manual. Meets with vendors, customers, and quality representatives to discuss and resolve quality problems as required.

Quality Assurance Specialist (Food Service)   Analyzes ingredients and finished products and checks standards of production, packaging, and sanitation. May be assigned to a particular type of product or food item.

Quality Control Manager (Food Service)   Travels to various units to inspect those units and make sure they adhere to company and state standards. Usually responsible for more than one operation.

Radiologic Technologist   Takes X-rays and administers nonradiologic materials into patient's bloodstream for diagnostic purposes.

Radiologist   Diagnoses diseases by obtaining and integrating medical images; correlates medical image findings with other examinations and tests. May recommend further examinations or treatments and confers with referring physicians.

Ramp Agent   Supervises baggage area to be sure baggage is sent to proper destinations.

Real Estate Fraud Investigator   Investigates allegations of illegal practices in real estate transactions.

Real Estate Manager (Food Service)   Supervises the negotiations for the acquisition and disposition of restaurant properties. Supervises staff engaged in preparing lease agreements, recording rental receipts, and performing other activities necessary to efficient management of company properties, or in performing routine research on zoning ordinances and condemnation considerations. Directs appraiser to inspect properties and land under consideration for acquisition and recommends acquisitions, lease, disposition, improvement, or other action consistent with the best interests of the company. Negotiates contracts with sellers of land and renters of property.

Real Estate Paralegal   Prepares loan documents, oversees transactions from beginning to end, drafts and reviews leases, works closely with escrow and title companies, reviews surveys, and prepares closing binders.

Real Estate Sales Manager   Creates revenue-generating ideas by strategically analyzing, planning, and implementing real estate initiatives targeting the builder and resale and rental categories.

Real-Time Reporter   Responsible for producing instant translation of shorthand into English, voice to print, via the court reporter's notebook computer.

Receiving Barn Custodian   Verifies credentials of persons at receiving barn and notifies stable attendants to bring animals to the barn for examination and inspection. Compares names of persons requesting admittance with list of names authorized.

Reception Manager   Supervises all activities of guest services, including registration of incoming guests and checkout of departing guests. Takes messages for guests and provides wake-up calls. Provides guests with information about functions at the hotel and about the general area where the hotel is located. Handles guest relations, problems with rooms, billing, or any other routine difficulty.

Receptionist   Greets people who come into an office and directs them to the proper department. May also answer the phone and do some typing. Learns the departments and key personnel in the company and the functions they perform.

Records Manager   Examines and evaluates records management systems to develop new methods or improve existing methods for efficient handling, protecting, and disposing of business records and information. Reviews records retention schedule to determine how long records should be kept.

Recreation Director (Cruise Lines)   Develops safe recreation programs suitable for a cruise ship. Ensures adherence to established standards and policies. Ensures staff is properly certified for instruction when needed. Makes recommendations to activities coordinator for recreation schedules.

Recreational Counselor   Conducts and supervises the recreational activities of inmates; promotes the emotional, physical, and social well-being of inmates.

Recreational Physical Therapist   Provides treatment services and recreation activities to individuals with disabilities or illnesses.

Recruiting Coordinator/Administrator   Works with the firm administrator and the recruiting or hiring committee to hire new attorneys. Coordinates Summer Clerk interviewing.

Regional Director   May oversee a group of regional managers. (See **Regional Manager**)

Regional Manager   Responsible for overseeing the activities of all operations in a particular geographical area of the country.

Regional Sales Manager   Recruits in-house personnel, recruits general agents, and assists when needed with training new sales staff with cold calling. Holds periodic sales meetings to strengthen competitive position and explain strategies for market penetration.

Regional Vice President (Food Service)   Deals with new business development; senior food service management contact, both internal and external; pricing analysis; food service business proposal development and presentation; and contract negotiations. Works on planning and achieving marketing objectives within the particular geographic territory.

Registered Dietitian   Ensures that nutritional needs of individual patients are being met and that all documentation related to patients' nutritional status is complete and accurate.

Registered Nurse   Evaluates, plans, and administers nursing care to patients. Provides prescribed medication and treatment. Monitors and records patient's condition and notifies physician when appropriate.

Registered Representative (Account Executive or Broker)   Buys or sells securities for customers. Relays the order to members of the firm who are stationed on the exchange floors; if the security is not traded on the exchange, sells it directly in the over-the-counter market. Advises customers on the timing of the purchase or sale of securities. Counsels customers about tax shelters, mutual funds, and other investments.

Registered Veterinary Technologist   Persons deemed eligible, by a governing or professional body, to be placed on a list of those who have completed a set of requirements needed to become a veterinary technologist. Being registered does not imply a legal right to perform certain veterinary technologists' duties.

Regulatory Auditor   Conducts audits and reviews of programs, services, functions, and processes to provide assurance to management that the firm is in compliance with policies, procedures, and administrative mandates.

Rental Sales Representative   Negotiates car rental rates with travel agents, corporate businesses, other commercial accounts, individual clients so as to remain competitive in the market.

Research Account Executive (Advertising)   Researches printed literature. Drafts reports from research. Gets competitive bids from suppliers. Sits in on planning sessions. Suggests new methods of data gathering. Helps design surveys.

Research Analyst   Evaluates research findings and determines their applicability to specific projects within the company. Recommends needed research projects. Compares research findings with similar studies or surveys to determine reliability of results. Uses statistical data and measurement to examine and apply findings.

Research Analyst (Financial)   Researches and sells research to institutional investors. Recommends stocks they believe should be bought and sold to portfolio managers.

Research Analyst of Foreign Trade Legislation   Keeps current on foreign trade legislation and stays abreast of its impact on foreign trade practices.

Research Assistant   Compiles and analyzes verbal or statistical data to prepare reports and studies for use by professional workers in a variety of areas. Searches sources, such as reference works, literature, documents, newspapers, and statistical records, to obtain data on assigned subjects. May interview individuals to obtain data or draft correspondence to make inquiries.

Research Chef   Creates new foods for restaurant chains, coffee shops, and food manufacturing companies; blends culinary training with a knowledge of food science. Understands food preservation, mass production, and the technical terms used by scientists and uses this knowledge in the recipes.

Research and Development Food Technologist   Applies leading-edge technology to food product and process development; develops methods to modify and/or improve existing products and/or processes. Works with production personnel to move new or improved processes from research and development into the production plant.

Research and Development Specialist (Food Service)   Conducts research on new product lines and equipment for the food service industry. May work with food products in test kitchens or with new equipment in food service establishments. Reports findings to manufacturers of food products and equipment and publicizes results in trade publications to inform the industry about the possible alternatives the findings may provide for food service professionals.

Research Director   May supervise a group of research projects at a given time. (See **Project Director**)

Research Manager   (See **Project Director**)

Research Veterinary Technician   Monitors and cares for the health of animals used in research to ensure they are properly treated. Assists researchers throughout the research process. Gathers data from the animals throughout the research process. Assists research scientists or veterinarians with diagnosing illnesses, prescribing medication, and performing surgery.

Researcher and Evaluator (Travel)   Investigates and evaluates public relations efforts of the organization. Responsible for making recommendations on public relations programs based on goals and objectives and competition's position in the marketplace. Evaluates needs for expanding public relations efforts. Researches and recommends best strategy.

Reservationist   Sells reservations and other travel products such as tours, hotel accommodations, car rentals. Operates computer reservations equipment. Assists passengers in solving their travel needs.

Reservationist (Cruise Lines)   Books cruises for individual clients and groups. Sells the cruise by telephone to inquirers. Explains details of the trip and accepts payment.

Reservationist (Hotel)   Responsible for confirming room reservations, either by mail or by telephone, and for writing or typing out reservation forms. Uses computer to keep guest reservations current and for billing procedures. May assist guests with other reservations for local transportation, dining, or entertainment, depending on the staff size of the hotel.

Reservations Manager   Supervises and coordinates activities of personnel engaged in taking, recording, and canceling reservations in front office of hotel. Trains front office staff. Reviews daily printouts listing guests' arrivals and individual guest folios received by room clerks. Approves correspondence going to groups and travel agents to answer special requests for rooms and rates. Evaluates computer system and manual record procedures for efficiency.

Reserves Accountant   Monitors reserves accounts to ensure compliance with reserve and clearing balance requirements.

Resident Manager (Hospitality)   Lives on the premises to manage the day-to-day operations of a hotel or other lodging facility.

Respiratory Physical Therapist   Evaluates, treats, and cares for patients with breathing or other cardiopulmonary disorders.

Restaurant Manager   Responsible for efficiency, quality, and courtesy in all phases of a food service operation. In large organizations, may direct supervisory personnel at the next lower level. In smaller operations, might supervise kitchen and dining room staffs directly. Knowledge of the responsibilities of all restaurant staff is essential to this position.

Retail and Cashier Fraud Investigator   Investigates allegations of and source of loss prevention in a retail operation. Educates and advises management on risks; identifies and reports criminal opportunity through lack of internal control and/or weak policies regarding cash and merchandise transactions.

Revenue Agent   Plans and conducts on-site examinations and investigations of individuals and small businesses to determine their federal tax liability.

Revenue Officer   Collects delinquent taxes owed and secures delinquent tax returns where taxpayers have failed to file. Conducts research, interviews, investigations, and financial statement analysis for assigned cases. Counsels taxpayers on their tax obligations.

Riddler   A wine cellar worker responsible for ridding bottled wine or champagne from settling sediment through the manual or automated operation consisting of turning inclined wine or champagne bottles on a daily basis to induce the sediment deposit to consolidate and slip into the neck of the bottle.

Roasting Cook   Responsible for all meat preparation that is made to order. Also responsible for all items that are deep-fried, shallow-fried, sautéed, or broiled.

Robotics Technician   Performs the work of an electronics technician, specifically on various types of robotic devices. (See **Electronics Technician**)

Rooms Attendant   Coordinates service for a block of rooms in a hotel. Ensures that room service operations are running smoothly. Arranges for any special requests from guests concerning accommodations. Checks the room rack and key rack frequently. Oversees the operation of switchboard and messages going to guests.

Rooms Division Supervisor   Directs all activities involved with the rooms division of the hotel, including staffing, housekeeping, occupancy, service, and promotion.

Rounds Cook   Replaces any member of the kitchen brigade who may be absent from each station. Must be efficient and versatile in cooking techniques.

Sales Assistant   Responsible for successful management of a selling area. Involves supervision of a selling area and customer service functions. In a large department store, may also direct inventory control and merchandise presentation and be responsible for increasing the sales growth and profitability of an area.

Sales Associate   Provides customer assistance in selecting and purchasing merchandise; furnishes information to customers about goods for sale. Collects payments. Might also schedule delivery or installation.

Sales/Field Representative (Electronics)   Advises customers on installation and maintenance problems and serves as the link between the manufacturer and the customer.

Sales Fraud Investigator   Investigates allegations and sources of illegal sales practices.

Sales Manager   Coordinates sales distribution by establishing sales territories, quotas, and goals, and advises dealers and distributors concerning sales and advertising techniques. Directs staffing, training, and performance evaluations to develop and control sales programs. Prepares periodic sales reports showing sales volume and potential sales. May recommend or approve budget, expenditures, and appropriations for research and development work.

Sales Manager (Food Service)   Responsible for the development and operation of the sales department. Maintains files on past group business. Works with the social director and promotion office on contacts and may do some traveling to other areas to bring new business into the establishment. Also trains and supervises sales representatives and some account executives.

Sales Manager (Retail)   Oversees the various sales departments in wholesale and retail companies. Directs promotional sales campaigns for their merchandise or services.

Sales and Marketing Specialist (Food Service)   Plans, researches, promotes, and sells products to the food service industry.

Sales Representative   Secures orders from existing and potential customers by means of visiting the customer facility or calling by phone. Follows up on quotations submitted to customers. Submits weekly activity/call reports concerning customer quotes, orders, or problems. Provides a territory sales forecast on a monthly basis.

Sales Representative (Computer Systems)   Calls on prospective clients to explain types of services provided by establishment, such as inventory control, payroll processing, data conversion, sales analysis, and financial reporting. Analyzes data processing requirements of prospective clients and draws up prospectus of a data processing plan designed specifically to serve client's needs. May also sell computers and related equipment directly.

Sales Representative (Hospitality)   Follows initial lead on a prospective client. Responsible for explaining hotel's services to government, business, and social groups to generate interest in the facility as a site for a major function. Sales representative conducts cold calls as well as calls to a selected prospect list. The sales representative may pass the interested client on to an account executive, who will actually set up, service, and maintain the account.

Sales Secretary   Types drafts of newsletters; keeps track of company's dealings with outside printers, suppliers, and creative people. Types, files, answers telephones, and routes mail. Takes orders, books events, or handles whatever customer request comes in for the product or service being sold.

Sales Supervisor   (See **Sales Manager**)

Sales Trainee (Hospitality)   Usually begins with front office experience to learn client relations and total product line offered by the hotel. May go on sales calls with sales representatives or assist an account executive with servicing an account.

Sales Trainee (Insurance)   Attends sales strategy sessions as an observer, or shadows an experienced agent on calls. Assists established agents to service accounts.

Sauce Cook   Responsible for all preparation of sauces to be used on main items on the menu. In a medium-sized operation, the sauce cook is also the Sous-Chef.

Schedule Planning Manager (Travel)   Approves and enforces scheduling recommendation for all air traffic coming into and going out of the airport.

School Director   Plans, develops, and administers education programs. Confers with administrative personnel to decide scope of programs to be offered. Prepares schedules of classes and rough drafts of course content to determine number and background of instructors needed. Interviews, hires, trains, and evaluates work performance of education department staff. Assists instructors in preparation of course descriptions. Prepares budget for education programs and directs maintenance of records of expenditures, receipts, and public and school participation in programs.

School Director/Administrator   (See **School Director** and **Administrator**)

School Director (Vocational)   Directs and coordinates schools with vocational training programs. Confers with members of industrial and business community to determine worker training needs. Reviews and interprets vocational educational codes to ensure that programs conform to policies. Prepares budgets and funding allocation for vocational programs. Reviews and approves new programs. Coordinates on-the-job training programs with employers and evaluates progress of students in conjunction with program contract goals.

School Nurse   Nurse who specializes in the practice of professional nursing that advances the well-being, academic success, and lifelong achievement of students.

School Secretary   Handles secretarial duties in elementary and secondary schools; may take care of correspondence, prepare bulletins and reports, keep track of money for school supplies and student activities, and maintain a calendar of school events.

Script Writer   Provides the creative support in a telemarketing agency. Writes all material that is to be read by the telemarketing representative.

Seafood Cook   Prepares all seafood dishes, mousses, soufflés, etc. Also prepares the fish for cold display or for hors d'oeuvres and then sends to the Garde-Manger for final decoration.

Secret Service Agent   Protects the president and vice president of the United States, along with their families. Protects the coins and securities of the government by enforcing laws pertaining to counterfeiting.

Secret Service Uniformed Officer   Provides security through a network of vehicular and foot patrols, fixed posts, and canine teams at White House buildings in which the presidential offices are located and at the main Treasury Building and the Treasury Annex in Washington, D.C.

Secretary   Performs secretarial duties for a supervisor. Takes and transcribes dictation with speed and accuracy. Maintains correspondence and data files, arranges appointments, answers routine inquiries, and handles general office duties. Often assists in performing administrative details using initiative and judgment. Requires thorough knowledge of company policies, the organization, and how to operate in the channels of the organization. As part of the management team, must be ready to make decisions and provide relevant information to staff members on a daily basis.

Secretary (Food Service)   In large food service operations, performs a variety of administrative duties; works with customers on group business and with vendors on orders and supplies. Frees the employer to work on other areas outside the property.

Securities Sales Representative   Develops financial plans based on analysis of clients' financial status, and discusses securities investment options, which usually include stocks, stock options, mutual funds, exchange-traded funds and bonds. Relays buy or sell orders to securities exchanges or to firm trading departments.

Security Access Manager   Serves as the process owner for all ongoing activities that provide appropriate access to and protect the confidentiality and integrity of customer, employee, and business information in compliance with organizational policies and standards.

Seller's Agent   A real estate agent employed to work in the best interests of the seller in a real estate transaction.

Sell-Side Research Analyst   Responsible for studies of specific sectors and specific analysis of individual companies, with a strong emphasis on providing detailed and unbiased analysis. Prepares written research reports for the firm's sales force.

Senior Accountant   (See **Accountant**)

Senior Account Executive   (See **Account Executive**)

Senior Analyst (Marketing)   (See **Market Research Analyst**)

Senior Claims Examiner   (See **Claims Examiner**)

Senior Consultant   (See **Consultant**)

Senior Copywriter   (See **Copywriter**)

Senior Drafter   Gives final approval to the plans drawn up by other drafters before presenting the plan to client. (See **Drafter**)

Senior Legal Assistant   Oversees the work of paralegals and legal assistants in the firm. (See **Paralegal** and **Legal Assistant**)

Senior Revenue Agent   Administers tax examinations of large corporations, dealing with issues such as tax shelters, mergers and acquisitions, and global operations.

Senior Sales Representative   Is in charge of finding, building, and maintaining client relationships to achieve company's sales target. Conducts client consultations, strategic planning, and program analysis.

Senior Systems Consultant   Provides specialized advice on programming languages and documentation. Maintains up-to-date knowledge of all programming languages. Makes provisions for the orderly processing of changes, updatings, and modifications of programs. Coordinates all company programming efforts. (See **Systems Consultant**)

Senior Systems Engineer   Provides systems engineering support on large-scale systems, major system elements, and/or interfacing systems. Develops strategic and implementation plans for large-scale information systems. Develops system architecture and design in software, hardware, and communications interface requirements.

Senior Underwriter   (See **Underwriter**)

Sensory Analyst   Provides food marketing and food sensory research to national and international clients across a spectrum of manufacturing, major food market research companies, and food customer marketing and consulting companies. Utilizes new technology and methods to help clients succeed in development of food products and services.

Sensory System Development Specialist   Creates systems within a research and development firm or testing laboratory for using sensory testing in the development of new flavors, ingredients, and recipes.

Sergeant   In the U.S. Marine Corps and U.S. Army, a noncommissioned officer of the fifth grade, ranking above a corporal and below a staff sergeant.

Serology Specialist Conducts laboratory analyses of body fluids. Performs extensive chemical tests to determine content level of drugs or alcohol.

Service Representative Goes out into the field upon customer's request to service problems with purchased equipment. May diagnose the problem, correct it, and test the equipment to see if it is working properly. Reports problem to research and development. Tells owners and dealers about new products, service techniques, and developments in maintenance.

Service Technician (Electronics) (See **Service Representative**)

Show Manager Plans and manages events or trade shows for an organization. Identifies event locations, develops budget for functions, acquires event permits, secures speakers, and sources products for display.

Skip-Tracing Assistant Organizes information for researchers. Locates people who have moved hastily or have secretly fled without giving notice and absconded to avoid paying debts.

Small Animal Veterinarian Doctors trained to protect the health of both animals and people. Work with small animals to evaluate animals' health, diagnose and treat illnesses, provide routine preventive care (such as vaccines), prescribe medication, and perform surgery. Although small animal veterinarians typically work with small companion animals such as cats and dogs and other non-farm animals, they are trained to perform a variety of duties on a wide range of animals.

Small Business Manager Oversees the entire operation of a small business, ranging from planning, marketing, staffing, and budgeting to ensuring compliance with industry standards.

Social Event Planner Organizes all aspects of social events, ranging from wedding receptions, yacht parties, and product launches to corporate group tours.

Social Secretary Arranges social functions, answers personal correspondence, and keeps the employer informed about all social activities.

Software Developer Develops computer software to run a robotics system.

Software Engineer Analyzes users' needs; designs, constructs, and maintains generic computer applications software and specialized utility programs.

Software Support Specialist Provides technical assistance to business professionals and consumers. Integrates computer skills, customer support experience, and related education to exceed technical, business, and customer requirements. Works closely with people to develop solutions to their problems.

Software Support Technician Handles telephone calls from customers on software, such as Microsoft Office and Novell GroupWise. Answers software questions, solves problems, and devises solutions based on the customers' needs.

Sommelier Works with the chef to devise harmonious pairings of wine and food. Crafts the restaurant's wine list, trains staff in wine service, and assists diners with choosing wine.

Soup Cook Responsible for all soups, both cold and hot, plus garnishes, stocks, etc.

Sous Chef Principal assistant of the Chef de Cuisine. In a large operation, will assist the Chef de Cuisine in general administrative and supervisory duties and will implement every order given. Must have the same professional background as the chef but not necessarily the same number of years of experience.

Spa Chef A chef who specializes in the design and preparation of menus for health-conscious guests. Creates menus that promote well-being and good nutrition for spa guests.

Spa Director Implements marketing and promotion programs and supervises staff. Ensures safety and security for spa guests and employees. Manages budget. Has working knowledge of benefits and protocols of spa therapies.

Spa Technician Member of the spa technical services team, consisting of aestheticians, massage therapists, nail technicians, and hair stylists.

Special Agent Combines accounting knowledge with law enforcement skills to investigate such financial crimes as tax evasion and money laundering.

Special Events Coordinator Performs basic function of the meeting planner and also is directly responsible for the advertising and promotion of the event, for the budget for the event, and for identifying the appropriate target market. Works with the press and media on promotion. Acts as the liaison between all participating parties.

Speaker Person elected by an organization to present its views, policies, or decisions.

Special Events Coordinator Organizes sales and marketing for special events; serves as the liaison with vendors. Performs office management functions and manages budget. Manages final event operations.

Speech–Language Therapist Works with people who have trouble speaking clearly or cannot make speech sounds. Helps people with oral disabilities that prevent eating or swallowing without difficulty.

Sponsorship Sales Representative Makes sales calls in person, by telephone, or via the Internet to solicit sponsorship support for a variety of programs, events, and services.

Sports Agent Represents professional athletes, officials, or coaches and oversees all aspects of their career, particularly their contracts with teams and the companies whose products they endorse.

Sports Broadcaster Reports the sports news on television or radio.

Sports Events Planner Schedules and organizes sporting events. Coordinates building staff, promoters, and facility management and is often in charge of the event itself.

Sports Safety Coordinator Maintains necessary certifications and licenses. Stays current on liability concepts and performs duties to eliminate possible questions of negligence. Provides emergency response care.

Sports Team Promoter Works to build interest in a team and keep it in the public eye; sells licenses to produce team-associated products. Opens new markets. Develops promotions to attract the attention of the public, media, and corporations.

Sportswriter Covers sporting events for newspapers and magazines, from national monthlies to small-town papers.

Stadium Manager Oversees and directs the operation of the stadium, which includes conducting lease and rental negotiations, administering contracts, and performing promotional activities. Supervises maintenance forces and coordinates event preparation.

Staff Accountant   Oversees the general ledger of a firm. Reviews cost center and chart of accounts structure. Makes recommendation as to cost center/account structure which will identify the nature of expenses to their proper areas; assists in controlling annual expenditures. Reconciles daily cash flow statements and reconciles to monthly bank statements. Reconciles payroll and cash disbursement accounts. Reviews accounts payable aging and vendor statements for problems.

Staff Veterinarian   Works under the supervision of the Director of a department, clinic, or other veterinary service operation. Assists with teaching and training technical staff, investigative staff, and students. Supervises animal care technologists, technicians, and volunteers. Assists with the monitoring of compliance to regulations governing the use of animals in research.

State Travel Director   Promotes visitor traffic within the destination, whether for pleasure, business, or convention purposes, and from within or from without the state.

State Trooper   Ensures public safety and patrols state and interstate highways.

Station Manager   Supervises a car rental business.

Statistical Typist   Works in all types of businesses typing statistical data from source material such as company production and sales records, test records, time sheets, and surveys and questionnaires.

Steganographer   Is skilled at overlaying one set of information on another. Responsible for discovering the presence of hidden data within a text.

Stenographer   Takes dictation in shorthand of correspondence, reports, and other matter, and operates typewriter to transcribe dictated materials.

Stockbroker   Looks after clients' investment portfolios, buying and selling shares to try to make clients get the best return on their money.

Stockbroker Assistant   Assists stockbrokers with helping clients buy, sell, and arrange a wide range of banking and financial services, from loans to mutual funds.

Store Manager   An executive responsible for the profitable operation of the store. Has broad merchandising responsibilities, develops staff, contributes to the store's public relations effort, and supervises the maintenance of the store. Spends significant amount of time on the selling floor and supplies other areas of management with detailed information on the operation of the store.

Storeroom Supervisor (Food Service)   Responsible for supervising, receiving, inspecting, counting, and storing all food and other articles delivered to the storeroom. Responsible for filling out all requisitions and, under the instructions of the house auditor, for keeping a journal in ledger of all goods received and delivered. Records names of purveyors, the costs and descriptions of articles, and other required information. Supervises monthly inventories with the auditor.

Substance Abuse Specialist   Provides individual and group counseling in correctional institutions and for prerelease and other alternative detention programs.

Superintendent of Service (Hospitality)   Responsible for overseeing all functions providing guest services in the hotel. This may include the front office and housekeeping as well as food service operations. Ensures quality service while keeping informed about any client-centered problems that may affect new or repeat business. Solves problems related to guest services.

Supervisor (Banking)   Responsible for improving the overall productivity of a department or area, motivating staff, and staying within budget. Oversees production, product development, marketing, and systems functions in the bank.

Supervisor of Gate Services   Observes staff to ensure that services to passengers are performed courteously and correctly. Supervises and coordinates the activities of staff engaged in admitting passengers to airplanes and assisting passengers disembarking at terminal exits of commercial flights. Reviews flight schedules, passenger manifests, and information obtained from staff to determine staffing needs. Recommends alternate procedures if needed. Evaluates performance of staff.

Supervisor (Telemarketing)   Manages groups of telemarketing communicators and is directly responsible for their performance. May also be responsible for training and scheduling of staff.

Support Administrator   Oversees support service functions for the wide range of operations departments that support the firm, such as sales, finance, IT, trade, and customer service operations.

Support Engineer   Communicates with corporate customers via telephone, written correspondence, or electronic mail or in person regarding finding solutions for technically complex problems.

Support Specialist   Assists users with their computers when the computers malfunction.

Surgical Technician   Assists surgeons and anesthesiologists before, during, and after surgery. Works under the supervision of registered nurses and operating room technician supervisors.

Surveyor   Interviews people and compiles statistical information. Asks questions following a specified outline on questionnaire and records answers. Reviews, classifies, and sorts questionnaires. Compiles results in a format that is clear and concise and highlights findings relevant to the objective of the survey.

Switch Technician   Maintains all aspects of a mobile switching center, including software upgrades, circuit board replacement, hardware installation, and other duties necessary for continuous operations and availability of a switching center.

System Integration Specialist   Responsible for installation of new software versions/releases. Provides software maintenance. Performs advanced problem diagnosis and resolution. Uses performance reports and metrics to identify improvement opportunities.

Systems Administrator (Word Processing)   Responsible for systems maintenance and management and systems analysis and design.

Systems Analyst   Prepares detailed instructions for assigned programming systems or components, enabling qualified personnel to proceed with implementation. Evaluates procedural and/or programming systems required to operate and support programs and systems. Solves the problems of adapting computer hardware and software to end users' needs. Determines how the company can save money by adapting existing equipment. Coordinates and supervises the efforts of many computer professionals. Maintains quality control by assessing the system once it has been implemented.

Systems Consultant   Advises clients on developing, implementing, and maintaining automated programs for business and for in-house use; on selecting hardware, writing software, and consulting with user/client when special programs must be developed. Writes the codes that make up a computer program, tests the programs, debugs them (eliminates errors), and sometimes writes the accompanying documentation that tells others why the program was written the way it was.

Systems Designer   Works with analyst on the feasibility and workability of a conceptual design by taking technical specifications prepared by the analyst and designing system components to meet the stated need. Prepares instructions for programmer implementation.

Systems Programmer   Prepares the computers to understand the language that the applications programmers will be using and tells the computers what peripheral equipment, such as printers and automatic teller machines, it will be controlling.

Systems Technician   Electronic technician who specializes in computer systems, including digital computers, video processors, tape units, buffers, key sets, digital-display equipment, data link, and related equipment.

Systems Trainee (Banking)   Works in programming or part of a systems team project, refining the use of current equipment or developing systems for as yet unmet needs.

Tax Accountant   Prepares federal and state income tax returns using compliance software. Provides assistance and support on all tax-related audits.

Tax Examiner   Responds to taxpayers' inquiries about their tax returns, as well as contacts them by mail or phone on a wide range of tax issues. Reviews tax returns for accuracy and completeness, codes returns for computer processing, and helps provide e-help and e-services for taxpayers who file tax returns online.

Tax Law Specialist   Provides expert advice on a range of corporate tax issues; may specialize in international tax law. Interprets the tax code and regulations to produce annual tax forms and publications.

Tax Specialist   Guides and assists taxpayers by conducting out-reach programs for individuals, or working through state and private "partners" who deal with specific taxpayer segments.

Teacher Librarian   Responsible for promotion of school-wide information literacy across all year levels and areas of curriculum. Assists staff and students to become independent users of online library resources through class and/or individual instruction.

Teaching Nurse   Works in the classroom and the practice setting to prepare and mentor current and future generations of nurses. Designs, implements, evaluates, and revises academic and continuing education programs for nurses.

Team Leader (Floor Supervisor)   Responsible for supervision of a floor in a hotel. Oversees the maintenance and upkeep, the repair and security of all rooms on an assigned floor. Supervises housekeeping staff assigned to that floor and coordinates the group to work efficiently. Submits work reports to Executive Housekeeper if requested.

Technical Analyst   Reviews, analyzes, and evaluates information systems operations. Is familiar with standard concepts, practices, and procedures within the information systems field.

Technical Graphic Designer   Uses graphic design technology and computer software to produce diagrams and layouts. Produces graphic design work for sales, advertising, and public relations materials.

Technical Manager   Manages internal procedure prioritization, development of prototypes, and outside relationships. Schedules and organizes development, testing, and documentation processes. Writes and updates functional and featured plan specifications and descriptions.

Technical Prosthetist   Takes digital images of a person's limb or torso to which a prosthesis will be fitted.

Technical Sales Representative   Makes cold calls to companies of all sizes to explore and develop opportunities in the information security section within a specialized solution set.

Technical Secretary   Assists engineers or scientists. In addition to the usual secretarial duties, may prepare much of the correspondence, maintain the technical library, and gather and edit materials for scientific papers.

Technical Support Specialist   Uses specialized technical knowledge to provide computer support. Addresses problems users have with connectivity when the user cannot reach data or gain access to it. Assists with sourcing missing data.

Technical Writer   Writes or edits technical materials, such as reports of research findings, scientific or technical articles, news releases and periodicals, regulations in technical areas, technical manuals, specifications, brochures and pamphlets on speeches, scripts on technical subjects.

Techno Chef   Chef specializing in food product design through the practice of blending culinary arts and food science techniques, practices, and standards.

Technology Account Consultant   Spends majority of time on customer sites; provides a range of consultancy services, including implementation of large-scale systems under guidance from a technical architect.

Technology Business Developer   Provides technology solutions to diverse businesses; analyzes business requirements; solves software problems.

Technology Financial Analyst   Formulates and presents timely investment opinions and recommendations based on a thorough knowledge of the technology industry business and develops a depth of knowledge about technology companies sufficient to form opinions about investment strategies.

Technology Project Manager   Provides support for client applications and serves as a liaison for the development, implementation, and maintenance of existing, new, or enhanced systems. Manages multiple large or regional projects, products, and clients by tracking resources, prioritizing projects, and providing guidance to staff and clients as needed.

Telecom Facility Examiner   Examines telephone transmission of activities to determine equipment requirements for providing subscribers with new or additional telephone services.

Telecom Line and Cable Worker   Installs and repairs transmission lines; inspects and tests transmission lines and cables; analyzes and records the results.

Telecom Network Engineer/Planner   Creates network engineering plans; designs monitors and provisioning elements in the local telecommunications network. Plans and designs timely, cost-effective relief and modernization projects for the local network.

Telecommunications Specialist   Manages and organizes communication computer systems (radio, telephones, computers, and other types of communications systems) activities. Evaluates communication requirements. Conducts training for telecommunications personnel.

Telecommunications Technician   Works on cable television plants' communication lines and fiber-optic lines.

Telemarketing Center Manager   Responsible for executing the program once components have been assembled and the script written. This involves either making or receiving the calls in a way that achieves each client's objective.

Telemarketing and Collections Investigator   Investigates allegations of telemarketing and collections fraud.

Telemarketing Communicator   Delivers what everyone else sells. Coordinates or manages the allocation of the product to the proper sales and delivery channels.

Telemarketing Representative   Sells a product or "qualifies" customers for the field sales force by telephone.

Telemarketing Trainer   Instructs communicators about the product or services and how to use the scripts. Trainers also teach telemarketing efficiency, listening skills, and sales techniques.

Test Engineer   May develop and support testing tools. Designs test objectives and test facility requirements, writes test agenda, conducts tests, troubleshoots test cell problems, analyzes test data, and writes test reports.

Test Kitchen Chef   Consults on food trends and helps clients hone in on current trends to create new food products. May review and test industrial kitchen equipment.

Ticket Agent   Sells tickets to airline passengers at the airport and city ticket office; promotes and sells air travel; gives air travel and tour information; makes the flight and tour reservations; computes fares; prepares and issues tickets; routes baggage; and prepares cash reports.

Ticket Sales Representative   Processes ticket orders; takes customer calls; processes payments, printing, and mailing tickets; maintains and updates client records in customer database.

Tour Director   Conducts the actual tour. Accompanies travelers as an escort throughout the trip. Solves problems and settles complaints. Has alternative plans set for the group so that tour will be successful even under adverse conditions. Coordinates the group to stay together and encourages questions about the area being visited.

Tour Escort   Assists passengers; generally assists with tours; accompanies the tour from start to finish; often handles large sums of money; makes necessary changes in group's accommodations or itinerary as needed.

Tour Guide   Does complete narration; has specialized knowledge of a particular region or country. Is hired to accompany a tour only while it visits the area of special expertise.

Tour Operator   Puts together all the elements of a trip: transportation, accommodations, meals, sightseeing, and the like; negotiates rates and block space; coordinates details of the itinerary; markets the product.

Tour and Travel Account Executive   Responsible for the development and service of group tour business coming into the hotel. Brings travel and tour groups to the hotel. Consults with the tour operators and travel agents and collaborates with the hotel staff to find the best strategy for servicing the group.

Tourist Information Assistant   Provides information and other services to tourists at state information centers. Greets tourists, in person or by telephone, and answers questions and gives information on resorts, historical sights, scenic areas, and other tourist attractions. Assists tourists in planning itineraries and advises them of traffic regulations. Sells hunting and fishing licenses and provides information on fishing, hunting, and camping regulations. Composes letters in response to inquiries. Maintains personnel, license sales, and other records. Contacts motel, hotel, and resort operators by mail or telephone to obtain advertising literature.

Trade Account Executive   Records the value of goods sold and purchased abroad by residents of the home country.

Trade Show Event Planner   Specializes in planning all aspects of trade show events. Coordinates design of the floor plan, booth pricing, inspection of facility, signage in the exhibit hall, and distribution and allocation of booth spaces.

Trader   Matches buyers and sellers of securities.

Traffic Coordinator   Coordinates with customs broker on import entry preparation on a daily basis.

Traffic Manager   Negotiates price and service issues of all modes of transportation carrier contracts and determines the appropriate transportation mode to be utilized. Develops, maintains, and disseminates logistical data.

Traffic Officer   Directs and controls the flow of traffic for both motor vehicles and pedestrians. Enforces parking regulations. Tracks stolen or wanted automobiles. Investigates traffic accidents. Provides motorist assistance, escort duty, crowd handling, and traffic rerouting.

Training Assistant   Assists in all functions for a training program.

Training Manager   Develops ongoing training programs for new and experienced personnel. Conducts training seminars.

Writes and coordinates training manuals, working with specialists for specified details. Prepares training videotapes and/or films; maintains library of video and film training aids. Notifies employees of training sessions. Introduces topic specialists at the beginning of the program and the program agenda. Develops means of measuring the effectiveness of programs through testing.

Training Specialist   Develops and conducts training programs for specialized functions within the company upon the approval of the training manager. (See **Training Manager**)

Training Supervisor   May supervise training manager(s) as well as the entire training function for the company. Responsibilities may include overseeing training programs at various divisions and performing all budgetary responsibilities pertaining to the programs. Also may evaluate existing programs and make recommendations for modifications or new or additional programs. (See **Training Manager**)

Translator   Translates written messages from one language to another.

Transportation Analyst   Identifies opportunities for savings with package carriers. Helps manage relationships with third-party distribution service companies and provides distribution administration support. Develops, maintains, and communicates key reports and tracking metrics.

Transportation Manager   Responsible for all aspects of transportation including inbound, between facilities, and outbound. Supervises various functions and personnel. Negotiates rates with warehouses and transportation companies. Plans, monitors, and implements the distribution department's fiscal budget. Establishes the most beneficial routing of company shipments for satisfactory customer service. Determines price levels. Plans for the department on a quarterly, yearly, and five-year basis.

Transportation Security Administrator   Responsible for security relating to civil aviation, maritime, and all other modes of transportation, including transportation facilities. Leads security at airports, at ports, and on the nation's railways and public transit systems.

Transportation Specialist   Advises industries, business firms, and individuals concerning methods of preparation of shipments, rates to be applied, and mode of transportation to be used. Consults with clients regarding packing procedures and inspects packed goods for conformance to shipping specifications to prevent damage, delay, or penalties. Files claims with insurance company for losses, damages, and overcharges of shipments.

Travel Agency Manager   Supervises the day-to-day operations of the agency. Prepares sales reports and dictates office policies. Decides on promotion and pricing of packages. Supervises, hires, and trains employees. Attends trade shows to keep informed on latest computer systems, rates, and promotions being offered by the airlines, hotels, and other related services. Initiates advertising for the agency and keeps budget.

Travel Agent   Plans itineraries and arranges accommodations and other travel services for customers of the travel agency. Plans, describes, and sells itinerary package tours. Converses with customers to determine destination, mode

of transportation, travel dates, financial considerations, and accommodations required. Books customer's mode of transportation and hotel reservations. Obtains travel tickets and collects payment. May specialize in foreign or domestic service, individual or group travel, or specific geographical areas.

Travel Counselor   Advises clients on best ways to travel, destinations, costs, and safety issues. Offers advice to clients on packages available, preparation for a trip, or availability of transportation or accommodations. Researches information requested by the client.

Travel Director   Client contact person who actually goes out with the incentive groups and on-site, coordinating sightseeing trips and troubleshooting.

Travel Editor   Buys articles submitted by freelance writers; selects unsolicited articles for publication; selects letters from readers to publish. Replies to readers' letters of comment or criticism. Works with layout and makeup of travel pages. May assign staff to stories almost anywhere in the world. Reviews manuscripts submitted by travel writers for content and readability. Chooses manuscripts for publication.

Travel Secretary   Coordinates all aspects of the travel function. Researches options to maintain an economical, efficient travel program. Schedules personnel for approved travel on corporate jets. Schedules personnel from approved travel authorizations on commercial flights. Makes hotel reservations. Performs clerical and secretarial duties pertaining to all travel arrangements.

Travel Specialist   Develops specialized expertise about a particular area of travel. May work for a travel agency, tour operator, publications department, or other related areas using information mastered about a specialized area of travel. May specialize in a geographic area, type of destination, or any other specific area in the travel industry.

Travel Writer   Provides practical guides, directories, and language books and brochures. Contributes feature stories to travel sections of large newspapers.

Treasurer   Directs and coordinates organization's financial programs, transactions, and security measures according to financial principles and government regulations. Evaluates operational methods and practices to determine efficiency of operations. Approves and signs documents affecting capital monetary transactions. Directs receipt, disbursement, and expenditures of money or other capital assets.

Treasurer/Controller   Has combined responsibilities of both the Treasurer and the Controller. (See **Treasurer** and **Controller**)

Trust Officer   Manages money and securities as well as real estate and other property. Decides how assets will be managed.

Undercover Agent   Someone, usually a law enforcement agent, who pretends to be someone else to obtain information for an investigation.

Underwriter   Reviews applications, reports, and actuarial studies to determine whether a particular risk should be insured. Specializations are usually in life, property, and liability, or health insurance.

Underwriter Specialist   Specializes as an underwriter in life, property, and liability, or health insurance. (See **Underwriter**)

Underwriter Trainee   Assists the underwriter. Usually spends much time on the telephone gathering information and verifying what has been reported before the underwriter makes final decisions. (See **Underwriter**)

Underwriting Supervisor   Oversees the underwriting department. Ensures staff is working within appropriate guidelines and regulations when reviewing submitted materials. Evaluates performance of the staff and hires new underwriters as needed.

Unit Manager   Representative of a food service contractor who is permanently assigned to one particular client installation.

Urban Planner   Works with city or state officials to produce plans for future building and construction projects. Must be able to project an area's future population and its needs and design facilities to meet those needs.

U.S. Capitol Police Officer   Protects life and property; prevents, detects, and investigates criminal acts. Protects members of U.S. Congress and their families. Enforces traffic regulations throughout a large complex of congressional buildings, parks, and thoroughfares.

U.S. Citizenship and Immigration Services (USCIS) Investigator   Reviews applications for visas, determines whether aliens may enter or remain in the country, and gathers all information for administrative hearings and criminal prosecution of immigration law violations.

U.S. Customhouse Broker   Provides for clearance of foreign import and export shipments passing through U.S. customs.

U.S. Marshal   Responsible for executing and enforcing commands of federal courts; processing federal prisoners; seizing property under court order; and protecting federal judges, witnesses, and juries.

Vegetable Cook   Prepares all garnishes, and side dishes such as potatoes, other vegetables, egg dishes, etc.

Vending Manager   Independent businessperson who places own machines in various installations in a community or facility. Responsible for locating new machine sites, developing good public relations for the firm by handling complaints, maintaining quality control of the product and proper functioning of the machines. Handles cash funds and keeps required records.

Veterinarian   Doctors trained to protect the health of both animals and people. Work with large and small animals to evaluate animals' health, diagnose and treat illnesses, provide routine preventive care (such as vaccines), prescribe medication, and perform surgery. Like physicians, some veterinarians specialize in areas such as surgery, internal medicine, ophthalmology, or dentistry. May focus on regulatory medicine, public health, or research.

Veterinary Anesthetist   Under the supervision of a veterinarian, chooses the type and dose of anesthesia appropriate for the specific animal procedure, based on the animal's species, breed, and weight and other significant factors. Responsible for preparing and administering the anesthesia. Monitors the anesthetized animal to ensure it responds appropriately pre- and post-medical procedure.

Veterinary Assistant   Supports the veterinarian and/or the veterinary technician in their daily tasks. May perform kennel work, assist with restraining and handling of animals, feeding and exercising animals or performing clerical duties. Unlike the veterinary technician, there is no credentialing exam for the veterinary assistant.

Veterinarian Assistant   Manages veterinarians office functions including answering phones, greeting clients, scheduling appointments, ordering supplies, managing billing and overseeing the budget. Works with sales representatives and manufacturers. Maintains client records.

Veterinary Assistant/Lab Tech Surgery   Administers anesthesia, works as a circulating nurse and anesthesiologist during surgery, recovers the animal and provides post-operative care.

Veterinary Behavior Technician   Specialists with behavior certifications responsible for preventing behavior health problems in animals. Train and manage animals in developing healthy behavior patterns.

Veterinary Dental Technician   Performs routine dental services in animals including preventive or therapeutic dental procedures. Recognizes signs of dental problems and treats the problem. Administers drugs and other remedies for dental problems. May perform orthodontic procedures. Removes or reduces teeth as a treatment for canine or feline aggression.

Veterinary Hospital Manager   Responsible for quality of veterinary medical services administered. Manages the business functions of the practice including day-to-day operations such as human resource management, staff scheduling, inventory control, and budgets. Manages compliance with regulatory and legal issues. Oversees promotion and marketing activities and facilities design services. Manages client relations.

Veterinary Intern   Graduate of a veterinarian program required to complete one to two years of experience working in general veterinary practice settings. Veterinarians who want to specialize, must become board certified and complete a three to four year internship with specialization.

Veterinary Medicine Doctor   Specializes in diagnosing animal health problems. Vaccinates against diseases. Medicates animals suffering from infections or illnesses. Treats and dresses wounds, sets fractures, performs surgery and advises owners about animal feeding, behavior, and breeding.

Veterinary Nurse   Performs diagnostic lab tests and assists the veterinarian to produce diagnostic radiographs. Places animals in protective area for surgery recovery and administers and monitors progress of recovery. Dispenses medication to animals under direct supervision of the veterinarian. Admits and discharges animals attending surgery. Assists veterinarians during consultations, examinations, and treatments. Provides information on nutrition, parasite control, and animal behavior.

Veterinary Surgery Technician   Prepares animals for surgery by pre-anesthetic administration-clipping and scrubbing animals, administers anesthesia. Acts as the operating room nurse and surgical assistant. Provides post-operative care as needed. Sets up and breaks down surgical facilities including cleaning and disinfecting.

Veterinary Technician   Assists the veterinarian in surgical procedures, laboratory procedures, radiography, anesthesiology, prescribed treatment and nursing, and client education. An experienced veterinary technician may discuss a pet's condition with owners and train new clinic personnel. Almost every state requires veterinary technicians to pass a credentialing exam which can vary from state to state.

Veterinary Technologist   Performs many of the same duties as a veterinary technician. May also assist veterinarians as they work with other scientists in medical related fields such as gene therapy and cloning. Some find career opportunities in biomedical research, wildlife medicine, the military, livestock management or pharmaceutical sales. Like veterinary technicians, veterinary technologists are required by almost every state to pass a credentialing exam, which can vary from state to state.

Vice President   Plans, formulates, and recommends for approval of the President basic policies and programs which will further the objectives of the company. Executes decisions of the President and Board of Directors. Develops, in cooperation with the President and supervisors, an annual budget, and operates within the annual budget upon approval. Recommends changes in the overall organizational structure to the President. Approves public relations programs.

Vice President of Account Services   Oversees the promotion, sales, and service of a product line to a variety of customers within a defined geographical area. Develops and seeks out business of a highly complex nature and of importance to the company. Ensures efficient servicing of all accounts, once obtained. Prepares programs for training and development of the field managers and other new and experienced personnel.

Vice President of Communications   Ensures the development and execution of advertising, public relations, public affairs, and member relations programs, together with effective internal and external communications to promote understanding, acceptance, and support of corporate activities and objectives by employees and the subscribing public.

Vice President of Finance   Acts under authority and responsibility delegated by corporate executive office. Conducts management studies, prepares workload and budget estimates for specified or assigned operation, analyzes operational reports, and submits activity reports. Develops and recommends plans for expansion of existing programs, operations, and financial activities.

Vice President of Healthcare Administration: Plans, directs, coordinates and supervises the delivery of health care. Some are specialists in charge of a specific clinical department or others are generalists who manage an entire facility or system.

Vice President of Human Resources   Develops human resources policies and programs for the entire company. The major areas covered are organizational planning, organizational development, employment, indoctrination and training, employee relations, compensation, benefits, safety and health, and employee services. Originates human resources practices and objectives that will provide a balanced program throughout all divisions. Coordinates implementation through human resources staff. Assists and advises senior management of human resources issues.

Vice President of Marketing (Hospitality)   In addition to overseeing the sales function, also coordinates the advertising, public relations, publicity, and community relations for the hotel. (See **Vice President of Marketing**)

Vice President of Marketing/Sales   Represents the marketing function's needs in the development of corporate policy.

Formulates sales goals, marketing plans, and strategy, and directs the execution of these areas for the achievement of corporate marketing objectives. Manages the sales force to achieve marketing and sales goals for assigned products.

Vice President of Merchandising   Manages several divisions of merchandise. Responsible for planning and giving buyers both fashion and financial direction. Plans sales, inventory, and marketing by store, based on the turnover desires. Plans markups and ensures that inventory supports sales efforts.

Vice President of Operations   Directs the formulation of corporate policies, programs, and procedures as they relate to distribution, operations, research, production, engineering, and purchasing. Maximizes group and divisional short- and long-range growth and profitability.

Vice President of Production   Plans, directs, and controls production and related support functions to provide timely manufacturing and delivery of output at lowest possible costs. Manages, controls, and reviews all assigned resources: staff, technical, material, and financial. Manages budgets and expense control to ensure effective meeting of operating objectives.

Vice President of Sales   Responsible for the selling of the output of several different manufacturing facilities. Must develop effective sales policies that result in each plant's producing the optimum profit. Determines final prices and works closely with the sales staff; the production, scheduling, and traffic staffs; and research and development personnel. After the initial sale is made, the sales staff assumes continuing sales effort to such accounts.

Vice President of Training and Development   Responsible for leading the design, development, and implementation of a comprehensive training and development system that supports key operational initiatives and drives business outcomes. Areas of responsibility include instructional design, video communication, vendor integrity, multimedia technical development, and coordination of training services and support.

Visiting Nurse   A nurse who is paid to visit the sick in their homes.

Vocational Counselor   Provides educational programs in vocational specialties; determines learning needs, abilities, and other facts about inmates. Provides other career training through work programs.

Voice Writer   A court reporter who repeats the testimony into a recorder by speaking into a handheld mask, called a stenomask, which contains a small microphone.

Volunteer Coordinator   Responsible for all aspects of volunteer programming, including planning and implementing the volunteer program or service being provided.

Wage and Salary Administrator   Maintains files of updated job descriptions. Ensures that responsibilities are appropriately compensated according to established standards. Participates in and reviews local and national salary surveys to set current salary standards and pay rates for each position within the organization. Processes salary increases or other changes for personnel according to established policies.

Waiter   Responsible for serving food and drink. Provides customer service by greeting customers and asking for customer feedback on satisfaction with food, drink, and customer service.

Warden   Responsible for overall supervision and administration of correctional facility; plans, directs, and coordinates programs.

Warehousing Agent   Transports shipments and materials to and from receiving area, staging area, or other area as designated.

Warehousing/Operations Manager   Determines and develops distribution strategies and practices that will support the corporate objective. Responsibilities include identifying areas within the company that offer some opportunity for improvement; optimizing investments in all locations, in inventory, facilities, and people; and matching the corporate distribution support capabilities to the outgoing marketing, business, and operational needs. Makes use of financial and computer expertise in evaluating projects and allocation of resources.

Web Designer/Developer   Designs, creates, produces, and maintains Web pages using relevant software packages.

Web Programmer   Designs and develops applications and scripts for the World Wide Web; works in the programming languages common to the Internet and World Wide Web; provides programming that makes Web pages interactive.

Web Site Manager   Oversees the Internet Web site of the organization. Manages database development, tech programming, Web site design, and daily operations. Directs the activities of other Web site staff, including the Web developer, Web author, Web administrator, or Webmaster.

Web Storefront Designer   Develops e-commerce store Web site design to include site design software, shopping card software, secure credit card processing, and site hosting.

Webmaster   Designs and implements internal and external Web pages and applications. Converts documents into HTML (Hypertext Markup Language) or other complex programming language. Determines user's needs, strategies, and goals and develops Web pages that meet that need.

Window Trimmer   Displays merchandise in windows or showcases of retail stores to attract attention of prospective customers. Originates display ideas or follows suggestions or schedule of manager. Arranges mannequins, furniture, merchandise, and backdrop according to prearranged or own ideas. Constructs or assembles prefabricated displays.

Wine Portfolio Consultant   A professional salesperson with an established clientele. Guides and recommends wine cellar selections suited to individual needs of independent restaurants and hotel and chain restaurants.

Wine Steward   A professional with vast knowledge about wine and wine culture. Makes suggestions on the menu or by request about which wines would enhance specific meals. Administers scheduling of all bar personnel, both on regular shifts and for catering work, and keeps records of their hours. Responsible for hiring, firing, and training all bar personnel; keeping customer account files; maintaining liquor and wine storage; and setting standards and ensuring that they are maintained.

Wine Taster   A taster who evaluates the quality of wine.

Wine Tasting Specialist   Wine taster expert at identifying wine varieties, qualities, and proper food and wine pairings.

Winemaker/General Manager   Responsible for all facets of the wine-making process, from deciding what grapes to use and when to harvest them, to determining when to bottle and ship the wine.

Wire Transfer Specialist   Provides support to customers using wire transfer products, including the Internet and software-based applications. Demonstrates an understanding of all associated tasks that apply to operating the wire system and performing end-of-day accounting entries.

Word Processor   Uses computers and specialized word processing equipment to enter, edit, store, and revise correspondence, statistical tables, reports, forms, and other materials. Word processing systems include keyboard, a cathode-ray tube (CRT) for display, and a printer. Some equipment also has telecommunications hookups and scanners used to obtain information for manuscript preparation.

Work-at-Home Scam Investigator   Investigates allegations of fraud committed in the promotion or implementation of work-at-home opportunities.

Zoo Animal Attendant   Monitors the health and daily activity of animals in a zoo. May assist with designing and building habitats, care for the plants around the exhibit area, or repair existing enclosures. May work closely with the zoo director on conservation, reproduction, and research projects. Gathers information to help protect and preserve rare endangered species. Gives presentations to the public. Educates the general public about wildlife conservation and animals' natural habitats.

Sources: Career Paths, Job Titles and Salaries (General/All)

http://www.bls.gov/oes/current/oes_alph.htm
Bureau of Labor Statistics
Occupational Employment Statistics
Alphabetical List of SOC Occupations

http://online.onetcenter.org/find/result?s=all%20job%20titles&a=1
O*NET Online
Occupations Matching "all job titles"

http://www.avma.org/careers/default.asp
AVMA-American Veterinary Medical Association Careers

Bibliography

American Culinary Federation (ACF)
ACF Certification Levels, 2005
180 Center Place Way
St. Augustine, FL 32095
http://www.acfchefs.org/Content/NavigationMenu2/Careers/
   Certification/default.htm

American Veterinary Medical Association (AVMA)
1931 North Meacham Road
Suite 100
Schaumburg, IL 60173-4360
http://www.avma.org/

CareerBuilder.com
Corporate Headquarters
8420 West Bryn Mawr Avenue
Suite 1000
Chicago, IL 60631
http://www.careerbuilder.com/default.aspx?cbRecursionCnt=1
   &cbsid=ef6d48df9f6e4765af669a4fe63f09ea-308252388-
   wr-6&ns_siteid=ns_us_g_career_builder.com

Career Guide to Industries (CGI), 2008–2009 Edition
U.S. Department of Labor
Bureau of Labor Statistics
Office of Occupational Statistics and Employment Projections
Suite 2135
2 Massachusetts Avenue, NE
Washington, DC 20212-0001
http://www.bls.gov/oco/cg/

Cedar Valley College
Careers in Criminal Justice
3030 North Dallas Avenue
Lancaster, TX 75134
http://www.cedarvalleycollege.edu/FutureStudents/
   DegreesandCertificatePrograms/TechnicalDisciplines/
   CriminalJustice/CareersinCriminalJustice/default.aspx

CollegeBoard AP Central
2005 The College Board
45 Columbus Avenue
New York, NY 10023-6992
http://apcentral.collegeboard.com/apc/Controller.jpf

Culinary-Careers.org
107 SE Washington Street
Suite 500
Portland, OR 97214-2205
http://www.aboutus.org/Culinary-Careers.org

Data Dome, Inc.
Workforce Trends
1050 Lindbridge Drive, NE
Atlanta, GA 30303
http://www.blogcatalog.com/blogs/
   data-dome-inc/posts/tag/workforce+trends/

Occupational Outlook Handbook, 2008–2009
U.S. Department of Labor
Bureau of Labor Statistics
Office of Occupational Statistics and Employment
   Projections
Suite 2135
2 Massachusetts Avenue, NE
Washington, DC 20212-0001
http://www.bls.gov/OCO/

Overview of BLS Statistics by Occupation
U.S. Department of Labor
Bureau of Labor Statistics
2 Massachusetts Avenue, NE
Washington, DC 20112-0001
http://www.bls.gov/bls/occupation.htm

O*NET OnLine
U.S. Department of Labor
National O*NET Consortium
2005 Frances Perkins Building
200 Constitutional Avenue, NW
Washington, DC 20210
http://online.onetcenter.org/

Vault, Inc.
150 West 22nd Street
New York, NY 10011
http://www.vault.com/wps/portal/usa

Wet Feet.com
The Folger Building
107 Howard Street
Suite 300
San Francisco, CA 94105
http://www.wetfeet.com/

The Wall Street Journal Career Journal
Executive Career Suite
4300 North, Route 1
South Brunswick, NJ 08852
http://cj.careercast.com/careers/jobsearch/results

Index

Note: Page numbers in **bold** refer to glossary definitions. Page numbers in *italics* refer to entries in the job descriptions index.